W9-DJO-093

Praise for Tyler Kepner's

K: A HISTORY OF BASEBALL IN TEN PITCHES

"You will love every single word of *K: A History of Baseball in Ten Pitches*. . . . I've never read a better love letter to the sport."
—Mike Vaccaro, *New York Post*

"No one celebrates the details of the game quite like Kepner . . . like Michelangelo explaining the brush strokes on the Sistine Chapel."
—*Newsday*

"A fascinating tour of the sport as seen from the mound."
—*The Washington Post*

"I've been a student of pitching for more than forty years, and Tyler Kepner has captured the essence of the craft with fascinating stories and insights on every page." —Orel Hershiser,
1988 National League Cy Young winner and World Series MVP

"An exceptionally well-written treatment of a significant part of American social history from the nineteenth century to today."
—*The Washington Times*

"[A] spirited romp through the history, folklore, and science of America's pastime." —*Booklist* (starred review)

"Tyler Kepner knows his stuff—by which I mean the plethora of possible assaults on the strike zone that have created the modern game: splitters, spitters, sinkers, sliders. *K* is an education in the history, mechanics, and language of pitching and as rich with detail as the craft it describes. This is inside baseball at its best. A must-read for any fan who aspires to be in the know." —Jane Leavy,
New York Times bestselling author of *Sandy Koufax: A Lefty's Legacy* and *The Big Fella: Babe Ruth and the World He Created*

"Kepner puts a new spin on baseball's history that will have even the most avid fans entertained as they learn something new in each chapter." —*Publishers Weekly* (starred review)

"Analytical and anecdotal, insightful and entertaining, *K* is a welcome addition to the baseball bookshelf." —Bob Costas

"[An] instant classic. . . . [Kepner] deftly weaves all these voices into a seamless narrative. . . . *K* is even better than I'd hoped, and I suspect it will now take its place on all the lists of essential baseball books." —Rob Neyer, Casey Award–winning author of *Power Ball: Anatomy of a Modern Baseball Game*

"A gripping tour through the most elemental component of baseball. . . . Kepner has worked magic." —*Kirkus Reviews* (starred review)

"For decades as a catcher and broadcaster, I've been fascinated by the craft of pitching. Tyler Kepner brings the pitchers—and the pitches—alive as few others ever have, with a fresh and informative trip through the history of the great American game." —Tim McCarver, Hall of Fame broadcaster and two-time All-Star and World Series champion

"I never expected to learn so much about events I've covered and people I've known for years. With lively stories from first page to last, Tyler Kepner brilliantly traces the evolution of each pitch in gripping detail, from the earliest days of baseball through today. If you love baseball, you'll gain a whole new understanding of the game." —Joe Buck, Emmy Award–winning broadcaster for Fox Sports

TYLER KEPNER

K: A HISTORY OF BASEBALL IN TEN PITCHES

Tyler Kepner started covering baseball as a teenager, interviewing players for a homemade magazine that was featured in *The New York Times* in 1989. He attended Vanderbilt University on the Grantland Rice–Fred Russell sportswriting scholarship, then covered the Angels for the *Press-Enterprise* (Riverside, CA) and the Mariners for the *Seattle Post-Intelligencer*. He joined *The New York Times* in 2000, covering the Mets for two seasons and the Yankees for eight and serving as the national baseball writer since 2010.

K

A HISTORY OF BASEBALL
IN TEN PITCHES

TYLER KEPNER

ANCHOR BOOKS
A Division of Penguin Random House LLC
New York

FIRST ANCHOR BOOKS EDITION, MARCH 2020

The Library of Congress has cataloged the Doubleday edition as follows:
Name: Kepner, Tyler (Baseball writer), author.
Title: K : a history of baseball in ten pitches / Tyler Kepner.
Description: First edition. | New York : Doubleday, 2019 |
Includes bibliographical references and index.
Identifiers: LCCN 2018016158
Subjects: LCSH: Pitching (Baseball) | Pitchers (Baseball) |
Baseball—United States—History.
Classification: LCC GV871 .K46 2019 | DDC 796.357/22—dc23
LC record available at https://lccn.loc.gov/2018016158

Anchor Books Trade Paperback ISBN: 978-1-101-97085-0
eBook ISBN: 978-0-385-54102-2

Author photograph © Eric Broder
Book design by Michael Collica

www.anchorbooks.com

Printed in the United States of America
10 9 8 7

For Jen

"We're not leaving in the seventh-inning stretch, are we?"

Contents

Introduction

The kid hung in there as a rookie for the Mets: 11 wins, five losses, a 4.04 earned run average, and 170 strikeouts. But the next year he struggled, and then he got hurt, and soon he was traded to the A's and the Twins. Finally he landed with his hometown team, the Phillies, where he stayed for many years, except for one season with the Indians.

He retired with a record of 350–182, for a .658 winning percentage. He won five Cy Young Awards, made eight All-Star teams, and struck out 4,819. He was clearly one of the greatest pitchers in baseball history.

———

This was my life plan in 1986. I was eleven, the oldest a kid can be before reality invades his dreams. I can still throw strikes reliably for the New York media team in our annual games against Boston, and I can spin a loopy little curveball. My arm is never sore, because I don't throw hard and never have.

Before my lack of speed mattered, though, I believed in that hand-written stat sheet. I found it in a notebook a few years ago, in a box at my parents' house. By then I was deep into this project, exploring the history and stories behind every pitch, from Christy Mathewson's fadeaway to Clayton Kershaw's slider. Seeing my scribbles through the prism of actual history, it struck me that, for some pitchers, real life surpassed my wildest ambitions.

In my childhood baseball fantasy, where I could do anything I wanted, I still won fewer games than Greg Maddux. I had fewer strikeouts than Nolan Ryan, a lower winning percentage than Roy Halladay, fewer All-Star selections than Randy Johnson, fewer Cy Young Awards than Roger Clemens. I spoke with all of them, and hundreds more, for this book. I wanted to know how the masters did what they did, how they learned and applied their best pitches.

Stardom is at their fingertips, literally. That's the mystery and the madness of the craft. Even the slightest adjustment of a pitcher's fingers can turn an ordinary pitch into a major league weapon. If your body and brain can withstand all the failure, you'd be foolish to ever quit the job.

The pitcher is the planner, the initiator of action. The hitter can only react. If the pitcher, any pitcher, finds a way to disrupt that reaction, he can win. You need a little luck and relentless curiosity.

By watching baseball up close for so long, and getting to know the men who play it, I can see that I was never like them. My fingers move better on a laptop than they do on a baseball, and I'm lucky I found a skill that allows me to move within their world. But I still wish that my younger self had recognized the baseball for the amazing plaything it is, diving and darting and sailing and sinking, with no instruction manual.

In a different Pennsylvania town in the 1980s, another right-hander got it. Mike Mussina grew up in Montoursville, high in the mountains near Williamsport. On cold days he would throw against a cinder-block wall in his basement from about 30 feet away, under a dropped ceiling about six feet, eight inches high. He liked to experiment, and while he couldn't come up with much, he knew what he was missing and how he could find it.

"Listen, I didn't leave high school with a fastball, curveball, slider, change, sinker—I had a fastball and a lazy curveball, that was it," Mussina told me in the summer of 2016, over lunch at Johnson's Café in Montoursville, where he still lives. "I came from small-town America. I didn't see anybody else that did anything that I wanted to be able to do. But when I got to college and got to pro ball, now there's other guys out there—*Man, that's a pretty good slider, I wonder how he does that? That's a pretty good curveball, I'd love to be able to do that.* And so you're looking at other people, you're stealing ideas and seeing if you can do it."

The Orioles drafted Mussina in the twentieth round out of high school, in 1987, but he wanted to learn more, on and off the mound. He hates to travel but chose Stanford University and graduated in three years. The Orioles chose him again in 1990, this time in the first round, and the next year he was in the majors. He stayed for 18 seasons by constantly evolving.

Mussina doubts that many pitchers will last as long as he did, because there's less incentive to innovate. Pitchers throw harder, but they're not trained or expected to work deep into games. If they were, he believes, they'd have to develop more pitches to keep the same hitters guessing. Then, as their best stuff fades with age, they'd have other pitches to use.

If a starting pitcher does his job, Mussina believes, he should win half his starts. That was his logic long before he finished with 270 victories in 536 starts. But there's a catch: the quality of a pitcher's stuff will vary from game to game. In a few starts it will be crisp; in a few others it will be flat. Most of the time, he'll have just enough to compete.

What made Mussina great, his peers believed, is that he always had so many options, so many different pitches to grind his way through a start when he wasn't at his best. This is how he described his thought process:

"Boy, there's so many variables involved in the equation that you can't even discuss it, almost," he said, then does so at length. "It's not like there's nobody on base every time—there's guys in scoring position, nobody out, crowd's going crazy. You think, 'OK, I screwed up, we can't go with A. What's B, what's C, what's D?'

"Who's hitting? Is he hot or cold? Where are the base runners? What's the situation? Where are we in the game? Are we on the road? Are we at home? Is it nighttime? Is it daytime? What has he done the other two at-bats? Let's say it's the seventh inning. Where he's at in the box? How'd he look taking that pitch, or how'd he look fouling that pitch off?

"There's all these things going on in your head. And then you take in all this outside input and you say to yourself, 'Yeah—but I don't feel good with that pitch.' Because your brain tells you, 'Look, you should throw this,' but I haven't thrown one of those for a strike in four innings. Eventually you just have to have enough balls to say, 'Screw it, I've got to do it the way I should do it, and whatever happens, happens.' I can't just throw fastballs because he knows I don't have a good enough changeup today, or he knows I don't feel good with my slider today. He doesn't *really* know that. All he knows is that I have these five pitches I can throw. He doesn't really know that I don't feel good about this one. He may know that I don't *look like* I have great command because I have three walks already and I usually don't walk anybody, but he doesn't know that I don't feel good with my changeup—so let's throw it anyway.

"That's the kind of stuff you think about, and it's not planned. It's just experience. You just have to do it. But there's so many variables. We could talk for months about variables when you're trying to figure out what to throw."

———————

Those variables consumed me for three years. Wherever I went, in my travels as the national baseball writer for *The New York Times,* I sought people who could help me tell the story of every pitch. How did the great ones learn? How did their pitches move? When and why did they use them? What made them work?

I settled on 10: the slider, the fastball, the curveball, the knuckleball, the splitter, the screwball, the sinker, the changeup, the spitball, and the cutter. Mussina, who taught me more about pitching than anyone else I covered in 12 years as a beat writer, isn't sure there are only 10.

"There might be 10 defined, different things," he says. "But every guy that throws it is different. My sinker and Kevin Brown's sinker aren't the same. Not the same pitch. When it's going through the strike zone and the hitter's trying to hit it, my sinker and his sinker are not doing the same sinking. My curveball and somebody else's curveball? They're not the same. They may be technically the same, but when it's going through the hitting zone and somebody's trying to hit it—to the guy in the box, it's not the same. Mo's cutter and my cutter aren't the same thing. I call it that and he calls it that, but it doesn't do the same thing. So is there really a limit, a number, to how many pitches there are? Like I said, I was out there trying to invent stuff."

There is, indeed, no limit to the kinds of options available to a pitcher, or how he can use them. Lance McCullers Jr., who called Mussina one of his favorite pitchers to watch, threw 24 curveballs in a row to close out the American League Championship Series for Houston in 2017. He knows the spin rates of all his pitches, and studies their movement on an X-Y axis after every start. But by reading his stuff in the moment, he pumped curve after curve with a pennant on the line. There was no rule against it, only convention.

"No one would be like, 'Oh my gosh, he threw 24 *fastballs* in a row,'" McCullers told me later, clutching a champagne bottle in the clubhouse. "No one would say that. But this game continues to evolve. A couple of years from now, it may not be so crazy to think about."

The pitches are the DNA of baseball, the fundamental coding of the game. Joe Maddon, the Cubs' manager, says the sport could easily be called "pitching," because the pitcher controls everything. He is the most influential player on the field, by far, but he can't play every day. That factor, more than any other, makes baseball so interesting.

A major league pitcher is part boxer and part magician; if he's not punching you in the face, he's swiping a quarter from behind your ear. If you ever square him up, you'd better savor it. Even in batting practice, the world's best hitters tap harmless grounders and punch lazy fly balls. In the heat of competition, every hit is an exquisite anomaly.

———

Playing baseball—as a pitcher or a hitter—eventually just got too hard for me. I played through high school, but by then I was well into this career. In seventh grade, I started jotting down my thoughts and opinions about the game, copying the pages and stapling them into a magazine. From early 1988 through early 1995, I published 11 issues a year, every month except January, so I could study for exams. I conducted my first interview—with Pat Combs, a Phillies pitcher— the day after my fifteenth birthday.

The press box was the ultimate learning lab. Instead of asking pitchers how I should grip a slider, I asked writers how they crafted their stories, how they asked the right questions, how they found their ideas. Sometimes, they reported on me. One winter day in 1990, the ABC affiliate in town, WPVI, sent its human-interest correspondent to meet me at school and drive me home for a feature story. His name was Tug McGraw.

"Is that Joe in front of us?" he asked on our drive.

"Joe?"

"Joe Mama!"

Tug was a scamp, an affable rascal who named his pitches and wrote a children's book, *Lumpy,* from the perspective of a baseball. In second grade, when the teacher told us to write a letter to a famous person, I wrote to Tug and invited him to my birthday party. He didn't come, alas, but he did send back an autographed photo with the inscription, "Best of luck in school and sports, pal." He also returned the letter and signed that, too. Always with a smiley face.

Digging through files at the Hall of Fame library in Cooperstown, New York, I found a column on McGraw from 1977 by Bill Lyon, an elegant writer for *The Philadelphia Inquirer* who inspired and mentored me. He spoke with McGraw about the art of pitching, and McGraw held a baseball as they talked. His passion all but singed the yellowed newsprint.

"You know, if somebody called me at four in the morning and said, 'Hey, let's go out and play some catch,' I'd do it," McGraw said. "I love this little thing."

If there's anything in life more endearing than enthusiasm, I've never found it. I've seen a lot in baseball, and I'm proud to say I'm not jaded. Neither are the hundreds of folks who gave me their time and insights for this book. We all love this little thing, this miracle: baseball.

Tyler Kepner
Wilton, Connecticut

K

THE
SLIDER

A Little Bitty Dot

I can pinpoint the single happiest moment of my childhood. On October 8, 1983, when I was eight years old, the Philadelphia Phillies beat the Los Angeles Dodgers to win the National League pennant at Veterans Stadium. Everyone in the stands chanted "Beat L.A.! Beat L.A.!" On our way home, my dad let me honk the horn of his Chevette, like the other revelers on Broad Street. It was the best traffic jam ever.

Steve Carlton won the game, just as he had won the World Series clincher three years earlier, when I was too young to notice. In between he claimed his fourth Cy Young Award, a record at the time, leading the majors in wins and strikeouts and mesmerizing me completely. When I had tickets on his day to pitch, I would scramble to the front row near the first base dugout to watch him get loose, staring up in awe. He would bring his hands together, dip them down by his belt, and then raise them up near his head. He'd drop them lower as he turned, hiking his right knee up around his chest. For a moment, he'd curl the ball in his left hand, down behind his left thigh, before whipping it up and around for the pitch. Power and grace, personified.

I would imitate this windup at home, in the mirror, where I could be left-handed, too. I pitched like Carlton in Little League, right down to his facial twitches. I collected every baseball card that ever featured him, scoring his rookie card for $75 from a cash-strapped friend who had just gotten his driver's license. Thirty-two has always been my favorite number. I named the family dog Lefty.

I met Carlton in 1989, his first year of retirement, at a charity signing at the Vet. I had just finished my middle school baseball career,
and he signed my jersey, right above the 32 on the back. I didn't tell
him that I wanted to be a sportswriter.

For most of his career, Carlton didn't talk to the media at all. To a
young fan, that only added to his mystique. He loosened up later in
his career, but not much. When I started this project, I wanted to talk
to Carlton more than anyone else. We connected by phone, and this
is the first thing he said: "So you're writing a book. Don't you know
people don't read anymore?"

If that was a brushback pitch, I ducked.

"Well," I replied, "my first goal in life was to be you, and that didn't
work out. So I'm going with my strengths."

He laughed and then talked for a while about the slider, the pitch
he threw better than anyone else.

"I always had a little bitty dot on the ball," Carlton said. "If it was
big as a quarter or half a dollar, that was a ring, or a circle, and hitters
could see that. When I threw it, I wanted the spin real tight on it, so
the ball is blurry like a fastball and you can't see the dot. The intent is
to fool the hitter as long as you can, so he has to commit to a fastball,
so he has to come out and try to get it, because he can't sit back on
a fastball and hit it. You have to commit to the fastball—and that's
where you want him."

———————

The slider is faster than the curveball and easier to control, with a
tighter break, shaped not like a loop but like a slash, moving down and
away toward the pitcher's glove side. The trick, as Carlton said, is in
the disguise, making a hitter swing over a pitch he thinks is a fastball.
A dot—formed by the side-spinning rotation of the seams—would
seem to telegraph the pitch. But some hitters call it a myth.

"I never saw it," says Matt Williams, who had 7,000 at-bats in the
major leagues. "Guys have said, 'Well, all you have to do is look for the
red dot and you'll know that it's a slider.' You've got a fifth of a second,
right? I couldn't do it."

He is hardly alone. Batters hit just .233 in at-bats ending with sliders in 2017, their worst average against any pitch. The Pirates' Chris Archer, who has one of baseball's best sliders, gave a simple reason why: "Of all the true breaking balls—slurve, curve, slider—it looks the most like a fastball for the longest."

The origins of the slider, as we know it now, are murky. In 1987, hundreds of former players responded to surveys for a book called *Players' Choice*. They answered many questions, including the best slider of their day. Pete Donohue, a three-time 20-game winner for the Reds in the 1920s, could not give a name: "We didn't have one when I pitched," he replied.

Hmm—but what is this pitch, if not a slider? "It was a narrow curve that broke away from the batter and went in just like a fastball," said the great Cy Young, describing a pitch he threw in a career that ended in 1911.

Contemporaries of Young, like Chief Bender, an ace of the early Philadelphia A's, probably threw it, too. Bender's name virtually demanded he not throw straight, and he was, you might say, the chief bender of pitches in his era. Listing his repertoire for *Baseball Magazine* in 1911, Bender first mentioned his "fast curves," which would seem pretty close to what we now call a slider. George Blaeholder and George Uhle, whose careers ended in 1936, were early pioneers. Blaeholder, who pitched mostly for the Browns, had sweeping action on his fastball that was said to baffle Jimmie Foxx. Uhle, a 200-game winner, developed the slider late in his career, after his prime with the 1920s Indians. It startled Harry Heilmann, a Detroit teammate who was hitting off Uhle in batting practice.

"What kind of curve is that?" Heilmann asked.

"Hey, that's not a curve," Uhle replied. "That ball was sliding."

Waite Hoyt, an admiring teammate and the ace of the fabled 1927 Yankees, compared its action to a car skidding on ice. He added the pitch himself and credited Uhle for inventing it. Uhle told author Walter Langford that, as far as he knew, he threw it first.

"At least I happened to come up with it while I was in Detroit," he said. "And I gave it its name because it just slides across. It's just a fastball you turn loose in a different way. When I first started throwing it, the batters thought I was putting some kind of stuff on the ball to make it act that way."

Red Ruffing used a slider in his Hall of Fame career, which included four 20-win seasons in a row for the Yankees from 1936 through 1939. In that final season, the National League MVP was the Reds' Bucky Walters, a former third baseman who had learned a slider a few years earlier from Bender, a fellow Philadelphian. Walters led his league in all the major categories in 1939, and the next year lifted the Reds to their only World Series title between the Black Sox and the Big Red Machine—a span of 55 seasons.

In 1943, another MVP threw the slider: the Yankees' Spud Chandler, who shut out the Cardinals to clinch that fall's World Series. Chandler had learned the pitch from Ruffing, whose influence Rob Neyer and Bill James cited as a reason the slider soon made a breakthrough. The other factors, they said, were Walters's success and the fact that the pitch now had a name; it was not just another breaking ball. After three years at war, Ted Williams noticed the trend:

> We began to see sliders in the league around 1946 or 1947, and by 1948 all the good pitchers had one. Before that there were pitchers whose curves acted like sliders. Hank Borowy threw his curve hard and it sank and didn't break too much, so it acted like a slider. Johnny Allen's was the same way. Claude Passeau's fastball acted like a slider.

Williams called the slider "the greatest pitch in baseball," easy for a pitcher to learn and control. He worried about grounding the slider into the infield shift, reasoning that the only way he could put it in the air was by looking for it. Most hitters are late on the fastball if they sit on the slider, but Williams was not like most hitters. He batted .419 off the Browns' Ned Garver and .377 off the Tigers' Jim Bunning, who otherwise thrived with sliders.

"The big thing the slider did was give the pitcher a third pitch right away," Williams wrote in his book, *My Turn at Bat*. "With two pitches you might guess right half the time. With three, your guessing goes down proportionately."

Williams believed the popularity of the slider helped drive averages down. Bob Feller, the best pitcher Williams said he ever saw, had fiddled with the slider in 1941, and perfected it by the time he returned from the war. Mixing a slider with his devastating fastball and curve in 1946, Feller struck out 348—then considered an American League record. He described the pitch like this:

> It can be especially effective for a fast ball pitcher because it comes up to the plate looking like a fast ball. It has less speed, but not enough for the hitter to detect the slightly reduced speed early in the pitch.
>
> The slider darts sharply just before it reaches the plate, away from a right-handed hitter when thrown by a right-handed pitcher. It doesn't break much—four to six inches—but because it breaks so late, the hitter has trouble catching up to it.
>
> I didn't invent the slider—I merely popularized it. The pitch has been around since Christy Mathewson's time.

The slider's transformative power showed up in Feller's statistics, and in his clubhouse. Phil Rizzuto said that in his rookie season, 1941, the only pitcher he faced who threw sliders regularly was Al Milnar of the Indians. Feller was on that team, and so was Mel Harder, who taught the slider a few years later to Bob Lemon, who went on to the Hall of Fame. The logic behind the pitch was so easy to understand, and the pitch itself so simple to learn—generally, but not always: off-center grip, pressure applied to the middle finger, and possibly a late, subtle wrist snap—yet there remained an odd kind of backlash against it into the 1950s.

Pitchers threw fastballs and curveballs, sometimes a trick pitch like a knuckleball, and a spitball if they could conceal it. The conventional wisdom was that learning a slider would harm a pitcher's curveball. A curveball demands a different arm action—wrapping the wrist and pulling hard, straight down, to generate furious topspin. Throw too many sliders and you might lose the feel for staying on top of the curve.

"If you have a good curve, it's foolish to add the slider," said Sal Maglie, a curveball master who was turned away from using a slider by Uhle for that reason. "But all the young pitchers today are lazy. They all look for the easy way out, and the slider gives 'em that pitch."

Maglie said this in 1962, in an *Esquire* article that included his assertion that Roger Maris had feasted off sliders while blasting 61 homers the year before. To Maglie, expansion and "all the second-line pitchers in the league throwing sliders" had added at least 10 homers to Maris's total. The pitch was widely derided as a "nickel curve"—a breaking ball, yes, but a cheap knockoff of the real thing. That term is long gone, but "cement mixer," which describes a lazy and obvious slider, persists today.

The critics of the slider were blind to its impact. In his book *Head Game,* Roger Kahn asserted that the slider "saved major league baseball from becoming extended batting practice" after the offensive boom of the 1930s. That era had its masters—Lefty Grove, Dizzy Dean, Carl Hubbell—but few others were much better than ordinary. The slider gave pitchers a weapon they could learn and control with relative ease, a pitch that looked like a fastball much longer than the curveball did.

"I could always tell a curveball from a fastball in the first 30 feet of flight," Stan Musial told Kahn. "I picked up the speed of the ball and I knew who was pitching and I put the two of them together and I'd know just what the ball was going to do. Break or hop. The slider was tougher. I got my share of hits off sliders. But during the years I played for the Cardinals, the slider changed the game."

Musial played from 1941 through 1963. By then, a contemporary from his playing days, Johnny Sain, was an avid teacher of the pitch, winning pennants and building 20-game winners with startling regularity.

———

Sain did not invent the slider in his long career as a pitcher and a coach, or use it very much as a pitcher. But he probably studied and imparted the principles of spin better than any coach ever has. Forever curious, Sain was the leading pitching mind of his era. He had seen the slider's rise, understood its impact, and spread its gospel like nobody before him.

"He was a genius in his field," says Roland Hemond, who hired Sain to instruct his White Sox pitchers in the 1970s. "Johnny Sain was a master."

Sain is remembered best for a rhyme—*Spahn and Sain and pray for rain,* a shorthand version of a poem by Gerry Hern, the sports editor of *The Boston Post* in 1948. Sain and Warren Spahn were the aces of the Braves' staff and carried the team to the pennant, the culmination of a three-year run in which Sain completed 62 of his 65 victories. He began the 1948 World Series by shutting out Feller and the Indians, the highlight of an unlikely 11-year playing career.

"I spent four years in the lowest minor leagues, the D leagues, and I never had overpowering speed," Sain told *The New York Times* in 1968. "So I kept practicing my breaking stuff, big curves and short ones. I started in 1936, and by the time I came up to the big leagues with Boston in 1942, I was throwing sliders."

Sain pitched mostly in relief that season, without distinction. He left for three years as a Navy pilot in World War II, spending the downtime building up his arm and experimenting with angles and pitches. He came back throwing breaking balls almost exclusively—90 percent of the time, he once guessed—and his creativity served him well when he moved into coaching, a fitting profession for the son of an auto mechanic. An open mind and skilled hands compelled Sain to innovate.

As a Yankees coach in 1961, he created a spinning device, first by impaling an apple with a television antenna. Sain could hold the antenna in one hand and twirl the apple with the other, tilting it this way or that to see the spin from various angles. He liked the idea so much that he transferred it to a baseball, drilling a wooden handle into the center and calling it The Spinner. Sain spent thousands of dollars developing his invention and sent it to the United States Patent Office. A Yankees pitcher, Luis Arroyo, called it the best tool he had ever seen.

"I'm most concerned about movement on the ball," Sain once said. "What makes it fool the hitter? Why does it do what it does?"

The Spinner showed pitchers how. Just by flicking their fingers on the ball as they held and moved the handle, they could see the way it spun. The more they toyed with it, the more knowledge they gained of their craft. Aspiring pitchers could purchase a Spinner by writing to Sain at PO Box 487 in Walnut Ridge, Arkansas. His pupils on major league teams could use them whenever they pleased, and if a pitcher got released, Sain often gave him a Spinner to take with him. Chances are Sain would soon follow him out the door.

As a coach, he bounced from the Yankees to the Twins to the Tigers to the White Sox, succeeding everywhere but doing so with independence that irritated the established order. He traveled with dozens of books and motivational audiotapes for his pitchers. He was their advocate, not the manager's friend, upending the logic of the day by emphasizing throwing—and experimenting with spin, even at moderate effort levels—over the rote running exercises that most pitchers hated.

"His big deal was turn and pull," says Jim Kaat, who thrived under Sain in Minnesota and Chicago. "So we would practice from 45 feet, straight backspin. Then he'd say 'turn and pull, turn and pull,' and it'd be like Mariano Rivera's cutter, and then we'd turn it a little more. He'd show us with the device. Every day we would throw.

"We'd play games—'OK, throw this as slow as you can and make it break as big as you can,' almost like Steve Hamilton's 'Folly Floater' [a version of Rip Sewell's Eephus pitch from the 1940s]. Then he'd say, 'OK, now let's put a little more velocity to it, let's see how short we can make it break and how hard we can throw it, without trying to muscle it.' He taught us how to make the ball do things. Velocity was never an issue."

The weapon most pitchers learned from Sain was not shaped like the arcing curveball, and certainly thrown much harder than the blooper Hamilton used for the Yankees in the 1960s. It had a two-plane break—over and down—which distinguished it from the cutter Rivera would perfect, which veered more than it broke. Yet it was not thrown as hard as the vicious sliders that Bob Gibson and Carlton were beginning to unleash on the majors.

Call it a short curve, or maybe a slurve, but basically it acted like a slider, and Sain's pupils used it to dominate the 1960s and early 1970s. All of these pitchers won 20 games under his guidance: Kaat, Whitey Ford, Mudcat Grant, Denny McLain, Jim Bouton, Al Downing, Jim Perry, Wilbur Wood, Stan Bahnsen. Later, as a minor league instructor with the Braves, Sain would mentor Leo Mazzone, who coached the celebrated Atlanta staffs of the 1990s. Tom Glavine always remembered Sain's advice on breaking balls: impart spin but think fastball, to protect your elbow through the delivery.

Too often, pitchers try to generate break with their elbows and forearms. The safer, more effective way is to do it with the wrist and hand. The former pitcher Jerry Dipoto, who would go on to be a general manager, remembers a daily drill that emphasized this. For 15 minutes every day, he and his Cleveland teammates had to throw all their pitches with a four-seam fastball grip. They would shape their pitches and create different breaks with their wrist, hand, and finger pressure.

"Creating break and spin is just about creating a fast hand," Dipoto says. "If you have a fast hand, you're gonna create movement. And the easiest way to work on training a fast hand is just by using it."

When the pitchers finally applied their grips, they would amaze themselves with the action they could impart. They would also know why they did it—and when a pitcher understands the way his pitch spins, Dipoto says, *it's on*. The pitchers had a name for this daily exercise in the art of the spinning baseball. They called it the Johnny Sain Game.

———

Bob Gibson decided to become a professional athlete at age 11, in 1947, the year Jackie Robinson joined the Brooklyn Dodgers. Gibson had lost his father before he was born, and his brother, Josh, who was 15 years older, helped raise him. Josh built a pitching mound at Bob's elementary school, and while he knew sports, he did not know a slider. Bob, therefore, did not know it either. He just threw it better than anyone ever had.

"I thought it was a curveball, because I didn't really understand the dynamics of all those pitches," Gibson says. "Since day one, I had always thrown a slider, and as I got bigger and stronger, I threw it harder. But I always threw it the same way."

His Triple-A manager for the Cardinals, Johnny Keane, told Gibson that the pitch he called a curveball was actually a slider. To be a curveball, he would have to start with his hand on top of the ball, and deliver it with a rolling wrist. Gibson could do that, but, he says, "it was slow and just kind of a flopper."

That was not his pitch. His pitch was a sharp, darting missile at 92 miles an hour, held with his index and middle fingers together between the seams, at their narrowest point, and his thumb on the seam below.

"It didn't really break that big, it was just really hard," Gibson says. "And I thought the harder I threw it the better it'd be, and that was true."

In popular lore, Gibson's heat and competitiveness are often mistaken for head-hunting. Yet he played 17 years and never led the league in hit batters. His slider was a big reason for the 102 he did hit, and the many close calls.

"Guys used to laugh at me all the time when I said they hit themselves," Gibson says. "They go, 'Yeah, right.' But no, they would. Because when you go guessing for a ball outside and you go out there to get it, especially with that slider out there a lot to right-handers, they would start out there to get that ball. Well, if I threw a fastball inside, especially a two-seamer, it's gonna hit them. And I wouldn't acknowledge, 'Oh, I'm sorry.' I would never acknowledge that. I just said, 'Gimme another ball, let's go,' so they thought I was throwing at everybody. And that was OK."

The Hall of Famer Billy Williams, who hit left-handed, handled Gibson fairly well. He liked the ball down and explained that Gibson's slider would sometimes drop squarely into his bat path. If he could extend his arms, Williams had a chance. That's how he hit 10 homers off Gibson, the most by any opposing hitter.

"But *here*," Williams adds, placing his hand a few inches from his belt, "you've got to get out in front. He'd throw a fastball to get you out in front, and you're way out here."

That pitch, the one that tied up lefties, was Gibson's stiff-wrist slider, which acted like a cutter and shattered many bats. He would break his wrist for a more sweeping slash away from righties, holding them to a .204 average, with a .287 slugging percentage, across 17 seasons.

Gibson's masterpiece was 1968, when he resolved to use the slider more, especially to left-handers, with catcher Tim McCarver's encouragement. Gibson authored one of the greatest seasons a pitcher has ever had, going 22–9 with a 1.12 earned run average, the lowest ever. He completed 28 of his 34 starts and was never removed from a game in the middle of an inning. He set a World Series strikeout record in Game 1 against Detroit, with 17, and overall went 7–2 with a 1.89 ERA in the World Series, twice winning MVP.

Baseball lowered the mound after the 1968 season, from 15 inches to

10, but Gibson kept on winning, adding another Cy Young Award in
1970. The change in the mound did not affect him much, because he
threw from a three-quarters angle and could easily adjust the angle of
his slider. Over-the-top pitchers with curveballs were more vulnerable.

There was a cost to Gibson's signature pitch: constant pain. Gibson
does not believe he was tougher than modern pitchers, but he pitched
with discomfort that would not be tolerated today, when injuries are
more definable. On game days when his elbow really ached, Gibson
would take Butazolidin after his warm-ups. Butazolidin, commonly
used on horses, has since been banned by the FDA.

"My elbow was sore all the time, and it was sore basically from that
stiff-wrist slider, because that's really hard on your elbow," Gibson
says. "The one where you break your wrist and the break is a little bit
bigger, that's not nearly as hard on your elbow as that stiff-wrist. It's
like holding your fingers on top, with your thumb on the bottom, and
rotating it like you're going to turn the doorknob, just with those three
fingers. And if you do that, you can feel tension on your elbow—and
you can imagine, throwing that 91, 92 miles an hour, what your elbow's
going to feel like afterwards.

"And I threw a lot of 'em."

———

A young pitcher on those Cardinal teams noticed the slider's toll on
Gibson. He decided he wanted no part of it. Steve Carlton never hurt
his elbow throwing a baseball, and he remains very proud of that. Even
as a boy, he refused to accept the idea that pitching had to be painful.

"Kids are invariably thinking if they're gonna make the ball spin a
particular way, they have to force the ball to spin," Carlton says. "So
they're gonna be twisting their hand and doing crazy things to it to
get it to spin, to break. That just goes along with being a kid, because
they don't know, so they think they have to do it this way.

"Even when I was a kid, I held my curveball and threw it. I didn't
twist it. I never twisted it. Even on the curveball, it was just hold it
and throw it. And that's why I had a good one: I never hurt my arm.
Never had elbow problems."

That curveball was good enough—with a fastball, naturally—to get Carlton to the majors at age 20. He was so proud of his curve that before he had even made the majors, after a spring training game, Carlton challenged McCarver to call more breaking balls when behind in the count. They were shaving at the time, towels around their waists, and McCarver—already a five-year veteran—admonished the kid, loudly. But Carlton was probably right.

(McCarver would find, over decades of close friendship, that Carlton had an unusual but accurate sense of things. In the mid-1970s, as they prepared for a long drive on a hunting trip, McCarver noticed that Carlton had packed a caulking gun in the trunk. McCarver teased him about it, but Carlton didn't care. Somewhere near Mitchell, South Dakota, in 20-degree weather with snow falling, a pheasant flew into the radiator of Carlton's Chevy Blazer. The car was leaking antifreeze. Carlton stopped, removed the bird, found the caulking gun, and used it to plug the leak. Years later, he sold the Blazer with the caulking still in the radiator. "Lefty," McCarver told him, "I'll never question anything you do again.")

For all of his intuition, though, Carlton was not above asking questions. He pitched with Gibson on two pennant-winning Cardinal teams, watching and learning what to do and what to avoid. McCarver had encouraged Carlton to develop a pitch that moved laterally, because his fastball was straight and his curveball dropped straight down, as if from 12 to 6 on a clock. Carlton asked Gibson how he threw his slider.

"He said he kind of got it out there and turned it at a particular time; it was a timing element," Carlton says. "And he had a great slider—but his elbow always bothered him. I thought, 'I don't want to do that.' I didn't want to turn my hand, like turning-a-doorknob kind of thing. That puts a lot of pressure on the ulnar region of the elbow."

Carlton started experimenting with a cutter, offsetting his fingers on the fastball to get side-to-side action. What he really wanted, though, was two-plane movement: *"cut, cut, cut—and then drop,"* as Willie Stargell would one day describe it to him. All through the 1968 season, Carlton toyed with the shape of the pitch and his angles of release. As Gibson fashioned a performance for the ages, Carlton went 13–11. He was an afterthought in the World Series, mopping up twice in blowouts.

That off-season, the Cardinals played an exhibition series in Japan. They would face Sadaharu Oh, the left-handed slugger who stood at the plate like a flamingo and smashed 868 career home runs. They did not understand that Oh and the Japanese would take the exhibitions seriously.

"We thought everybody was gonna just play pat-a-cake, have some fun and have a beer," Carlton says. "It wasn't like that. They came out swinging. They're trying to kick our ass. So we had a clubhouse meeting without the coaches and the managers: 'We gotta step it up a little bit.'"

Oh hit a home run off Carlton; maybe two. Desperation was his inspiration.

"I told Timmy, 'I gotta break this out against Oh because I can't move him off the plate,'" Carlton says. "He picked that leg up and he was pretty tough at the plate. My first throw I threw it at his ribs and it kind of unsettled him. He kind of flew back. After he got that leg up, he just kind of jumped out of the way and it came over for a nice strike. That was a pretty good test right there, the first one I ever threw."

At spring training the next season, Carlton told the pitching coach, Billy Muffett, that he planned to use the slider quite a bit. Muffett was unsure; some teams, like the Dodgers, did not want their pitchers throwing sliders at all, for fear of elbow trouble. But as the season progressed, Carlton used it more and became a star: he struck out 19 Mets in a game that September and nearly won the league's ERA title, at 2.17.

He loved the pitch, sometimes too much. The next August, after McCarver had been traded, Carlton was 6–18 when he took the mound at Dodger Stadium. Joe Torre asked to catch him that night, with a plan to call only fastballs. Carlton obliged, shaking off Torre just once, for a slider that turned into a homer by Andy Kosco. It was the only run he allowed in a 2–1, complete game victory.

Carlton abandoned the pitch in 1971—"Steve Ditches 'Made in Japan' Slider," a *Sporting News* headline said—and while he won 20 games, he was not much better than he had been the year before. Unwilling to meet his demands for a $10,000 raise the next spring, the Cardinals traded Carlton to the Phillies for Rick Wise. By the time the Cardinals reached the postseason again, in 1982, Carlton had finished four Cy Young Award–winning seasons.

For the first, in 1972, he was reunited with McCarver, his personal catcher for much of the decade. The two were an unlikely pair— Carlton silent with the press, McCarver loquacious—but McCarver earned Carlton's respect with his tactics at bridge, the card game. McCarver's knack for remembering cards impressed Carlton, who figured he could apply the same skill to remembering pitches.

The 1972 season was Carlton's answer to Gibson's 1968. Only once before had a pitcher won at least 27 games with 30 complete games, 300 strikeouts, and an ERA under 2.00—Walter Johnson, in 1912, when his Washington Senators won 91 games. The 1972 Phillies won just 59.

Carlton never threw a no-hitter, but the best of his six career one-hitters came that April at Candlestick Park, in his third start for the Phillies. He allowed a leadoff single to Chris Speier and no other hits, facing just 28 batters, whiffing 14, walking one and needing only 103 pitches. He threw 20 sliders, 17 for strikes.

"It was freezing that night," McCarver says. "Worst playing conditions imaginable, but it didn't bother Steve. Nothing bothered him. Nothing. Impervious to outside pressures."

The slider was back, forever. All along, Carlton was determined never to hurt his elbow. He made every start for the Phillies for 13 years, and McCarver said he never met anyone stronger from the forearm to the hand. Dick Ruthven, a teammate, would ask Carlton how he threw the slider.

"I hold it like this," Carlton would say, "and I throw the shit out of it."

Carlton laughed as he told the story; it was a joke, but basically true. He would hook his wrist to set the pitch, holding his index and middle fingers less than a quarter-inch apart, angled diagonally across the stamp on the sweet spot. He wanted to feel as if he were holding the outer third of the ball and applying pressure equally with the two fingers. His thumb provided more pressure on the bottom seam, and he released the ball off the inside of his index finger.

"The slider's tough because the hitter has to come out and get it, because it looks like a fastball," Carlton says. "So he has to start swinging, and then it starts breaking. So that's where you get the check swings. Then you throw your fastball behind that, and then he's behind it, because he's coming out. He's waiting for another rhythm to it."

When Carlton pitched, McCarver said, the two most important people on the field were third baseman Mike Schmidt and the first base umpire—Schmidt to field the ground balls pulled by right-handers, and the umpire to call strikes on their check swings. The pitch was his ultimate finisher.

Carlton would do this well past his thirty-fifth birthday. His four best strikeout rates (8.5 or more per nine innings) came from 1980 to 1983, his age 35–38 seasons. It was the payoff from his punishing daily workouts with Gus Hoefling, a strength coach who came to Philadelphia when the Eagles traded for quarterback Roman Gabriel, his star pupil, from the Rams in 1973. Carlton was already a black belt in Shotokan karate and found, in Hoefling, a martial arts guru who could help him ward off the dangers he had seen in St. Louis. Carlton would churn his elbow in buckets of rice or ball-bearings. He did pushups with his fingertips. Gibson had told him, "If you throw, it's gonna hurt." Carlton wanted to be indestructible, with Hoefling's help.

"We gained strength in areas that most people didn't know how to exploit as trainers," Carlton says. "We went after weak tissue all the time, which would be the ulnar regions. We made that stronger, more able to take the stress. That was the whole idea."

Walter Johnson had held the career strikeout record at the end of every season from 1921 through 1982. But in 1983, the year of that pennant-clinching victory over the Dodgers, Carlton was the all-time king. Nolan Ryan took over for good the next season, but right to the end, at age 43 in 1988, Carlton's elbow withstood all those sliders. He finished with 329 victories and 4,136 strikeouts, and his 709 starts are the most among left-handers in the history of baseball.

———

For much of Carlton's prime, American Leaguers had their own version of a merciless left-handed slider: Ron Guidry's. Even when hitters knew he would throw it, Guidry could still frustrate the hell out of them.

"What drove me nuts was his slider would start in the strike zone, and by the time I would swing at it, it almost hit my back foot—*and I knew it was coming*," says Paul Molitor, who had 3,319 career hits. "I'd see Graig Nettles take two steps toward the third base line. He got the sign from the shortstop and I'd look and see him move over. So I knew it was a slider, I knew where it was going, and I still swung."

Molitor faced 14 pitchers more often than he faced Guidry. Yet Guidry struck him out more than anyone—20 times in just 74 plate appearances. Molitor is in the Hall of Fame and Guidry is not. But for Guidry's first 10 full seasons in the majors, no pitcher won more games.

From 1977 to 1986, Guidry earned 163 wins for the Yankees. He was third in that span in strikeouts, just behind two Hall of Famers (Nolan Ryan and Carlton) and just above two others (Phil Niekro and Bert Blyleven). Guidry, in his time, was in the pantheon of greats, Carlton in different-colored pinstripes.

"Their sliders would come with such late break and with such force," says Ken Singleton, who faced both in their primes and hit .180 against them. "Other guys would throw sliders and they would hang, you could see them, you could hit them. I was a good breaking-ball hitter, too, but theirs had such velocity, such late break, that by the time you committed, it wasn't where it was supposed to be."

Their careers unfolded differently. Carlton had 57 victories by his twenty-sixth birthday; Guidry had none. He had pitched college ball in his beloved home state of Louisiana and then struggled to assert himself in the majors. After a bad Guidry relief outing in August 1976, a raging George Steinbrenner offered this morale-booster: "You will never be able to pitch in this league."

The remark infuriated Guidry, because Steinbrenner said it in front of the Yankees' general manager, Gabe Paul. But it would have been accurate had Steinbrenner added "unless you develop a slider." Until he did, Guidry really was going nowhere. He knew he had to find a second pitch, and quickly.

"All I knew was, 'OK, look, I'm here, this is where I want to be, I can't waste time,'" Guidry says. "I had to learn everything I needed to in a short time."

Guidry's flat breaking ball fooled no one, and he had abandoned his high school curveball because it did not work with his mechanics. Guidry's left arm looked like a catapult as he delivered a pitch, and he could not throw a curve from that slot.

But frustration with a bullpen role turned into opportunity. Guidry learned pitching philosophy from one Yankee reliever, Dick Tidrow— "pitch 'em low, bust 'em high"—and learned his slider from another, Sparky Lyle, who threw with the same over-the-top technique.

Lyle had come to the majors with the Red Sox. As a farmhand, he became intrigued by the slider when Ted Williams, then a spring training coach, told him it was the best pitch in baseball. Williams told Lyle how a slider spins, but said the rest was up to him.

Lyle would lie in bed with a ball in his hand, wondering how to do it. He was in Double-A, living in a converted garage, and awoke at three one morning with the answer. Like Paul McCartney dreaming the melody for "Yesterday" and bolting to a piano to preserve it, Lyle dashed outside and tried his new slider against the wall of the garage. It was such an easy game to play.

Lyle introduced the pitch in a bullpen session the next day, drilled his catcher in the foot, and knew he had a keeper. The next season was his first of five for the Red Sox until 1972, when they traded him to the Yankees for a utility man named Danny Cater. A half century after the Babe Ruth sale, the Red Sox still hadn't learned. Lyle went on to win a Cy Young Award for the Yankees and teach Guidry his best pitch.

"Don't let it fly at the end," Lyle told him. "Pull it down."

By using the same arm action, Guidry could mimic Lyle while throwing the pitch harder than his mentor. Guidry was just 5 foot 11, 161 pounds—a whippet, Singleton called him—and could not relate to the pain that bigger men like Gibson endured from the slider.

"Nothing happens to the elbow," Guidry says. "I mean, it's almost the same as throwing your fastball. It's all thrown with your wrist; it was not done with your elbow. If you find any pictures, you'll see my elbow and Sparky's elbow, they're basically in a straight movement. Our arms are not bent to be able to throw it."

Guidry would need surgery to remove a bone chip from his elbow in 1989, and he never pitched again. But by then, he had done enough to one day have his number 49 retired by the Yankees. He made four

All-Star teams, set the team's single-game strikeout record (18), and followed Lyle as the AL Cy Young Award winner in 1978.

Guidry went 25–3 that season, beating the Red Sox at Fenway Park in a one-game playoff for the division title. Danny Cater had long since retired.

————

U.S. Route 167 passes through Lafayette, Louisiana, Guidry's hometown, and winds north through the state past Ruston, the hometown of another All-Star pitcher born in 1950: J. R. Richard. His first target was not a catcher's glove.

"How I got started, I used to kill birds and rabbits with rocks," Richard says. "My thing was just to throw, throw, throw every day. I would get a pocket of rocks and just go out to the woods throwing."

Sometimes Richard would tape rags together, or throw tennis balls. But mostly he threw those rocks. He did not play organized baseball until he was 15 years old. He threw four pitches, he said: fast, faster, fastest—and a slider he learned from a pitching manual he found along the side of U.S. 167.

"In the country, sitting on the porch every day, twiddling your thumbs, sometimes you just take off and go for a walk," he says. "Basically just something to do to keep you busy, if you weren't working in the fields. There was divine intervention."

Richard picked up the manual and took it home. He was not much of a reader then, and would travel many more roads before devoting his life to the Bible. At 15, that pitching book was his scripture, its descriptions and illustrations his guiding lights. The slider had been a completely unfamiliar pitch until he found the book. He absorbed its lessons and improvised on his own.

"We had a rock in the country called a coal rock, which was a round rock, and I used to practice a lot with that and see the movement of the rock, see what it was doing," Richard says. "A lot of stuff I learned on my own. The fastball came naturally."

Richard's high school slider had a wider, slower break than the one he featured in the majors. But it still left an indelible impression on those who saw him at Lincoln High in Ruston, where he never lost a game. The Astros made him the second overall pick of the 1969 draft.

"If you ask me who had the best slider I ever saw, it would probably be J. R. Richard," says Pat Gillick, the Hall of Fame executive who scouted for the Astros in the 1960s. "I was down there when we signed him and I thought he had the hardest slider, and the hardest slider to pick up, that I can ever remember."

In 1971 Richard tied a record for strikeouts in a major league debut, with 15 in a complete game victory in San Francisco. Willie Mays struck out three times. It was an early glimmer of overpowering talent, and the start of an exhilarating and tragic career.

Richard took years to gain footing in the majors, then broke through with a run of extraordinary seasons before it all ended, abruptly, at age 30. All of this was true for Sandy Koufax, too, and while everything else was different—their stuff, their throwing hand, their race, their teams' visibility and levels of success—people speak of Richard with the same kind of reverence they do of Koufax.

"Nobody struck me out," says Dusty Baker, but Richard did— 24 times, more than any other pitcher Baker faced in his 19 seasons. "They had him and Nolan, both of them were nasty. But J.R. was the nastiest. He was 6 foot 8, big old hands; the ball looked like a golf ball in his hands. He had a big Afro and he pulled his hat way down, so you couldn't see his eyes, and he was kind of wild. Boy, he was nas-*tee!* And the nastiest part about him is you know it's 60 feet, 6 inches from the mound, right? He was throwing from about 50 feet. You had no time to pick up the ball."

For the entirety of his career, Richard was the tallest pitcher in the major leagues. He could hold eight baseballs in one hand, as he demonstrated for a 1979 *Sporting News* story that called his slider "the best 'out pitch' any man possesses today." Richard threw it nearly as hard as his 98-mile-an-hour fastball, often with better control.

By 1980 he was coming off consecutive seasons of 300 strikeouts, a feat that had been achieved by just three others: Rube Waddell in the 1900s, Koufax in the 1960s, and Nolan Ryan, his new Astros teammate, in the 1970s.

Ryan had just become baseball's first $1 million–per–year player, yet it was Richard who started the All-Star Game for the National

League at Dodger Stadium. He did not allow a homer through the season's first three months. He was holding hitters to a .168 average. And he would be bathed in the California sunlight, with hitters in shadows, when the game began at prime time in the East.

In the top of the first inning, Richard faced Reggie Jackson with a runner on third and two outs. He had just brushed Jackson back with a high fastball, running the count to 3–1. Working from the windup, Richard rocked back and lifted his left knee almost to his chin, turning and whipping his right arm through the air. Jackson swung hard, and the slider fooled him so badly that he lost his balance, his body whirling completely around, his back foot becoming his front.

On the ABC telecast, Keith Jackson said the slider measured 94 miles an hour. "If it was," said Don Drysdale, the Hall of Fame pitcher in the booth, "it was one of the quickest sliders known to mankind."

Jackson bit on another slider, this one in the dirt, striking out to end the inning—and that was as good as it would ever get for J. R. Richard. He would pitch in the majors only one more time.

Richard had complained of a stiff, dead arm in the first half, but his performance showed no decline. On July 14, back in Houston, he struggled to read the catcher's signs, and moved slowly. He left in the fourth inning and was placed on the disabled list.

This was the summer of "Who Shot J.R.?," the cliffhanger from the TV show *Dallas*. The comparison was irresistible—and misguided. Houston's J.R. mystery was not some manufactured drama. Richard's complaints were real. In late July he was diagnosed with a clot in the artery leading to his right arm. Doctors told him it was stable, and cleared him for supervised workouts.

At the Astrodome on July 30, with the team on the road, Richard began to sweat profusely, yet his arm had gone cold. He made a few throws and collapsed to the turf onto his left side. His ears rang. He lost feeling on the left side of his face. A blood clot in his neck had begun to cut off circulation to his brain.

Richard suffered a series of three strokes, underwent surgery, and never made it back to the majors. He battled depression, lost his fortune, and was homeless by the mid-1990s, often sleeping under a bridge at Fifty-ninth and Beechnut Streets in Houston.

"I had some people I knew when I was playing ball and I would go to their house and wash my clothes and eat, maybe spend a night or two, but some of those people had families and I did not feel right just coming in," he says. "So I would go under the bridge, and that's it. Everything became a point of survival. You're trying to survive; you have no transportation, no food, no finances. You ask yourself a lot of times: Where do I go from here? You don't have an answer."

Richard would connect with a local pastor, find work with an asphalt company, and receive help from the Baseball Assistance Team. The details are a bit hazy—Richard says that he lost brain cells because of his stroke, which still affects his reflexes on his left side and, sometimes, his speech. But he walks a lot, loves to fish, and is skilled at cooking baby back ribs. He says life is good.

And he can still remember his days of dominance.

"It was grand, to be in control," Richard says. "I felt like I was the baddest lion in the valley."

———

There was no magic moment in the development of Randy Johnson's slider. He knows that he was seven years old when he started playing baseball, in 1971, the same year Vida Blue rose to stardom for Johnson's hometown Oakland A's. Blue was also left-handed, so maybe he inspired Johnson, but he is not really sure. It was all so long ago, Johnson said in 2015, just before his induction to the Hall of Fame—and anyway, Blue did not throw a slider then.

Johnson could flip knuckle-curves as an amateur, but mostly he needed only a fastball. More important, though, was his ability to consistently harness the power of his 6-foot-10 frame. J. R. Richard led his league in walks three times by his age-28 season, and so did Johnson.

His first season in professional baseball was 1985. Johnson made eight starts for the Jamestown (New York) Expos, going 0–3 with a 5.93 ERA and more walks than strikeouts. He did not have his slider then because he was simply trying to survive, mechanically. Two years later, at Class AA Jacksonville, he pitched 140 innings—with 128 walks and 163 strikeouts. Jim Fanning, a former Expos manager, came to watch him.

"He wanted to know, 'What's wrong, is everything OK?'" Johnson says. "I go, 'Yeah, why?' He said, 'Randy, you could strike out 12 in six innings, but you could walk seven in three.' That's what I was dealing with, the inconsistency. I didn't need to be able to strike out 12, I just needed to be able to throw strikes. I couldn't repeat that, and as a professional athlete, it's frustrating when you know that you can do it, but you can't do it *today*—and you can't figure out why."

Around that time, Johnson learned his slider; he does not know precisely how or when. It was all a blur in the early years, a long slog with the Expos and the Mariners to unlock his potential. With his fastball and slider, Johnson had two luxury sports cars—but what good were they if he kept running them off the side of the road?

By 1992, Johnson had made an All-Star team, thrown a no-hitter, and averaged a strikeout per inning over two full seasons with Seattle. He was also coming off a season of 152 walks, a figure unequaled for more than a decade before, and more than a quarter century since. In his zest to overpower hitters, Johnson would speed up his delivery and overthrow his fastball. Calling for sliders, catcher Scott Bradley found, tended to calm things down. Johnson was a different beast to corral, and it gnawed at him.

"It bothered Randy that every other pitcher would go over scouting reports, and for some reason, because he was big and had control problems, they'd pretty much say, 'OK, Randy, just throw strikes, just get the ball over,'" says Bradley, who caught Johnson in his first three years with Seattle. "I think he was kind of self-conscious. If everybody else was going over scouting reports, he wanted to be a pitcher just like everybody else."

Sometime during the 1992 season, Johnson was scheduled to throw a bullpen session before a game against the Rangers at the Kingdome. The Mariners' bullpen was then located down the right field line, beyond the visitors' dugout, which Johnson passed on his walk there. Rangers pitching coach Tom House had gone to USC, like Johnson, and asked if he wanted to watch Tex throw in the Rangers' bullpen. Tex was Nolan Ryan. Johnson said yes, and it changed the course of his career.

"We've seen some things that you've been doing," House told Johnson, who demonstrated his mechanical flaw for me, many years later, in a boardroom at Chase Field in Phoenix. He rose from a table and faced a wall.

"I was landing *on the heel* of my foot, so I'd be spinning and I would lose my arm angle," he said, unfolding his frame toward another wall on his right. "Now look where that's going—all my momentum's kind of going off to the side, and my arm angle's dropping. You need to be consistent with your arm angle in order to throw a strike.

"But if you land *on the ball* of your foot, now all your momentum's landing on the ball and you'll go straight."

Johnson would demonstrate this lesson dramatically later that season, against Ryan and the Rangers in Arlington, when he struck out 18 in eight innings (and 160 pitches). But the off-season brought despair when Johnson's father, Bud, a police officer, died on Christmas. The change in mechanics, and the clarity of purpose he gained from the death of his father, set Johnson on a new career path.

"I got help mechanically, didn't have to struggle as much, and it was a little bit more fun," Johnson said. "And because it was fun throwing strikes, I was able to dig down deeper and pitch with a chip on my shoulder because of my dad dying. So I used my emotions and pitched with anger."

Everyone feared him. Johnson's physical presence was intimidating enough—the pterodactyl wingspan, the low-three-quarters delivery, the mullet and the mustache and the scowl. Add in a focused rage, and his fastball/slider combination was all but impossible to solve.

"He was gonna bully right-handers in with the fastball and slider, and bully left-handers away with the fastball and slider," says Mark Grace, who was 1-for-10 off Johnson until becoming his teammate in Arizona. "He didn't really need to pitch in. His weapons were so ridiculously good that he didn't really need to change his location. You knew where he was going with it and you still couldn't hit it."

Tony La Russa, who managed many games against Johnson, said there was no better pitch in his era than Johnson's slider, which Tim Raines nicknamed "Mr. Snappy." Gary Sheffield, the most dangerous right-handed pull hitter of his time, could not solve it.

"He throws it out like a slingshot, and it comes down on your back leg," says Sheffield, who hit .209 off Johnson. "By the time the ball gets to the plate, you think it's a strike, but it's bearing down on you.

Because he's so tall, you can't judge if the ball's close to you or not. And once you go forward on a cutting slider, it's hard to hold up."

Johnson won four Cy Young Awards for the Diamondbacks, part of a five-year stretch in which he averaged almost 350 strikeouts per season and beat the Yankees three times in the 2001 World Series, a year in which he struck out a mind-bending 419 hitters, postseason included. He reached 300 victories with the Giants in 2009 and made his final start two months before his forty-sixth birthday. Johnson— a right-handed hitter—lunged at a curveball in the dirt from the Astros' Roy Oswalt. His bat went flying and Johnson grabbed his left shoulder, seized by immense pressure. He struggled to get the ball to the plate in his warm-ups for the top of the fourth, allowing two home runs and a single before fielding a bunt by Oswalt. Johnson threw wildly to first and winced: he had torn his rotator cuff.

Surgery would have ended his season and career. It was not an option.

"I didn't want to go out that way," he says, so he came back, 10 weeks later, as a reliever. His arm was shot but his spirit still burned. "You tell players: 'You don't know when your last game is. You're a superstar now, you're in the limelight, but you don't know what's gonna happen today—and it may not even happen on the field. It could happen on the way to the ballpark, anything. Play the game.'

"It took me forever just to get to the major leagues and feel like I could compete. So when I could, I relished the moment."

John Smoltz, who entered the Hall of Fame with Johnson in 2015, also had a wipeout slider. Two, actually: one before his 2000 Tommy John surgery, and one after. The first he learned from Leo Mazzone, who passed on the principles he learned from Johnny Sain in the Braves' farm system: think four-seam fastball, then turn and pull. When Smoltz's rebuilt elbow made turning the ball too painful, he changed its position in his hand—"I call it, like, putting the ball on a 45-degree angle," he says, "so when you throw it, it's already coming out cut."

After shoulder surgery in 2008, that slider was about all Smoltz had left. Released by the Red Sox the next summer, he got his final job because the Cardinals believed in his slider. Smoltz pitched well for a few starts and made his final appearance as a reliever in the playoffs. His fastball did not have its old extension, those explosive last few feet. But at 42, he could have kept pitching. He trusted his slider that much.

"I could have been that guy that just pitched with sliders," he says. "I could have been the Larry Andersen if I wanted to. That's just not who I am. I did not want to be hanging around if I didn't feel like I had the arsenal. I didn't want to be a specialist."

Smoltz did not need the work. He'd had a Cooperstown career as an elite starter and closer, and that was enough. For pitchers like Andersen, Jeff Nelson, and so many others, life as a slider specialist was a necessity, and a fine way to make a living. Together, Andersen and Nelson pitched for 32 years, almost entirely as setup relievers, and combined to hold right-handers to a .214 average.

They both improved their sliders by closely observing Hall of Famers at work. Andersen was already in his ninth season when he joined the Astros in 1986 and saw the power of Nolan Ryan's high leg kick. Andersen found that the higher he lifted his leg, the harder he threw his pitches. Nelson, who came up with the Mariners, admired Dennis Eckersley, the closer for the division-rival A's. He wore 43 in Eckersley's honor and tried to mimic his arm angle.

"He always threw three-quarters," Nelson says. "Once I started doing it, my fastball moved a lot more, my velocity stayed the same—but my breaking ball was huge."

Nelson also threw hard and had no fear of pitching inside. It was all to set up his sweeping slider, down and away from right-handers, taught to him in the minors by coach Pat Dobson—who had learned his on the 1968 Tigers from Johnny Sain. Nelson used his slider to humble some of his era's Hall of Fame right-handed hitters: Ivan Rodriguez hit .121 off Nelson, Frank Thomas .161, Paul Molitor .188, and Cal Ripken .200.

When Andersen talks to young pitchers, he tells them, "Don't make it break, let it break." He said he kept a loose wrist, put his fingers together, held a four-seam grip off-center, and pulled down on the side—a simple-sounding trick and a good cover for a wily craftsman.

Andersen was a master of disguise off the field, so mischievous

that the Phillies once gave away plastic masks of his face for a summer Halloween promotion. His longevity—17 seasons—was all about
deception and guile. Hitters knew he threw sliders, but which one?

"I was a three-pitch pitcher with three sliders," Andersen says. By
altering the pressure of his fingertips or the position of the ball in his
hand, he could spin out a cutter, a slider, or a slower slider. And when
those pitches abandoned him at the biggest moment of his Phillies
career—two outs, bottom of the tenth, one-run lead, Game 5 of the
1993 NLCS in Atlanta, Ron Gant at the plate—he improvised.

"He has thrown him three straight sliders," said McCarver, in the
CBS booth, "and if there was ever a time to make sure that if a hitter
beats you, he's gonna beat you with your best pitch, this is it."

Catcher Darren Daulton did not want to be beaten with anything,
and another slider, he was sure, would fly a long way off Gant's bat.
Daulton had a different idea: a changeup with a split-finger grip, the
emergency lifeline Andersen had never come close to perfecting.

"He called that and my jaw hit the ground on the mound," Andersen
says. "But why not? I threw it, it started off the plate away and came
down to the outside corner, and Jerry Crawford rung him up."

It was the fiftieth and final save of Andersen's career.

———

The Phillies would win the pennant but lose the World Series to
Toronto. By 2008, their city's streak without a major sports title had
stretched to 25 years. It ended, at last, with a slider from a different
right-handed reliever.

Brad Lidge had converted every save opportunity for the Phillies
in 2008. He had done so largely with his slider, a pitch he had never
even tried to throw until well into his professional career. The pitch
had not always worked: three Octobers before, needing one out to send
the Astros to the World Series, Lidge had thrown a flat slider that the
Cardinals' Albert Pujols obliterated into the Texas night.

But it had been the right pitch, Lidge was sure. The first time he
had ever faced Pujols, he ended the game by striking him out on a
slider, on the front end of a strike-him-out/throw-him-out double play.
It was the very first save of Lidge's career.

Earlier in the playoff at-bat, he had fooled Pujols with a slider, and his plan was to throw an even better one the next time, reasoning that a pitcher's stuff should get nastier the longer an at-bat lasts. But the added pressure undid Lidge: he wanted to make Pujols "swing and miss even worse," and so his legs uncoiled too quickly, his arm lagged behind a bit too long, and the slider hung in the strike zone, begging to be crushed. Pujols obliged.

Now, in Game 5 of the World Series, before another home crowd ready to explode, Lidge faced a similar challenge in Eric Hinske of the Tampa Bay Rays. Hinske was no Pujols, but his best skill was enough to ruin everything: Hinske could demolish a fastball. He had shown this the game before, with a homer to straightaway center off Joe Blanton. The blast was inconsequential—the Phillies won easily, to take a three-games-to-one lead in the series—but Lidge noticed the type of pitch Hinske had hit.

That bit of intelligence underscored what Lidge knew from his own history with Hinske. It was brief—just four pitches in June 2005—but memorable. The first time Lidge had faced Hinske, who then played for Toronto, he struck him out on a slider to end a game, just as he had done with Pujols. But the next night, Hinske, a left-handed hitter, scorched Lidge's first-pitch fastball off the right field wall.

Lidge processed all this as Hinske came up as a pinch hitter. The tying run stood at second base. Lidge did not think about Pujols, but the circumstances were the same: failing to clinch in Game 5 would send the series, and the momentum, back to the other team's park. The Phillies' pitching coach, Rich Dubee, and catcher, Carlos Ruiz, met Lidge on the mound. The infielders also huddled there, with second baseman Chase Utley stationed just behind Lidge's left ear. Utley was in perfect position to shout at Lidge if he chose the wrong strategy.

"If we would have said fastball," Lidge says, "he probably would have been like, 'Wait, wait, wait! Let's think about this.'"

Utley said nothing; Lidge's plan was to not throw another fastball until 2009.

"The last time I threw this guy a fastball, he crushed it off the wall," Lidge told Dubee. "We're going all sliders here."

If Ruiz gave him a sign, Lidge does not remember it. Maybe Ruiz patted the ground—signaling location, not the type of pitch—but

Lidge was committed to the pitch that had made him a star. If Lidge had never learned the slider, and had stuck with the curveball as his off-speed pitch—well, his elbow would probably have blown apart. But even if he had managed to stay healthy while throwing a curve, the best he could have been was a setup reliever, a middle man. Without the slider—without a true swing-and-miss weapon—Lidge never would have found himself on the mound at the end of a World Series.

As a boy in Colorado, he rarely found himself on the mound at all. Lidge did not pitch until his sophomore year at Cherry Creek High School, and then just occasionally, because he had shown a strong arm on throws from the outfield. As a senior, he lost his starting outfield spot to a sophomore, Darnell McDonald, who would go on to play in the majors. Lidge's only chance to play varsity was to pitch.

He took to it instantly, his velocity rising from about 83 miles an hour to 91 with a few weeks of instruction. Lidge also spun a curveball, just to have something slower to drop into the strike zone. But in Colorado, a poorly located curveball can hang in the thin air and be hit a long way. The rush of the fastball made pitching fun.

"Something just felt right with rearing back and throwing the ball as hard as I could," Lidge says. "That felt even better than hitting a home run for me."

Drafted by San Francisco in the 42nd round—teams now stop at 40—Lidge instead chose the University of Notre Dame, down at sea level, where his curveball had a much sharper break. Still, he had only a rudimentary understanding of the pitch, and it was not what got him drafted again. A fastball, by then touching 97, enticed the Astros to choose him in the first round in 1998.

The problem in pro ball was that Lidge needed something else. He was a starting pitcher then, and because starters face more hitters than relievers do, they need more options—at least three, generally. Lidge tried a changeup but never mastered it, and the more he used his curveball, the more his elbow swelled. He threw 74 innings, total, in his first three minor league seasons.

Somehow Lidge had never tried the slider. He had heard it could be more effective than the curveball, because it was thrown harder, but he feared that tinkering with a new pitch would distract him from perfecting his curve. He did not attempt a slider until his third spring training, in Kissimmee, Florida, in 2001, when an Astros coach, Dewey Robinson, altered his arm angle to alleviate the pain.

Lidge was a bit of a short-armer, releasing his pitches closer to his head than most pitchers do. With his hand further away from his head, Lidge's arm felt better but his curveball suffered. He trusted Robinson, whose analytical approach appealed to Lidge and whose status, as the pitching coordinator for the farm system, made him familiar to Lidge and important to his future.

Throwing the slider as if making a comma with his index and middle fingers, Lidge found that the pitch had too much horizontal spin, staying on the same plane as the hitter's bat. He wanted something to make hitters miss, and Robinson encouraged him to stay on top of the ball for a deep, almost vertical break that Lidge could control by altering his finger pressure and the angle of the ball. They played catch for a week before trying the slider on a mound. Lidge spiked the first two in the dirt, but on the third try, *like that*, his muscle memory kicked in. Everything felt right.

"It was, I guess for lack of a better word, miraculous," said Robinson, a former White Sox reliever, in 2010. "I've never, ever had somebody pick it up so quickly and so devastating. It had this huge break, it was an instant swing-and-miss pitch, and it was thrown harder than anybody I've ever taught before or since."

In about 14 months, Lidge was a major leaguer, and on that chilly night in Philadelphia, at the apex of his career, he reached for the pitch Robinson taught him. Hinske dribbled the first slider up the first base line, a weak foul. He checked his swing on the second slider for strike two.

Lidge could make his slider dive away from a left-handed hitter. "A little bit of inside-out," he calls it, and sometimes his frustrated victims would tell Lidge his pitch was not a slider at all, because sliders from righties do not break that way. Further, they would say, the seams on Lidge's slider did not form a red dot. That was because he threw them with topspin—top-to-bottom rotation, not sideways—yet still threw them hard, about 84 miles an hour in 2008.

Lidge stared at Ruiz's target and held the final slider of the season in his right hand. He gripped it as he always did but tilted it a bit to the right, and made sure that his index finger would be the last to leave the ball.

"On the very last one, it was one of those deals where I gripped the ball and I could feel, like, the grip was just right when I came set," Lidge says. "There were two strikes and I was like, 'OK, this is the one.' I could really feel it the second I gripped it in my glove that everything was just where it needed to be, and that last slider was going to be a good one."

Hinske had no chance. The pitch dive-bombed into Ruiz's black Wilson catcher's mitt, far below Hinske's swing. Lidge leaped in the air, his arms outstretched, then fell to his knees and cried: "Oh my God, we just won the World Series!" A teammate, Jayson Werth, would tease him about that reaction, telling Lidge he seemed to be speaking in tongues. Lidge did not mind. His slider was the snapshot of triumph for a generation of Philadelphia sports fans.

———————

For all of these slider masters, though, there is still something missing about the pitch—respect, perhaps, or maybe widespread recognition. The curveball or the slider? When it comes to pitching, this is the Ginger or Mary Ann question.

"The curveball's so sexy, it's such a great pitch," says A. J. Ellis, a veteran catcher. "Broadcasters can recognize it and they really spice it up and describe it well. The whole stadium oohs and aahs. There's nothing better than seeing that guy jelly-legged, like he's drowning, as that curveball finishes its last 10 feet. It's a slow, slow, painful death."

Curvy, glitzy, and glamorous, the pitch is so perfectly Ginger that Tina Louise, the actress who played the stranded starlet on *Gilligan's Island,* actually dated Bo Belinsky, a playboy Angel of the 1960s who threw, yes, a curveball. The one described by Ellis belongs to the Dodgers' Clayton Kershaw, the ace of his era. Yet Kershaw's best pitch is actually the slider, his Mary Ann: alluring in its simplicity, comfortable and familiar but a knockout at the end.

Kershaw did not throw a slider at Highland Park High School in

Dallas. The summer after eleventh grade, he was the No. 4 starter on a junior national team behind future major leaguers Tyson Ross, Brett Anderson, and Shawn Tolleson. As a senior, he was the best high school pitcher in the country: undefeated with a 0.77 ERA and 139 strikeouts in 64 innings. The dominance foretold his success in the majors, after he had added the slider.

"His curveball *looks* the best, because everybody sees it on a GIF or on TV, that big break, guys turn the other way," says Anderson, his Dodger teammate in 2015, when Kershaw became the first pitcher in 13 years to strike out 300 hitters in a season. "But as far as hitter in, hitter out, the slider's his best pitch, because it looks so much like his fastball and he can throw it for strikes or he can get them to chase. The curveball is so big and there's so much break and it's so nasty that guys just take it automatically. It's tough to throw that pitch for a strike because there's so much movement."

That was Kershaw's problem in his last high school start before the 2006 draft. Without command of his curveball, he walked four hitters and gave up a home run. His failure was the Dodgers' gain, though, because six teams passed on Kershaw before the Dodgers grabbed him. Within two years, at age 20, he was pitching at Dodger Stadium. He struck out three in his first inning and started Game 1 of the NLCS the next fall.

Yet Kershaw's ascent was not as direct, or as easy, as those facts make it seem. Without the slider, it would not have happened.

"You adapt to survive, and that's basically what I was doing," Kershaw says. "I was kind of just putting along being mediocre, so I wanted to try to figure something out."

Kershaw? Mediocre?

"Yeah, I was," he insists. "Check the numbers. Check '08. Check the first half of '09."

In 22 games in 2008, Kershaw's ERA was 4.26. It was 4.34 by the end of May 2009, when the Dodgers played a four-game series at Wrigley Field. Four times already, Kershaw had lasted just five innings and thrown at least 97 pitches. Two other starts were headed that way before he was pulled in the fifth.

Kershaw was surviving, barely, but not adapting. He would snap off that picturesque curveball, hitters would stare at it for a ball, and Kershaw would fall behind.

"Eventually it got to the point where he was a one-pitch pitcher," Ellis says. "He was throwing a lot of heaters. Even though his fastball was elite, as it is today, guys are still able to hit a major league fastball, especially when they know it's all you can throw for a strike. And even if they weren't able to put it in play and hit it hard, they were able to foul it off because there were no speed changes, nothing that was throwing their timing off. They were on time for the fastball, so his pitch counts were getting out of control. It got to the point where a demotion to go work on some things—probably a changeup—was really strongly considered."

The slider saved him. Mike Borzello, a Dodgers coach in 2009, suggested Kershaw throw it while playing catch. Pitching coach Rick Honeycutt showed Kershaw a grip. Ellis, up for the weekend as an emergency third catcher, squatted behind the plate as Kershaw tried it out in the bullpen.

Ellis had caught Kershaw in the minors, and tried to nurse him through an awkward experiment with a changeup. This was different. The slider hurtled toward the plate on the same plane as the fastball for 58 feet—and then it bottomed out, below the hands, below the barrel. This is *usable*, Ellis thought, finally something besides a fastball that Kershaw could throw when behind in the count.

Kershaw had never tried the pitch before. He had never needed to. But just like that, he had it down.

"It's really tough to explain, because it's such a feel," he says. "You know when you throw it right. It's the same with any pitch. When it comes off your fingers the right way, you know it's the way it's supposed to. And when it doesn't, it feels that way instantly. With the slider, I kind of felt that right away. I felt when I did it right, and I felt when I didn't.

"Like the changeup, I still don't have that feel. It's still hard for me to figure that out, and I think it's just because it's such a feel pitch. The slider, it's more grip it and rip it."

Kershaw gripped it and ripped it and by 2011 had begun streaks unprecedented in major league history: four seasons in a row as the major leagues' ERA leader, and five in the top 3 in Cy Young voting.

He took home three of those awards, plus an MVP trophy. He earned a $215 million contract and built an orphanage in Zambia.

None of it would have been possible without the best pitch of baseball's best pitcher, the difference-maker for Gibson and Carlton and so many more, the spinner that changed the game.

THE
FASTBALL

Velo Is King

Every pitch is a decision. That is the beauty and the burden of the pitcher. Think there's downtime in baseball? Tell it to the man on the mound, all alone on that dirt bull's-eye. The catcher thinks along with him, back behind the plate, but the pitcher rules the game. Nothing happens until he answers these questions: Which pitch should I throw, where should I throw it, and why? It is an awesome responsibility.

"It's about being in control—who's in control of the game?" says Jamie Moyer, one of the nicest people you'll ever meet, whose competitive fire kept him pitching until the year he turned 50. "I don't want to sound brash or rude, but if they came to me at 3:00 and said, 'OK, tonight we're starting at 7:06,' I'd say, 'We'll start it when I'm ready to throw the first pitch.'"

With each pitch thereafter, the calibration changes—sometimes slightly, like the position of the sun, and sometimes seismically, like an earthquake. But it always comes down to the pitcher's internal computer, and his default setting is the four-seam fastball, thrown with the index and middle fingers separated slightly across the widest gap between the seams. As the backspinning ball hurtles through the air, four seams cycle through each revolution. It is the easiest pitch to steer, and gives the hitter the least time to react. Every pitcher, no matter what else he throws, understands this rule:

The best pitch in baseball is a well-located fastball.

"For sure it is, because if you can't do that then you can't use your other stuff, because you use that other stuff based on your fastballs," Madison Bumgarner says. "I don't throw a two-seamer. I feel like my curveball and slider/cutter—whatever you want to call it—are pretty close; some days one's better than the other. But the fastball's always got to be number one."

That is where Bumgarner turned in Game 7 of the 2014 World Series, when faced with a decision few others had ever confronted. Just six pitchers before and one since—the Cubs' Mike Montgomery, in 2016—had been in position for a Golden Pitch, a term used by the Society for American Baseball Research for a pitch that could win or lose the championship for either team. By definition, this spot arises only in Game 7 of the World Series, in the bottom of the ninth inning or later, with the visitors leading and at least one runner on base. Those precious pitches, loaded with cork, yarn, and possibility, can make the ballpark go silent or crazy.

For Bumgarner, the steely left-handed ace of the San Francisco Giants, there was no doubting his weapon of choice. There never is. His mind-set, and a deceptive delivery that offers hitters no basis for comparison, gives Bumgarner an extraordinary edge.

"The thing that's different about him compared to a lot of guys is there's conviction behind every fastball he throws," says A. J. Ellis, who faced Bumgarner more than any other pitcher across his first 10 years in the majors. "It might not go to the area he wants it to go all the time, but it comes with aggression, and it comes with conviction."

Bumgarner entered Game 7 in Kansas City in the fifth inning with a 3–2 lead. He had shut out the Royals in Game 5 and also beaten them in the opener, when he worked seven innings in a blowout and gave up just a solo home run. Here, Bumgarner retired 14 in a row after a leadoff single. Then the earth shook.

With two outs in the ninth, Alex Gordon looped a sinking liner to center field. It fell for a single, skipped past one outfielder, and squirted away from another. Gordon huffed his way around second, but left fielder Juan Perez, a former high school pitcher, fired a strong one-hop throw to shortstop Brandon Crawford. The third base coach, Mike Jirschele, wisely held Gordon at third, 90 feet from tying Game 7. The next hitter could win it with one swing.

It was Salvador Perez. It had to be. Bumgarner had pitched shutout ball in the 2010 World Series against the Texas Rangers, and again two years later against the Detroit Tigers. In his three games against the Royals, he had allowed only that solo homer—to Perez. If he struck again, Perez would ruin everything.

———

Fifty-two years before, in another Game 7 involving the Giants, Ralph Terry had faced this precise problem. For Terry, a Yankees right-hander, the predicament was even more acute. Just two years earlier, in 1960, he had become the first pitcher ever to allow a home run to end the World Series, by the Pirates' Bill Mazeroski in Game 7. Terry had warmed up five times that day on a steep bullpen mound down the left field line at Forbes Field. He was worn out when he finally got into the game, and could not adjust to the flatter mound on the field. His foot came down early, everything was up, and Mazeroski smashed a high, cutting fastball over the left field wall.

In 1962, though, Terry had seized Game 7 from the start. Like Bumgarner, he had thrown nine innings to win Game 5, but his team had lost Game 6 to force a decisive finale. Because of rainouts, Terry started on five days' rest for Game 7, and carried a 1–0 lead into the bottom of the ninth at Candlestick Park. After a leadoff single and two strikeouts, Willie Mays doubled to right.

Like Juan Perez, Roger Maris hit the cutoff man to keep the tying run at third. And like Salvador Perez, the next batter had already homered in the World Series off the pitcher he would face with Game 7 in the balance. It was Willie McCovey, and even with a base open, Terry told manager Ralph Houk that he wanted to pitch to him.

An intentional walk to McCovey would have loaded the bases for Orlando Cepeda, another future Hall of Famer Terry feared even more. He also knew that this strategy had backfired for the Dodgers in the playoff to decide the NL pennant; after an intentional walk had loaded the bases in the ninth inning, Stan Williams walked in the go-ahead run. With an NL umpire behind the plate for Game 7, Terry guessed, he would have little margin for error against Cepeda.

With so many factors to consider, Terry says his mind did not flash back to 1960, and the possibility that he might—*again!*—give up a homer to end Game 7. He had house and car payments back in New York, with a wife, one child, and a baby on the way. That was pressure enough.

"I thought about the money difference," Terry says. "The winners got $12,000 and the losers got $8,000. I was making about $40,000. We needed the money in those days."

Terry did think about the homer McCovey had pulled off him at Candlestick in Game 2. He had thrown a cut fastball, inside but low enough for McCovey to extend his long arms. Terry resolved to avoid that spot this time.

"I wanted it high, in here," Terry says, shaking his hand near the chest of his pinstriped jersey on Old-Timers' Day at Yankee Stadium in 2016. Terry noticed his second baseman, Bobby Richardson, shading McCovey to his left—too far, Terry thought, but he knew better than to challenge his infielders' instincts. "They know how your ball's coming out."

McCovey hit a line drive, right to the spot Richardson was standing.

"I saw some film later on, from behind," Terry says. "I came in, he leaned back and got on it with his hands and put a lot of topspin on it—*whack!* He really hit it hard, but I thought, 'I got a man over there somewhere,' and boy, it was right at him. It wasn't like he made a sensational play.

"It was a fastball—crowded him," Terry says, smiling. "And I said, 'Thanks, Abner Doubleday, for inventing the game with a second baseman.'"

———

The San Francisco Giants never did win a World Series until Bumgarner came around. By 2014, they stood to capture their third in five seasons, if only he could solve Salvador Perez. Bumgarner, too, remembered the homer from earlier in the World Series, but he did not change his plan of attack: fastballs with conviction.

While backing up the plate on Gordon's hit, Bumgarner and catcher Buster Posey talked briefly about Perez. He is naturally aggressive, a tendency that would only be heightened with a chance to hit a walk-off homer in Game 7 of the World Series. They could use that impulse against him.

"Perez is a good fastball hitter, but Bum is so good at elevating the ball when he wants to," Posey says. "We both felt confident that in that situation, we were going to try to play off of Perez's anxiousness. That's somewhat instinctual, to know the type of hitter and say we probably can expand here. Could he have still got a hit? Sure. But we felt like that was the best way to attack him. The fastball's a high-percentage pitch, probably the lowest risk, because you figure his command is gonna be the best as well."

Thirty regular starters threw harder in 2014 than Bumgarner, whose average fastball was 92.1 miles an hour. But his superior confidence in the pitch was deeply ingrained; he threw nothing else at South Caldwell High School in Hudson, North Carolina, but was still drafted tenth overall by the Giants, at age 17. With Gordon on third in Game 7, no other pitch made sense.

"It's a little bit of a pride thing," Bumgarner explains. "I'm not like all these young guys that come up here throwing 100, but I like my fastball and I like to throw it. So a little bit of that, and we knew he was going to be aggressive and chase. So if I could throw it up there, we had a good feeling about it.

"We could have thrown a curveball and bounced it in front of the plate, and I think we might've gotten him on that, too, but then you're putting a little bit more on Buster. I trust Buster, he blocks almost all of them for me, but you never know. What if it hits the corner of the plate and bounces over his head or something stupid like that? That's not the way that you want to blow the lead right there.

"Could have thrown him the cutter or whatever, but you're taking a chance on leaving something over the plate and hanging it, and then bouncing it again. So it was the easy decision for us."

Bumgarner's first pitch sailed up and away, letter-high at 92 mph, and Perez swung through it for a strike. For the second pitch, Bumgarner tried an even higher fastball, over the plate but even with Perez's neck. Perez didn't bite on that, but Bumgarner went up again with his third pitch, about shoulder-high. Perez took the bait for another swinging strike.

One more strike could end it now, and Bumgarner poked his left index finger to his left nostril, blowing a snot rocket to the ground. This seemed almost too easy. Would Perez be so antsy that he'd go for a pitch over the plate, but up by his helmet? No. He did swing at the fifth pitch, armpit-high, and fouled it back.

Two balls, two strikes, five fastballs in a row, all at 92 mph. The plate umpire, Jeff Nelson, pointed at Bumgarner. Posey balled his right hand into a fist between his legs, then pounded his glove and bent the top of the pocket. He sprang into a half-crouch as Bumgarner delivered his 291st pitch of the World Series, spreading his arms wide and stepping toward first in his smooth, unmistakable style. Posey held his target up around Perez's chest—and Bumgarner missed his spot.

The pitch split the plate, above the belt but not as high as Bumgarner had wanted it. The pitch Perez had hit for a homer, in Game 1, was low enough to be a called strike, Bumgarner thought. This pitch, he says, was just high enough to be a ball. "It wasn't a whole lot different," he conceded, but that little bit meant everything.

Bumgarner found one extra mile per hour for this pitch, at 93 mph, but Perez was still too eager. He popped it up, in foul ground, to third baseman Pablo Sandoval. Posey flung his glove and mask to the sky and embraced Bumgarner as teammates swarmed from all directions. Champions, again.

"I think I got too excited," Perez said the next spring. "That's why I swing at a lot of pitches up. But now I got experience. I know what happened."

A year later, Perez would follow Bumgarner as the World Series MVP, hitting .364 in the Royals' triumph over the Mets. By then, he had also had his rematch with Bumgarner, again with Posey catching, at the 2015 All-Star Game in Cincinnati. This time Bumgarner used all his pitches and struck out Perez on a curveball. Funny thing, though—the third strike skipped past Posey, and Perez reached first base safely.

Had that happened in the World Series, Gordon would have scored to tie the game. Instead, when it had mattered most, when the stakes were the highest they could possibly be, Bumgarner had chosen the fastball. He had chosen wisely.

Pitching has always been a delicate balance of velocity and command. More of one can mean less of the other. In the early days, the pitcher was merely a tool for initiating action, a delivery device to place the ball in a specific spot. Throwing too hard would impede that goal if pitchers were wild, overpowering, or both.

An 1864 article in the *New York Clipper*—cited by Peter Morris in *A Game of Inches,* a treasure of research from 2006—reminds umpires that the pitcher cannot lift his foot until the ball leaves his hand. The desired result, the story said, was less speed, greater accuracy, "and the transfer of the interest of a match from the pitchers to the batsmen and outerfielders."

Pitching then looked almost nothing like pitching now. In 1884, the National League finally allowed overhand pitching, from a six-foot-by-six-foot square, 50 feet from the plate. Try to imagine Randy Johnson pitching like that. He can't.

"You think you know something, and you go to the Hall of Fame and you see how the game started off," Johnson said, after a Cooperstown tour in 2015. "There was no pitcher's mound there. There was a box— *there was a box!*—and you could move from one side of the box to the other side of the box. I don't remember how big, but you could run in this box. Not that you're gonna run far, because it's a small box."

That is the origin of the term "back through the box," to describe a hitter lashing a ball straight over the pitcher's mound. Tony Mullane, a big winner for the Reds in the nineteenth century, was known as "The Apollo of the Box." The king of the box, in those days, was Old Hoss Radbourn, who was 59–12 with a 1.38 ERA in 1884. He logged nearly 700 of the 1,000 or so innings pitched by his Providence Grays.

"Radbourn was said to stand in the right-hand rear corner, turn his back on the batter similar to the way Luis Tiant did it in the 1970s, and then take a hop, skip and deliver his pitch from the left side of the box," wrote Craig R. Wright and Tom House in *The Diamond Appraised.* "His motion was much like a modern shot-putter's turn."

A Giants pitcher of the 1890s, Amos Rusie of Mooresville, Indiana, threw so hard that they changed the game to account for him. Rusie—known as the Hoosier Thunderbolt—led the league in strikeouts and walks by such a wide margin that a pitcher's rubber, located 60 feet, 6 inches from the plate, replaced the box for good in 1893. Strikeouts fell by 44 percent that season.

By then, a new pitching star had just begun to emerge: Denton True Young, known as Cy for a wheeling, cyclone-like delivery in which he hid the ball from the hitter. Big for his time—6 foot 2, 210 pounds—he set nearly every longevity record with a disciplined lifestyle forged on a farm in Ohio as a boy. As he wrote in *Sporting Life,* in 1908: "A man who is not willing to work from dewy morn until weary eve should not think about becoming a pitcher."

That quote is not inscribed on his annual award for pitching excellence, but maybe it should be. In any case, while Young did not specialize in strikeouts—he ranks first in innings pitched but twenty-first in strikeouts—he understood which pitch was most important.

"My favorite pitch," he said, "was a whistler right under the chin."

Young led the AL in strikeouts in 1901, the league's first season. Then Rube Waddell took over, joining the A's the next June. For the rest of the decade, no one came close to Waddell in strikeouts, or eccentricities. He was known for leaving the dugout during games to chase fire trucks passing by the ballpark. Sam Crawford, a hitting star of the time, told Lawrence Ritter in *The Glory of Their Times* that Waddell threw so hard, he would have to pour ice water over his arm before games. "I've got so much speed, I'll burn up the catcher's glove if I don't let up a bit," Waddell would say.

Fastballs inspire that kind of colorful imagery. As he built his legend in the Negro Leagues, in the 1920s and '30s, Satchel Paige mesmerized hitters with his "trouble ball," a general term for his two fastballs—a "bee ball" that stayed on a level plane and a "jump ball" he said rose as much as six inches. Paige was such a control artist, he was said to warm up with a stick of chewing gum for a plate; he practiced hitting the corners of the wrapper. It wasn't the only home plate substitute he could find at a drugstore.

In 1971, when Paige was elected to the Hall of Fame, he recalled his tryout for Bill Veeck with the Indians in 1948: "He asked me to throw at a cigarette as a plate, and I threw four out of five over it."

Other Negro League stars, like Smokey Joe Williams and Bullet Joe Rogan, had fastballs baked into their nicknames. (Williams inflicted so much soreness on his poor catchers' palms that he needed two catchers per game.) In scouting reports for the Hall of Fame, Buck O'Neil compared Williams to Walter Johnson and Rogan to Bob Feller. Johnson was known as the Big Train, and Feller as Rapid Robert.

From 1902 to 1948, Waddell, Johnson, Lefty Grove, and Feller took turns as the AL strikeout king, combining for 32 strikeout titles. (Dazzy Vance won seven in a row in the NL, for Brooklyn in the 1920s.) Grove did it in each of his first seven seasons with the A's, starting in 1925, and collected nine league ERA crowns. He built his speed by throwing rocks as a boy in Maryland, and a humorist of the time, Arthur "Bugs" Baer, said Grove could throw a lamb chop past a wolf.

"Did you ever see speed like that in a human arm?" marveled Connie Mack, owner and manager of the A's, in spring training of 1930. "Why, it gives you a sore arm to watch him, doesn't it?"

We'll never really know who was fastest, because it took until 1974 for radar guns to reliably measure velocity; Danny Litwhiler, a former major league outfielder, popularized their use while coaching at Michigan State. Before then, the best pitchers could do was engage in primitive speed contests; Feller threw fastballs alongside a moving motorcycle and tested himself on photoelectric Army devices. He claimed Johnson was fastest, anyway.

"Johnson was so great," Feller wrote in his memoir, "that he almost belongs in his own Hall of Fame."

————————

Let's face it: you'll never be Walter Johnson, but you do have a fastball. Pick up a baseball, throw it, and there it is. It is probably very slow, relative to major leaguers' fastballs, but whatever else you throw, this pitch will be your fastest and straightest. Typically, the catcher signals for it with the index finger, the ol' number one. If it's especially fast, it's a heater, but with apologies to Bruce Springsteen, it's never a "speedball"—and a hitter who swings and misses it doesn't really look like a fool, boy. When a hitter guesses wrong and swings hard at a puttering off-speed pitch, *then* he looks like a fool. If he can't catch up to a fastball, he's simply lost the game's most primitive one-on-one battle.

"George Brett hit some of the shots heard 'round the world off me," Goose Gossage says. "But, man, that was the greatest part of what I did, challenging those great hitters when they *know* it's gonna be the fuckin' fastball!"

Gossage remains as brash as his old fastball, slinging opinions with such unsparing force that the Yankees, in 2018, stopped inviting him to spring training. Win enough macho duels, though, and you also might develop a personality to match.

"There's no better feeling as a pitcher than to just tell the guy what's coming—'Here, fastball, get in the box, let's go,' and they still couldn't hit it," says Frank Tanana, the major league strikeout leader in 1975. "You can be loud when you have that kind of stuff, and have the immaturity to go with it."

By the end of his career, when he teased hitters with curveballs and changeups, Tanana was a changed man, a devout Christian with a gentle nature off the mound. (He would sign autographs with the inscription "Jesus Loves You!") But Tanana was tough enough to grind out 616 career starts, most without great stuff. Only 17 pitchers have ever started more games, mostly Hall of Famers but also a few like him: Tommy John, Jim Kaat, and Jamie Moyer.

No pitcher has ever allowed more homers than Moyer, and John once gave up 287 hits in a season while striking out only 65 (think about that). Kaat led his league in hits allowed three seasons in a row, but he also won 60 games in that stretch, including one in the World Series. All three pitched past their forty-fourth birthdays, sacrificing a few miles per hour for a lot of durability.

"Sometimes a dad'll come up to me and say, 'Hey, my son's a junior in high school and they've got him clocked at 91!'" Kaat says. "And I'll say, 'Really? Teach him how to pitch at 86.'"

Kaat wishes teams would take their hard-throwing prospects and tell them to work three innings without topping 90 miles an hour. (Think of the movie *Speed,* but on a mound.) Then, he believes, they would understand the art of their craft and learn to keep their best fastballs in reserve for critical moments, giving hitters a new and startling look. But times have changed.

"Somebody asked me, 'How many times in your career do you think you threw the ball as hard as you could throw it?' And I said zero," Kaat says, explaining that a showoff might get hurt and lose his spot on the staff. "We wanted to throw for rhythm and control and condition our arm that way."

There have always been exceptions, of course, pitchers who threw their hardest at all times. Nolan Ryan, the career leader in strikeouts and walks, exerted himself like a short reliever yet somehow threw more innings than anyone born after 1887 except Phil Niekro, a knuckleballer.

"I never had the ability to back off my fastball," Ryan says. "I always pitched maximum effort."

Ryan had a paper route as a teenager, rolling *The Houston Post* by hand every morning, which helped build his shoulder muscles. Then again, he flung the papers from the car window with his left arm, and we've never seen an outbreak of paperboys becoming strikeout kings. Ryan knew he was an outlier, crediting his ability to throw hard to God, and a perfect alignment of genetics and will. He actually expected Steve Carlton to wind up with the career strikeout record, guessing that Carlton would pitch longer because he was left-handed and famous for conditioning.

Before the 1980 season, when he left the Angels for Houston as a free agent, Ryan said he asked for only a three-year contract, to take him through age 35. He actually got a four-year, $4.5 million deal, making him the first player ever paid $1 million per season. But he had no idea he would keep pumping fastballs for well more than a decade.

"Power pitchers faded away once they got in their early thirties," he says, "and I had no reason to think I was going to be any different."

Ryan's elbow finally gave out at the Seattle Kingdome on September 22, 1993. Pitching for the Rangers, he served up a grand slam to Dann Howitt (the last of the five homers in Howitt's short career), and then departed before he could finish his last batter, Dave Magadan.

"I was like, 'Something's not right,'" Magadan says. "He was barely getting the ball to the plate. Howitt hit the grand slam, then I came up and it went ball 1, ball 2. He threw a strike, and I think at that point he walked off the mound. The trainer didn't even go out there. I was like, 'Oh, we might not ever see him again.' It was sad."

It was sad because there may never be another pitcher like Ryan, though today's all-out, all-the-time generation will try. More common, and more effective, was the artistic approach of Greg Maddux. In the rare times Maddux fell behind in the count, hitters knew they might get a fastball. But it was not the same fastball every time.

"It may be only a B.P. fastball," Tony Gwynn once wrote in a scouting report for ESPN.com. "He will take something off the pitch, make the hitter get out in front and force him to hit the ball weakly."

While this was not especially effective against Gwynn, who hit .415 off Maddux, it highlights the value in changing speeds and giving up power for command. In the 1960s and '70s, Catfish Hunter was a master of this for the A's and Yankees. Early in games, Hunter would nip around the edges of the plate to establish the umpire's strike zone. Then he would work the corners with precision, changing speeds on the fastball to bait hitters into weak contact. Hunter did not throw hard, but few have ever used a fastball better.

"He did not have any exceptional pitch," says Dave Duncan, who caught him with the A's. "He was exceptional because he could hit a gnat in the ass."

To Duncan, the pitcher most like Hunter was Tom Seaver, whom he coached near the end of Seaver's career with the Chicago White Sox. Jim Evans, an AL umpire then, tells a story that illustrates the way Seaver thought.

"I was working the plate in Detroit in 1985," Evans says. "We stayed at the Hyatt Regency in Dearborn; we generally didn't stay where the clubs stayed, but for some reason the White Sox were there. So I was sitting at the bar after the game, and Seaver tapped me on the shoulder: 'Hey, nice job back there tonight, thank you. I just think you missed one pitch.'"

It was a 1–1 fastball to Kirk Gibson in the middle innings, Seaver explained, and Evans had called it a strike. Nothing remarkable, Evans thought. So why, hours later, was it on Seaver's mind?

"I don't want you to call that pitch a strike," Seaver said, as Evans recalls it. "That was a mistake. I got it up too high, like a ball or two above the waist, and I don't want any batter to get used to swinging at that pitch. My fastball is still my best pitch, my bread-and-butter, but if I keep throwing that one up there, they're gonna kill me. I can't get away with that pitch, and if the umpire's calling it a strike, they're gonna start swinging at it and I'll get in trouble."

Command is not everything, but it matters more than sheer speed. The longtime pitching coach Don Cooper, who helped guide the White Sox to the 2005 title, ranks his priorities in this order: location, movement, velocity. A star pupil, Mark Buehrle, made more than 30 starts for 15 years in a row by following those principles. His fastball averaged about 86 mph.

"We're trying to turn guys into professional glove-hitters, because no matter what style you are, you still have to do that," Cooper says. "If you can do that with 95 or 96, even better. But the common denominator is hitting the glove."

The pitcher who tries too hard to reach back for more velocity often works against his interests. The veteran starter Dan Straily says he throws some of his best fastballs to pitchers, who pose such little threat that he simplifies his mechanics and hits his spot easily. When a power hitter comes up, though, pitchers often try to overdo it. With the Marlins in 2017, Straily said, he saw too many pitchers foolishly try to blow heat past Giancarlo Stanton.

"We faced a guy the other day: 90, 91, 90, 91, all on the corners," Straily said that summer. "Giancarlo steps in the box and it's 95, 96—but everything's right down the middle."

It is possible to be Picasso with a machine gun, as reliever Dan Plesac colorfully described Curt Schilling's fastball command to writer Jayson Stark. But such artistry and power form a rare combination indeed; nobody born between 1857 and 1985 can top Schilling's career strikeout-to-walk ratio of 4.38-to-1.

––––––––––

The Kansas City Royals visited Yankee Stadium in early May 2016. The last time they had been to New York, the previous November, they celebrated a championship at Citi Field. Chris Young had beaten the Mets in relief in the World Series opener, and pitched well in his Game 4 start in Queens. He was almost 37, but the Royals eagerly re-signed him for two years and about $12 million.

Young was something of an anomaly. A former Princeton center, he stands 6 foot 10 but threw his fastball below 90 miles an hour. Yet Young was still hard to hit, with a fastball that stayed true through the strike zone much longer than most pitchers' did. In the lingo of the game, Young had a sneaky fastball, good finish. His pitches had *life*—that final, forceful burst that both fools and overwhelms a hitter.

"Life, to me, is almost a mystical concept," says Alan Jaeger, a highly regarded pitching trainer in Southern California, speaking unironically. "Some people seem to have more life than others and they might be throwing the same velocity."

This night, though, Young's pitches were dead on arrival. The Yankees battered him for five home runs, and he was gone by the third inning. Young had not lost his ability to throw at his peak velocity. But his ERA was 6.68, and nothing was working. He didn't know it then, but Young would not win another start for the rest of his career.

"Last year I could throw an 86-mile-an-hour fastball with life and miss my spot, and the guy would swing and miss or foul it off," he said that night. "Now I throw it 89 without life, and they hit it in the stands. That's the difference. It's always been more about life than velocity. You can see it in their swings."

Life has long been used to differentiate fastballs—a tiebreaker, of sorts, for some of the greats. Luke Sewell, a catcher from 1921 to 1942, used it to distinguish Bob Feller from Lefty Grove.

"Grove's fast one actually was past the batter and into the catcher's mitt quicker than Bobby's," he said. "Feller's fast one, though, had more life to it."

Every hitter in the majors can handle velocity. Pitchers always have the advantage, on a pitch-by-pitch basis, because batters get three strikes and nobody hits .500. But give a hitter enough looks at a straight fastball, and he'll drive it somewhere hard. Gary Sheffield speaks for his brethren when he says, "If you ask any hitter, they would rather face a guy throwing 98 than a guy throwing 92 with filth."

Filth means anything deceptive—not just breaking balls, but

fastballs that move differently than most. With modern analytics, we know which pitchers are more likely to survive with high fastballs. We know that while J. A. Happ and Koji Uehara do not throw hard, their fastballs spin so much that they don't drop at the same rate as most pitchers' fastballs.

To hitters who see thousands and thousands of fastballs fall a certain way, a pitch with an unexpected trajectory can be baffling. You might yell at your TV when your favorite hitter swings through a high, slow fastball. But there's more in play than it seems.

"When they say 'He's got that good, riding fastball,' I just think it doesn't fall off," Jason Giambi says. "With most guys, gravity will kind of take hold of it. Some guys just get those extra rotations, whether it stays on their fingers a little bit longer, or they've got a release point so they get that true plane—it's what you want. I mean, no pitcher wants that ball to fall into the strike zone. If you can keep it riding high, kind of above that belt area, you're gonna get a lot of strikeouts."

You'll also get plenty of balls a hitter just misses. When a pitch lacks life, Mike Mussina says, it seems to just barely make it to the catcher, no matter how fast it might be. But when it's lively, it seems capable of carrying straight through the catcher, the umpire, and the backstop. Hitters can't do much with it, even when they connect.

"Something caused that guy to miss that ball by a sixteenth of an inch," Mussina says, "so it's a fly ball to center instead of a ball off the wall or a homer."

Don Sutton—the Mussina of his era—threw a level-plane fastball that Tim McCarver found impossible to hit squarely; he faced him 70 times, with two extra-base hits and countless pop outs. Jim Palmer, a contemporary, conceded that while fastballs might not rise, some simply do not sink. He adds, assuredly, "I could make the ball go up. Backspin."

For most of baseball history, the rising fastball was taken as fact. Bob Shaw, who pitched 11 years in the majors and beat Sandy Koufax in the 1959 World Series, wrote a pitching manual in 1972 that described how to throw a four-seam fastball. The pitch is easier to control, he writes, and the seams blend together visually, to make the ball look smaller.

"If you can apply enough spin and velocity while gripping the ball across the seams, you can overcome the downward force of gravity and make the ball rise," Shaw asserts. He adds, with no equivocation, that "throwing across the seams produces vertical or upward movement."

This is a fairly consistent theme for fastball pitchers, especially of Shaw's generation and earlier. Don't tell Bob Gibson a fastball can't rise.

"Ah, those are scientists," he says. "They also used to say it didn't break, too. Oh yeah, it goes up. They never had a bat."

In *Fastball,* an enchanting 2016 documentary directed by Jonathan Hock, Hank Aaron, Ernie Banks, and Eddie Murray insist the fastball can rise. In Jane Leavy's definitive Sandy Koufax biography, from 2002, Jim Bunning sneers at the theory that the rise on Koufax's fastball was an optical illusion: "Physics is full of shit," he says. Leavy also quotes Frank Robinson's advice for his Baltimore teammates before facing Koufax in the 1966 World Series: "If it starts at the belt, take it because it's going to choke you."

Pat Gillick, the Hall of Fame executive, swears that a fastball can rise. As a minor league pitcher for the Orioles in the early 1960s, he was teammates with Steve Dalkowski, the almost mythical left-hander who fanned 1,324 hitters (and walked nearly as many) in 970 minor league innings. Dalkowski never reached the majors, but Gillick—who became one of most astute scouting minds in baseball history—can still picture his hopping fastball. He says only one catcher, Cal Ripken Sr., could handle it.

"What was funny about him, he wasn't wild in and out, he was wild up and down," Gillick says. "You could tell Steve, 'Look, I want you to throw a pitch 58 feet,' and he would attempt to throw a pitch 58 feet and it would be over the catcher's head. The ball rose so much between the pitcher's mound and home plate."

It literally rose?

"Oh yeah, absolutely," Gillick insists. "Absolutely. Well, you know, when you hit a home run, you put backspin on the ball and the ball carries out of the ballpark. And he had so much spin on it, so much rotation on the ball, the ball just kept carrying and kept rising."

Don't take Gillick's word for it? How about the man who threw more innings and won more games than any lefty in history? In *The Head Game,* Warren Spahn tells Roger Kahn, "If you throw enough and put enough backspin on the pitch, you get a fastball that goes against gravity." Spahn compared a fastball's flight to an airplane lifting off. "If a physicist wants to argue," he concludes, "let's just say backspin levels off the baseball."

An actual physicist, Robert K. Adair, addressed the topic in his book, *The Physics of Baseball*, taking the wise approach of respecting the perspective of the men on the field while explaining what they actually see. Like the curveball, he explains, the hopping fastball makes a smooth arc—but gets half of its hop in the final 15 feet of its journey. By then, the hitter has begun his swing and cannot adjust.

"Such a hopping fastball, thrown with a lot of backspin, does not 'rise' in the sense that it increases its height above the ground as it passes the batter, but it does rise with respect to the trajectory it would have without the spin. . . . If the batter bases his swing on the trajectory of the ball with the lesser spin but the pitcher has put extra spin on the ball, he will complain that the ball 'hopped' right over his bat—and I would agree."

Adair would get no argument from Eddie Perez, a Braves catcher who pinch hit against Randy Johnson with two outs in the bottom of the ninth inning on May 18, 2004. Johnson had retired 26 in a row, but Perez was a nemesis who had several career hits off his fastball. With two strikes, Perez expected a slider.

The catcher, Robby Hammock, set his target thigh-high, on the inside corner. Johnson fired a laser above the belt, outside, close to 100 miles an hour. Perez swung hard in futility. Perfect game.

"Even if I was looking for that fastball, I wouldn't have hit it anyway," he says. "You see it as a strike and all of a sudden . . ."

Perez makes an upward slash with his right hand, like a stage actor taking a bow. You know, I remind him, scientists say that kind of movement is impossible.

"No, it goes that way, too," Perez says, and who am I to argue? I believe in science, but I'd like to believe in baseball mythology, too.

History remembers 1968 as the year of the pitcher. Denny McLain won 31 games, Bob Gibson had a 1.12 earned run average, Don Drysdale threw 58⅔ consecutive scoreless innings, and only one American League batter, Carl Yastrzemski, hit .300.

The season's strikeout leader is less celebrated: the Indians' Sam McDowell, with 283. He finished his first inning of the year by fanning the Angels' Don Mincher with a 3–2 slider. When Mincher came up in the third inning, McDowell ran the count full again. Mincher expected a slider, but McDowell, a tall lefty with the best fastball of his era, had other plans.

"I wanted a fastball up and in because the left-hander can't hit a ball up and in," McDowell says. "So I reared back and I was gonna throw as hard as I could, and it got away from me and hit him in the cheek. He immediately went to the hospital. I went and visited him and I was scared half to death. I never had that feeling in my life, and never want it again. It was total fear."

McDowell pitched 15 years in the majors, but by the end he had descended into alcoholism. He found sobriety in retirement and became a counselor, dedicating his life to helping the afflicted. He drew from that experience when I asked how it feels to unleash a fastball that crushes another man's face.

"You don't really focus on the injury as much, once everything quiets down and gets back to the game, because now you've gotta focus on what you're doing," he says. "But after the game's over with, I mean, it's just scary as hell. It's like—well, I won't say it's exactly like it, but one of the areas I work in is suicide prevention. And with each individual that's attempting suicide, while you're stabilizing him and getting him to come down so you can get him professional help, you're trained to be focused on what to say, how to say it, what your reaction should be to his reaction. But I know that in every case I've ever had, when it's all over with, and the individual is in the EMS or the ambulance, I just shake like you can't believe, from the fear."

Fastballs have the power to kill. It happened to Ray Chapman, a Cleveland shortstop, on August 16, 1920, when facing the Yankees' Carl Mays at the Polo Grounds. Chapman was a renowned bunter; he still holds the single-season record for sacrifice hits, with 67 in 1917. As he led off the top of the fifth, under overcast skies after light showers at game time, Chapman moved his back foot, perhaps preparing to bunt down the first base line.

Mays, a right-hander with a submarine delivery, noticed. He aimed his fastball up and in. Chapman, a right-handed batter, was not wearing a helmet—those would not come to baseball for three decades—and the ball struck his left temple. It caromed back to Mays, who thought for a moment that it had hit part of the bat. Mays tossed the ball to first baseman Wally Pipp, but in an instant, he knew what had really happened. Chapman slumped to the ground, blood pouring from his left ear. He staggered up, began walking to the center field clubhouse, flanked by teammates, then slumped as he neared second base.

As Mike Sowell recounts with gripping detail in *The Pitch That Killed,* Mays, in the immediate aftermath, pointed to a rough spot on the surface of the ball. The umpire, Tommy Connolly, examined it and tossed it out of play, unaware that he was, effectively, trashing the murder weapon. After the game, Mays would say the ball had been wet.

An ambulance took Chapman to nearby St. Lawrence Hospital, where doctors determined that Chapman had sustained a fracture extending 3½ inches to the base of his skull on the left side. A piece of bone, 1½ inches square, had pressed against his brain, which was shoved against the right side of his skull from the force of the impact with the ball. Blood clots had formed. Doctors operated for an hour and 15 minutes, but they could not save him.

Jack Graney, an Indians outfielder and Chapman's roommate, would go to his grave believing Mays had thrown at his friend on purpose. At the hospital, he had decried the danger of Mays's pitch.

"A batter has a chance to dodge the fastball thrown by an ordinary pitcher, but Mays has a freak delivery and his fastball has a sudden dip to it that never gives a batter a chance to dodge."

Mays learned of Chapman's death the next morning, when a Yankees secretary came to his apartment to tell him the news. Later that day, he gave a statement to John F. Joyce, the assistant district attorney:

It was a straight fast ball and not a curved one. When Chapman came to bat, I got the signal for a straight fast ball, which I delivered. It was a little too close, and I saw Chapman duck his head in an effort to get out of the path of the ball. He was too late, however, and a second later he fell to the grounds. It was the most regrettable incident of my career, and I would give anything if I could undo what has happened.

Joyce ruled the death accidental, closing the investigation and releasing Mays from custody. He interviewed no witnesses, and the ball itself was gone, "mixed in with the other baseballs removed from play that day," as Sowell writes. That in itself was somewhat rare in those days, and while lights were still years away, Chapman's death changed the game by showing the consequences of using dark or defaced balls. In 1924, the NL used about 54,000 baseballs. In 1919, the year before Chapman's beaning, it had used about 22,000.

Players today may know little, or nothing, of Mays and Chapman, but they don't need to. The threat of a fastball to the head, and what could happen, is understood as a workplace hazard. Giambi compares the rare fastball to the head to the every-play brutality of the NFL.

"You end up getting smoked and you're kind of out of it," he says. "Everybody hears the stories about guys getting their careers ruined, but I don't know—it's just one of those things you don't think about, I guess, like being a race-car driver and going fast. It's just part of the game."

If hitters cannot manage that fear, they cannot play. But pitchers must also find a way to cope with their power to inflict damage. Walter Johnson always understood that his pitches could be lethal, ever since his semipro days as a teenager out West. This is how a breathless fan described Johnson to the Senators in 1907:

"The boy throws so fast you can't see 'em . . . and he knows where he is throwing the ball, because if he didn't, there would be dead bodies strewn all over Idaho."

Johnson was in the majors by the end of that season, on his way to perhaps the greatest career any pitcher has ever had: 417 wins, a 2.17 ERA, 3,509 strikeouts, and a record 110 shutouts. If he had a weakness, Ty Cobb explained late in life, it was a fear of himself.

"I know Johnson was afraid he would hit and kill a batter," Cobb said in a 1958 *Sporting News* story. "When he saw me crowding the plate, he would steer his pitches a little bit wide. I got some hits off him only because I knew he pitched wide to anybody who crowded the plate off him."

As Johnson told writer F. C. Lane in 1925: "The bean ball is one of the meanest things on earth and no decent fellow would use it. . . . The bean ball pitcher is a potential murderer."

Johnson was plenty dominant and proved himself to his manager right away. So did Feller, another phenom, who said in his memoir that it would have been "outrageously criminal or immoral" to deliberately bean a hitter.

"If a manager had ordered me to stick a ball in a batter's ear," Feller wrote, "I would have told him to stick it in his own ear."

Yet for much of baseball history, pitchers often had to pass a manager's toughness test. Spahn starred in the Boston Braves' farm system in 1942, but the major league manager, Casey Stengel, ignored him because Spahn refused an order to throw at a hitter.

"Warren wouldn't knock a guy down like Casey said," Spahn's teammate Lew Burdette told the former commissioner Fay Vincent in *We Would Have Played for Nothing*, an engrossing oral history of the era. "He said, 'You're gutless,' and sent Warren back down to the minors."

Spahn pitched just four games for a bad Braves team that season, then left for three years in the military. He went on to win 363 games and help the Braves beat Stengel's Yankees in the 1957 World Series. Years later, Stengel finally apologized for the slight.

As the fastest pitch and the easiest to control, the fastball offered the perfect vessel for a primitive show of guts. As a rookie for the A's in 1967, Rick Monday took a fastball to the face from Gary Peters of the White Sox. Fifty years later, Monday could press his index finger on the point of impact, an inch or so to the right of his nose, and still feel pain. Just before he blacked out, Monday said, he could hear Chicago's manager, Eddie Stanky, screaming from the dugout.

"The next time I faced Peters was in Chicago again, and Stanky was yelling again: 'Knock him down!'" Monday says. "The first pitch was right here [close to his head] and I took it. Next pitch, I ducked—it was over my head and broke the bat."

After Monday swung at the next pitch, he says, he flung his bat at Peters to show he would not back down.

"Because they wanted to see, as a young player, how long it took you to get up, *if* you got up, and if you'd ever bother them again," Monday says. "It was a game about intimidation, and you'd get away with it."

Being mean was just part of a pitcher's job. Most did not want to cause injury, but these were hardened competitors with little to no financial security, fighting for their careers. A high and tight fastball had a clear purpose, with no apologies.

"I wasn't really throwing at them, but I didn't care whether I hit them or not," Bob Gibson says, distilling the intimidator's mind-set. "Today they dare you to come inside, and if you do, the umpire kicks you out of the ballgame: 'Oh, you're throwing at somebody!' No, I'm not throwing at him. If I threw at him, I would hit him."

Doug Griffin, a Red Sox infielder, took a Nolan Ryan fastball to his helmet in April 1974. Griffin would one day tell the *Herald News* of Fall River, Massachusetts, that it felt "like a train going through my head, a loud whistle," a sensation that lasted two weeks. He missed two months but singled twice off Ryan the next time they met.

To Ryan, inside pitching just isn't what it used to be.

"Well, I think it's been taken out of the game *a lot*," he says. "What we considered pitching inside versus what they think pitching inside is today is totally different. And it seems to me like a lot of pitching inside nowadays is cutters. So it's just changed; the game goes in phases like that."

Ryan cited the aluminum bat as a critical factor in the way pitchers learn to use their fastball. Ryan, who was born in 1947, never once faced a hitter with an aluminum bat. In the mid-1990s, when he served as a volunteer coach for TCU, Ryan was startled by its impact.

"I had trouble getting my pitchers to pitch inside," he says. "You could pitch inside and a guy can still hit the ball off the handle and be very successful, so a lot of pitchers didn't want to pitch inside."

Gossage sings lead in the chorus of former players lamenting what the game has become. But his crass language shouldn't obscure his points. The best lesson he ever received, he said, came from the man he called the greatest player he ever saw: Dick Allen, the AL Most Valuable Player for the White Sox in 1972, when Gossage was a 20-year-old rookie teammate. Throwing hard came naturally to Gossage; as a boy in Colorado Springs, he would kill rabbits and birds with rocks, just like J. R. Richard. But Allen taught him how to intimidate a hitter.

"He said the best thing you can do is knock one of those fuckers on their ass," Gossage says. "The rest of that bench over there is watching. They don't want any part of you. They know you're going to establish in.

"Dick taught me to pitch in, right here," Gossage continues, meaning the hitter's lead elbow, just above the inside edge of the plate. "He said, 'As hitters, we see this pitch and we panic, because it looks as big as a basketball, and we've got to get the barrel there and God can't hit it. We identify this ball away from us and we may be able to get a bat on it, foul it off, or hit a ball down the right field line. But this ball in here, we gear up, we see it, and we can't hold up.'

"The last thing these kids think about today is the first thing hitters used to think about: 'I might get knocked on my ass.' These guys would get killed today, because they don't even know how to get out of the way of a ball. They have no clue. And then they take exception to it and they stare out at the pitcher. Back in the day they would have gotten drilled."

Gossage says he hit only three batters on purpose: Andres Galarraga, whom he just didn't want to face; Ron Gant, who had admired a long foul ball; and Al Bumbry, who had taken out two teammates with hard slides. But when he beaned Ron Cey in the helmet in the 1981 World Series, leaving the concussed Cey in a heap at the plate, it jolted Gossage severely.

Like McDowell with Mincher, Gossage stayed in the moment; he was working, too busy to consider the consequences. But it took him a month or two into the next season, he said, to feel comfortable letting loose with his fastball.

"When he was laying in the batter's box, I thought he was dead," Gossage says, before pivoting to an essential truth that can never be legislated out of the game. "There are inherent risks in baseball."

————

One inherent risk is simply the act of throwing a baseball, repeatedly, at high speeds.

"It's definitely an unnatural motion—overhead, throwing like that, putting that kind of stress on your shoulder and elbow," Justin Verlander says. "I mean, the natural motion is softball, underhand. Those girls or guys throw every day, they throw 200 pitches a day, they practice as long as they want. We can't do that, because we get really sore."

Likewise, Mike Mussina is convinced that pitching overhand is unnatural.

"We don't walk around with our arms over our head," he says, drawing the same softball comparison as Verlander. "There's no unnatural stress throwing a ball underhand, but there's unbelievable unnatural stress throwing a ball overhand, and that's just how it is. So every pitch you throw is stress on your body that it really wasn't born to have."

In a 2015 study, doctors at Henry Ford Hospital in Detroit found that while high velocity does not, by itself, endanger the ulnar collateral ligament, throwing too many high-velocity pitches does. The study put the threshold at 48 percent; if you throw a greater percentage of fastballs than that, you're adding significant risk to your UCL.

A 2013 article in *Nature*, the weekly science journal, explained that while chimpanzees sometimes throw objects, only humans do so with high speed and accuracy. This ability helped early hunters survive—but the species of baseball pitcher was eons away.

"Paleolithic hunters almost certainly threw less frequently than modern athletes, who often deliver more than 100 high-speed throws over the course of a few hours," the study says. "Unfortunately, the ligaments and tendons in the human shoulder and elbow are not well adapted to withstanding such repeated stretching from the high torques generated by throwing, and frequently suffer from laxity and tearing."

Precisely, says Dr. Glenn Fleisig, the research director at the American Sports Medicine Institute. The motion itself is not the issue.

"Throwing overhand is natural; windmill pitching is not," he says. "You know what my proof is? Do you remember when your son was two and you rolled the ball to him, and he picked up the ball and kind of pushed it with his shoulder toward you? Did he do windmill pitching? No. Humans, especially males, we like to pick up things and throw them. If you and I went to the lake and were gonna throw a rock, I wouldn't do a windmill throw. I would do an overhand throw. And my friend who doesn't do any sports, if I gave him a rock, he'd still throw overhand. So, basically, throwing overhand has been around as long as people have, and throwing overhand is natural. Throwing balls and rocks and things, that's natural. But throwing 100 throws as hard as you can every fifth day is not natural. When there's too much of that, that's when the injuries happen."

Baseball America once ran a cover of Steve Avery—who starred for the Braves in the early 1990s before injuries hit—with his left arm painted gold. Some young pitchers are like that, born with the precious gift to fire thunderbolts, the separator between ordinary and special. The ordinary arm will never dispense thousands of pitches, and probably never get hurt. But a special arm is vulnerable, pointing its owner to glory, despair, or both.

Sometimes a pitcher does not even know what he possesses. That is how it was for Jarrod Parker the first time he threw a baseball 98 miles an hour. It was a rainy day, the first start of his senior year of high school in Indiana. Parker was already a pro prospect, and when he left the game, he looked at his father for a signal of how hard he had thrown on the scouts' radar guns. His father held up eight fingers.

"And I'm like: 'Eighty-eight? Well, it's cold, whatever, it's early,'" Parker said in 2014, in the Oakland Athletics' clubhouse. "And he was like, 'No—98.' It never feels that much different between throwing a pitch at 88 or 98. You can't see it."

Soon Parker was a top 10 pick in the nation, but his arm just could not withstand its own heat. He had Tommy John surgery in the minors to repair a torn ulnar collateral ligament. After two strong seasons for the A's, including a club-record 19 starts in a row without a loss, Parker tore his UCL again. As he tried to recover, he fractured his elbow. Twice.

How many kids dream of the chance to match up against Verlander in the playoffs, as Parker did twice? Without question, he made it. Yet his career also embodies the sad paradox facing developing pitchers: you've got to throw hard to get signed, but throwing too hard, too often, too young is a recipe for breakdown. As UCL injuries interrupt or end more and more professional careers, the majority of Tommy John surgeries—56.8 percent, according to a 2015 study cited in *The Arm*, Jeff Passan's brilliant exploration of the epidemic—are now performed on teenagers.

In the early 2000s, after the Red Sox fired him as general manager, Dan Duquette ran a youth sports academy in Massachusetts. While children of a previous generation typically played multiple sports, Duquette noticed that they now tended to play just one, because of pressure to make their high school team.

"As these kids specialize, they're trying to throw harder before they're mature enough to throw hard, before their bodies can withstand the stress of it," he says. "And they're throwing on a year-round basis. So the one thing that is clear is that you need a rest and recovery time after the season's over, and if you want to condition your arm for a long season, you should do a long-toss program before getting on the mound when the season starts."

Alan Jaeger, the pitching trainer who advocates long-toss programs, draws a direct correlation between that exercise and velocity. If someone can throw a ball 300 feet, Jaeger says, he can pitch at 86 to 92 miles per hour. At 350 feet, he insists, the corresponding velocity is 93 to 97.

"Think about everybody's arm as a treasure chest, and there's treasure in there based on their size and weight and DNA," Jaeger says. "We don't know what kind of treasure's in there, but we'd like to find out."

For most of baseball history, it was assumed that the foundation of that treasure—the fastball—could not be taught. To a large degree, that is true. How else to explain cases like Matt Bush, who was chosen first overall by San Diego in the 2004 draft, one spot before Verlander?

Bush threw 96 mph in high school, but the Padres took him as a shortstop—and Bush couldn't hit. He floated to the Rays' system and showed promise as a pitcher, but was sent to prison for more than three years after driving under the influence and nearly killing a motorcyclist at spring training in 2012. Three years later, at a work-release program in Jacksonville, he would pitch in the parking lot of a Golden Corral restaurant, using a concrete parking block to push off with his back leg. The ball exploded from his arm, with accuracy. The next year he was a vital member of the Rangers' bullpen, armed with one of the hardest fastballs in the majors.

"Velocity doesn't come from a program," says Roy Silver, a former minor leaguer who worked with Bush in that parking lot and signed him for Texas. "If you're an atheist, it comes from your ancestors; if you're not an atheist, it's God-given. This guy just spent four years in jail and he's throwing 100 in a big league game? Are you serious? These are freaks of nature."

One of the game's most dominant closers, Billy Wagner, threw 100 mph with the wrong hand. Wagner was always small, and when he was five years old, he was roughhousing with a bigger kid named Chip, tossing around a hat like a football. ("We didn't have a football," he explains. "We had a hat.") Chip fell on Wagner and broke his right elbow. Wagner threw left-handed while wearing a cast, then got the cast off and broke his right elbow again when he fell off the monkey bars. He kept throwing as a lefty. Things worked out.

"I can't do anything left-handed other than throw," Wagner says. "I can't hold a pencil. I almost poke myself in my eye with my left hand if I'm trying to eat. It's crazy. For God to bless me and say, 'Hey, you're gonna throw 100 miles an hour left-handed'—it's just not something that happens every day."

The majors' fastest pitcher, Aroldis Chapman, started on his path without even trying. As a boy in Cuba, he did not burn to throw fastballs for a living.

"I wasn't into baseball, it wasn't a big deal for me," he says, through an interpreter. "I was a first baseman, just kind of messing around a little bit. This coach decided to put me on the mound. They're all looking for pitchers, and one day he goes, 'Hey, Chapman, give it a try!' I wasn't really feeling it, but I was out there and I started throwing hard.

"The rest is history. No more first baseman."

In 2010, as a 22-year-old rookie for the Reds, Chapman threw a pitch 105 miles per hour, the highest ever recorded. He would soon have a tattoo of a flaming baseball with the digits "105" inked on the inside of his left wrist. In 2016, a month after recovering from a blown save to win Game 7 of the World Series for the Cubs, Chapman signed with the Yankees for five years and $86 million. He is, in the truest sense of the word, a trailblazer.

"One hundred miles per hour is the new benchmark," says Tom House, the former pitcher and coach who founded the National Pitching Association. "I think in the next five to eight years, most pitchers, to sign a pro contract, are going to have to show 97, 98, and touch 101, 102. That's where the research is going."

Research is the buzzword around Driveline's modest headquarters at an industrial park near Sea-Tac Airport. Hundreds of pitchers flock there every year, striding with purpose around the parking lots, holding kettlebell weights over their heads, or wiggling long sticks—called shoulder tubes, for warm-up and recovery—in front of their chests. Kyle Boddy founded Driveline in 2008, and takes the title of research and development director. He pitched in high school, but his arm always hurt and no one could tell him why. He worked as a software developer at Microsoft but was fascinated by the science of pitching, and probing the secrets to arm health and potential.

By now he has several units at his complex, including one to store Driveline's inventory of brightly colored PlyoCare balls, weighing 3.5 ounces to 4.4 pounds. (Standard baseballs are 5 to 5.25 ounces.) In another unit, while one pitcher works in a screened-in bullpen, others fire the weighted balls, from close range, at padded walls. Still another unit acts as a laboratory, with 12 high-speed cameras surrounding a mound, capturing biomechanical data while a cluster of computers tracks every movement in intimate detail.

Boddy's data points a clear direction for the game.

"We're reaching a point where the maximum velocity is around that 110 mile per hour mark, like 107," he says. "I just don't think people are going to throw much harder than that. But what you're going to see, and what we are seeing evidence of, is that there's this curve that gets shifted to the right where everybody throws 95 now. There's a stabilization. It creates a profile of a pitcher, like: 'This is what we want.' Front offices are so advanced, they know what will succeed at the big-league level."

Major league hitters are so advanced that they can handle a steady stream of fastballs. In fact, as pitchers throw harder, they also throw fewer total fastballs—a better fastball makes for better off-speed stuff, because the hitter must start his swing sooner and therefore has less time to react. But with an ever-growing pool of hard-throwing amateurs, the soft-tosser with guile is being naturally selected out of the game. Picture pro baseball as a carnival attraction with a sign at the entrance: YOU MUST THROW THIS HARD TO RIDE THIS RIDE.

"How many prospects do you see coming up that throw 88, 90?" says Trevor Bauer, the Indians right-hander and the first established major leaguer to train at Driveline. "Watch the Futures Game—there's not a single guy throwing under 94, and most guys are sitting 96 to 98. Sure, it's the Futures Game and you have one inning and all that adrenaline, but watch All-Star Games from the last five or 10 years in the big leagues. It's ridiculous. Average velo rises every single year. Doesn't seem to have any sort of limit on it right now."

Bauer threw 78 miles an hour as a freshman in high school in Southern California. He quickly grew tired of seeing harder throwers, with worse results, get more opportunities. Before his sophomore year, at the urging of a pitching coach, Jim Wagner, Bauer visited Ron Wolforth, who runs the Texas Baseball Ranch in Montgomery, Texas, and learned how to train to throw hard. Bauer went on to dominate college hitters at UCLA and was drafted third overall by Arizona in 2011. His journey to the majors made him a realist about breaking through the pro gates.

"It took a long time for people to realize that velo is king, at least in the draft process, amateur ball, and up into minor league ball," Bauer says. "Once you get to the big leagues and you're here, getting outs is king. But up until the big leagues, velo is king, and in the minor leagues, guys that have poor results but throw really hard get a lot more opportunities than guys that have really good results but throw 86, 88.

"A lot's changed in five or 10 years. You get to college and college coaches say, 'Hey, locate this, throw a changeup, let's get people out,' and you're like, 'OK, that's what it takes to be successful at this level'— but you didn't realize, because the information wasn't sitting there telling you, 'Hey, you're not going to get drafted unless you do *this*.'"

Throw hard, he means.

"So it's just taken a while for the research to be done, and for methods to be developed to train velocity reliably, and then for that information to be spread through enough high-level people that people start trusting it."

Now, some of the more progressive college programs, like Vanderbilt and Oregon State, use Driveline training techniques for their pitchers— weighted balls, long toss, and so on. More than 10 MLB teams have visited Boddy's complex in Washington, and major leaguers regularly consult with him, Wolforth, and others to rebuild their fastballs and learn to train with less soreness.

The coaches are learning, too, as the game rapidly evolves. Wolforth started his business in 1993, and a decade ago, he said, teams viewed him as a pariah. He could help pupils throw hard enough to get signed, but mainly built pitchers who could win teddy bears at carnivals, not actual games. In that case, he thought, what was the point?

"There was real criticism: you get a Wolforth guy in 2008, he's going to throw the ball through a car wash and not get it wet, but I'm not sure he could throw it over the white thing," Wolforth says. "And now, when we send a guy up, not only can they throw it over the white thing and throw it hard, but they can also recover, and their pitchability goes very high. We have shifted our emphasis and broadened it."

Today, Wolforth says, he spends more time teaching mechanics, secondary pitches, and command than teaching velocity. He consults with about half of the major league teams and has helped rejuvenate the careers of several wayward pitchers, including at least two former Cy Young Award winners.

When pitchers suddenly throw harder, Wolforth says, they must also learn the right way to decelerate in their follow-through; using Volkswagen Beetle brakes on a Maserati, he said, invites disaster. Wolforth believes that with a comprehensive, individualized program, all pitchers can find their maximum velocity. But that is only part of what they need.

"The radar gun doesn't tell us if they can pitch or not," Wolforth says. "It's a very simple, snap way to tell something, and sometimes it's not the best way, but people like it because it immediately gives you feedback and it's comparable."

With so many hard throwers, Tom House believes, the traditional starting pitcher, as we have long known the role, will soon cease to exist. Future staffs, he predicted, will be made up of 12 pitchers throwing three times a week, with nobody working more than 45 pitches per game or going more than once through the lineup.

To some extent, this is already happening. Only 15 pitchers worked 200 innings in 2017, matching the previous year for the fewest ever in a nonstrike season. The World Series teams got there without asking much of any individual pitcher—the Astros' innings leader (Mike Fiers, with 153⅓) did not even meet the minimum standard to qualify for the ERA title, and the Dodgers had just 12 games all season in which their starter threw 100 pitches, the fewest in the majors.

In 1976—in a 24-team league—47 pitchers reached 215 innings. By 2017, that number had fallen to zero across the game's 30 teams. With such an inventory of pitchers who can throw hard for short bursts, teams now build five- or six-inning starters and let relievers handle the rest.

"When I first got called up, the pitchers they were going with were guys that were 88 to 92, with sink and cut—veteran guys that could spot it up," says Brian McCann, the longtime catcher. "Over time, we've realized that the prospect in Triple-A that throws hard is a way more uncomfortable at-bat than the other guy."

The Reds' Joey Votto, who combines slugging and patience better than any modern hitter, says the velocity spike has led to more swings and misses, but also to more mistakes cruising down the middle, begging to be crushed for home runs. Max Scherzer, a dominant right-hander for the Nationals, says hitters know they can't string together singles against such overpowering stuff, so they tailor their swings to hit fly balls. They drive more misplaced fastballs into the seats and accept more strikeouts as a trade-off.

In 2002, the average fastball was 89 miles an hour. In 2017, it was 92.8 mph. With velocity, home runs, and strikeouts rising, pitchers' workloads are falling. It is not a healthy trend.

"These guys only know one thing, because organizations are telling them one thing: give me everything you have and we'll take care of the rest," John Smoltz says. "It's taking, on average, 25 pitchers per year per club, and no one's paying attention to it because their theory is, 'There's just so many arms, we don't need to.'

"I'm not stuck in the old school, but I'm saying, 'Whoa, let's slow the roll a little bit.' I maintain that in three to five years, this game will crash. If I'm right, the pitching cannot keep up, and/or fans are gonna go, 'Uncle, I can't take it, it's 10 pitchers a game, I can't take the pitching changes, I can't take the length of the games.' They're trying everything they can to speed up the game, but we're not gaining any speed-up time."

In 2017, batters struck out nearly 3,000 more times, while hitting roughly 2,000 more homers, than they had in 2014, the year that ended with Madison Bumgarner's flurry of fastballs to Salvador Perez. That means a lot fewer balls in play, and a lot more standing around. The average time of a nine-inning game reached three hours, five minutes in 2017, an all-time high—and the average fastball velocity rose for the seventh year in a row.

Those two trends are joined tightly together, another paradox in a sport full of them: when the fastball speeds up, the game slows down.

THE CURVEBALL

A Karate Chop with a Ball

Mike Montgomery's throwing program for the 2016 season began just before New Year's on Via Saludo in Valencia, California. He had no reason to believe that his work would stretch until November, to Ontario Street in Cleveland, where he would throw the most anticipated pitch in the history of the Chicago Cubs.

It was Montgomery's ninth professional season. He had reached the majors only a few months earlier, in June 2015 with the Seattle Mariners. He threw two shutouts for them but was otherwise ordinary. When his agent floated the idea of leaving for a $2 million contract in Japan, the Mariners seemed content to let him go. Their nonchalance bothered and inspired Montgomery. He would show them he was better than they thought.

First, though, Montgomery needed a catcher. He asked his mom, Jeannette, a former third baseman for the softball team at Cal Poly Pomona. She strapped on catcher's gear, caught her son's best fastball, and barked, "Is that all you got?" Montgomery, unnerved, tried other stuff, too.

"I would throw her my curveball and she would catch it," he said. "And I'm like, 'Man, maybe this pitch ain't that good then, if my mom can catch it.'"

As a boy, Montgomery had been drawn more to basketball than baseball. But his father, David, rooted for the Atlanta Braves, and he watched their games on TBS at the family's home in California. Montgomery liked the Braves' aces, Greg Maddux, Tom Glavine, and

John Smoltz. He was tall and lanky and left-handed—the only lefty in the family—and when spring came around, coaches told him to pitch. As a sophomore at Hart High School, he made the varsity with a fastball, a changeup, and a palmball that acted as a curveball; Montgomery used the high seams like training wheels, the ball rolling off his fingers for a slow, loopy break.

The Kansas City Royals signed Montgomery as the thirty-sixth pick in the 2008 draft, and his palmball/curve did not come with him. The pro balls were stitched tighter, the seams lower, and the old breaking ball barely moved. In time Montgomery would understand that pro balls—including the even harder version in the majors—were better for breaking balls, because they were not as loose and could thus spin more. With the Royals, though, his curveball was hopeless. The fastball/change combination got Montgomery to Triple-A, but his attempts at a curveball were laughable. Once, in Omaha, it bounced on the grass and ricocheted off the hitter's elbow.

Without a reliable third pitch, Montgomery lost his status as a top prospect. But when the Royals traded him to Tampa Bay before the 2013 season, Montgomery had a few things that would help him: a gregarious personality, an inquisitive mind, and no fear of throwing a lot. In 2014 he befriended a teammate, Nate Karns, and played catch with him every day. Karns showed Montgomery his grip for a spike curveball, in which the index finger is raised and curled, with the tip resting lightly on the leather; the middle finger and thumb do all the work. Montgomery modified Karns's grip, removing the index finger completely when he let the curveball go, and worked on the pitch relentlessly. A coach, Neil Allen, let Montgomery throw 40 or so curveballs in a row in the bullpen, just to get the feel.

With the curveball, feel is big. The fastball, like nearly every other pitch, is thrown with backspin. The curveball is thrown with topspin, the seams whooshing downward as the pitch tumbles to Earth. Only certain pitchers have the loose, easy wrist action to make a ball act that way.

"Being able to spin the ball, either you can or you can't," says Nolan Ryan, who may have thrown the most devastating curve of all. "If they don't really have that ability—yeah, you can teach them a curveball, but will it be an exceptional pitch? I don't think so. I think people either have that ability or they don't."

A quick wrist is critical to disguising the pitch. Since a curveball is thrown so differently on release—with the pitcher's hand facing his head, not facing the batter—it's easy to telegraph. If a hitter sees that hand position, he knows he'll get a curveball. He also knows it's coming if the ball pops up before plummeting down. The curveballs that go *out* and then tumble down, after an imperceptible wrist turn, work best.

"The way many of us were taught to throw the curveball was to mentally think fastball out of the hand," said Bryan Price, the longtime pitching coach and manager. "Even as you get up into what we call your power position, as your hand comes forward, it's in fastball position first, and then accelerates into curveball position. That gives you hand speed through the pitch and gives you a tighter spin, tighter break, and more deception."

Montgomery often struggled to control his curveball, but he always had the hand to impart spin. Andrew Friedman, who traded for Montgomery with the Rays, noticed the exceptional spin rate, and suggested he use it more. Montgomery was still not sure; he knew the curve was a separator—when he pitched well, that was usually the reason—but he could not trust it.

The Rays gave up on Montgomery before the 2015 season, his fifth at Class AAA. He would make 99 starts at that level, more than the combined total of Jon Lester, John Lackey, and Kyle Hendricks, three of the starters on the 2016 Cubs. But Montgomery used his apprenticeship wisely, as a laboratory for new grips and angles of release, trying to unlock the mystery of the pitch he knew he needed.

By the start of the 2016 season, he was ready, and his curveball was the difference. But he still needed more convincing.

"Monty, you have a swing-and-miss breaking ball," said Mel Stottlemyre Jr., the Mariners' pitching coach, after a side session in spring training. Montgomery insisted that his changeup was better and his curve was too erratic. "No, no, no," Stottlemyre continued. "Believe me, I've been around this game a long time—I'm telling you, your breaking ball is that good."

Montgomery was emboldened. On opening day in Texas, in relief of Felix Hernandez, he struck out the first batter he faced, Delino DeShields, on a wicked curveball. DeShields stared back at the mound, puzzled by a pitch he had not seen from Montgomery before. After another strikeout, Montgomery faced Prince Fielder, the dangerous left-handed slugger. He was nervous but confident. He aimed the curveball at Fielder's front shoulder and it dropped over the middle for a called third strike.

On the bench after the inning, teammates bombarded Montgomery with praise. He stopped doubting his curveball after that.

"Man, my curveball is good," he thought, "and I don't know if I even understand that it can get better."

The Cubs understood. They traded for Montgomery in July, encouraged by the curveball. All his years of tinkering were paying off: the data showed that Montgomery's curveball was spinning about 100 rpm more than it had the year before. Chris Bosio, the Cubs' pitching coach, echoed Friedman and Stottlemyre: that's your best pitch, so use it more. Montgomery would double his curveball usage, from 12 percent in 2015 to 24 percent in 2016. By the end of that regular season, opponents had a .103 average off Montgomery's curve in his career.

As the summer went on, Montgomery kept buying in. The statistics guided him. After every game, on his phone or in the Cubs' video room, Montgomery logged on to BrooksBaseball.net to learn how many inches, vertically and horizontally, his curve had moved, comparing his results to those of other lefties. He remembered how certain pitches had felt coming off his hand, and matched them up with the data. The numbers comforted Montgomery. They told him never to worry, even when his best pitch deserted him as he prepared for the biggest moment of his life.

Montgomery was not part of the plan for Game 7 of the World Series against the Indians. Joe Maddon, the Cubs' manager, wanted to use three pitchers—Hendricks, Lester, and Aroldis Chapman—to secure the team's first championship in 108 years. He tried, but all of them wobbled. Montgomery warmed up in the third inning, then again in the fifth, the ninth, and the eleventh. He had already pitched four games in the World Series, and he did not have much left. Not only was he tired—much like Ralph Terry in 1960—he was bouncing his curveball everywhere. He did not throw a single strike with it in warm-ups.

In the bottom of the tenth, after the Cubs had taken a two-run lead in the top of the inning, Maddon called for the right-handed Carl Edwards Jr. to close it out. With two outs and no base runners, Edwards allowed a walk to Brandon Guyer and a run-scoring single to Rajai Davis.

The Indians had come to the eighth spot in their order, where Coco Crisp had started and gotten two hits. But with one out in the top of the ninth inning of Game 7, the Cubs' Jason Heyward had stolen second and taken third on a throwing error by the catcher. Fearing a sacrifice fly, Indians manager Terry Francona removed Crisp from right field and replaced him with Michael Martinez, who had a much stronger throwing arm.

The threat passed. But with the Indians down to their last out of the season, it was Martinez coming to bat, with no position players behind him on the bench. Martinez had a .197 average and just six home runs in almost 600 career trips to the plate. Of all the position players in the last quarter century with as many plate appearances as Martinez, none had a lower OPS—on-base plus slugging percentage— than his .507.

Martinez was a major league hitter in name only, having gone almost seven weeks since his last hit. And his last hit *off a curveball*? That had come more than a year earlier, on September 6, 2015. In 11 at-bats since that had ended with a curveball, Martinez had struck out nine times.

Maddon did not know this specific information, offhand, as Martinez came to bat in the tenth. But he did know that Martinez would have no chance to hit a Mike Montgomery curveball. For Montgomery, the Cubs had distilled their scouting reports on the Indians' hitters this way: Can he, or can he not, hit your curveball? Martinez most certainly could not. Maddon knew that pitch could win the World Series.

"I love Montgomery's curveball in that moment," Maddon said later, and Montgomery loved it, too.

Yes, he had lost the pitch in the bullpen. But the positive

reinforcement that had washed over him all season, on the field and the computer screen, calmed any nerves he might have felt. He did not stop to imagine the scene back in Chicago, outside Wrigley Field, where throngs of revelers anxiously awaited that blessed "F" on the score strip of the famous red marquee. The final score would stay 8–7, Montgomery believed, if he simply threw that curveball, the fully formed version of the pitch he had thrown to his mom back home.

She was in the stands now, with Miguel Montero catching. Montero came to the mound and Montgomery asked, "What's the plan?" They both knew the answer, but Montero said, "Let me think about it," and trotted back to the plate. Later, Montero would tell his pitcher that of course he had no doubt: curveballs all the way. He just didn't want Montgomery to dwell on it.

But Montgomery already was, in a good way.

"I wasn't thinking about the World Series, really," he says. "I was just thinking about me being able to throw a strike in that moment. That's all I cared about. I knew all I had to do was throw strikes and just take my chances that that was gonna work. Obviously, I'm not gonna walk the guy; that's not gonna help us. If he hits a homer? I didn't even think about it. I just said: 'I'll just throw a strike and take my chances.' I have confidence as long as I throw it, especially to that batter, to Michael Martinez, that was the game plan: to throw a curveball in the zone for a strike. And sure enough I throw a perfect first-pitch curveball right in there. He took it for a strike, and at that point I knew it was over, because that was the biggest hurdle, throwing that first one for a strike in that situation. And from there on I was in control."

Only seven other pitchers had thrown a pitch that could win or lose the World Series for either team. Now Montgomery's first had been perfect. He had the right matchup, and he had the right weapon.

For the final curveball, the one that slayed the Billy Goat and brought a catharsis to millions, Montgomery set his sights on the middle of the batter's box on the first base side. Nearly seven months before, Prince Fielder had stood there in Texas and watched the pitch buckle into the zone for strike three. This one was not as sharp, a little lazier, but still low and tight enough that a hitter like Martinez could do nothing with it. He tapped it softly to third, where Kris Bryant scrambled in to scoop it. Bryant lost his footing but still fired across the infield to Anthony Rizzo, who made the catch and raised his arms in triumph. Rizzo stuffed the ball in his back left pocket and romped toward Bryant. Montgomery flung his glove in the air and embraced them. He got the glove back but never touched the ball again.

"When we had our parade, a couple of us went up to [Rizzo] and said, 'You know, that's supposed to be my ball, that was my first-ever save,'" Montgomery said. "But he had it because he presented it to Ricketts at that time. I'm OK with that."

Tom Ricketts owns the Cubs, so he got the curse-breaking curveball. Montgomery got a ring, a memory, and the certainty that his job is the best there is.

"I enjoy, obviously, being competitive—but I also enjoy just the creativity you can have being a pitcher, because you're the one in control," Montgomery said. "You're the one with the paintbrush. Everyone else is reacting to what you do."

The reaction to Montgomery's curveball was overwhelming joy, bottled up since 1908. By then the pitch had been around just 45 years, from its beginnings on a craggy beach in Brooklyn. Or so the legend goes.

———

If you had to group pitches into two categories, you would choose "fastball" and "other." The "other" makes pitching interesting. If the ball went straight every time, pitchers would essentially be functionaries, existing merely to serve the hitters. Long ago, that is just what they were, as the name implies. Think of pitching horseshoes: you're making an underhand toss to a specific area. That was pitching for much of the 1800s. For 20 years—1867 through 1886—batters could specify whether they wanted the pitch high or low. The poor pitcher was forced to comply.

Baseball might have continued as a test of hitting, running, and fielding skills had pitchers not discovered their potential for overwhelming influence. What if they could make the pitch behave differently? Long before cameras and websites could classify every pitch into a type, many of the offerings intended to deceive a hitter—in-shoots and out-shoots, in-curves and out-curves and drops, in the old parlance—were largely known as curveballs. The "other" was, simply, everything that wasn't a fastball.

In researching the history of curveballs at the Hall of Fame Library in Cooperstown, I was struck by how many people claimed to be the inventor. In 1937 *The New York Times* published an obituary of a man named Billy Dee of Chester, New Jersey, who was said to have invented the curveball in 1881. Dee threw a baseball with frayed seams and, intrigued by its movement, said he practiced and practiced until "I soon was able to loop the old apple without the benefit of the damaged seam." Sounds impressive—but what's this? A 1948 *Times* obituary of one George McConnell of Los Angeles, "an old-time Indian fighter" who "decided that the 'English' being put on billiard balls could be used with a baseball." That was in 1878.

There are many more such stories in the files and the history books at Cooperstown. Fred Goldsmith has a case, like James Creighton and Phonie Martin and Alvah Hovey and more. There's even a hoary old Ivy League debate from the 1870s: Did Charles Avery of Yale curve first, or Joseph Mann of Princeton?

Peter Morris untangles it all in *A Game of Inches,* quoting a letter from Mann to the *Times* in 1900 that sums it up neatly: "As long as baseball has been played and baseballs have had seams with which to catch the air, curve balls have been thrown."

Mann goes on to assert that, in spite of this, no one thought to use those curving balls for pitching until he did so in 1874. Then again, Mann admits he was inspired by watching Candy Cummings one day at Princeton. Mann said Cummings's catcher told him he could make the ball curve, though it did not do so that day.

Confused yet? The plaque in the Hall of Fame gallery for W. A. "Candy" Cummings boldly settles things in seven gilded words: "Pitched first curve ball in baseball history." The plaque dates this discovery to 1867, when Cummings was the amateur ace of the Brooklyn Stars. History should always be so easy.

The Cummings backstory is so indelible, so rich in imagery, that if it's not true . . . well, it should be. It has never been debunked and would be impossible to do so. Cummings is practically a charter member of the Hall, going in with the fourth class of inductees in 1939. His story links the discovery of the curveball to the curiosity of a 14-year-old boy on a beach in Brooklyn. What could be more American than that?

Here is how Cummings described it for *Baseball Magazine* in 1908:

> In the summer of 1863 a number of boys and myself were amusing ourselves by throwing clam shells (the hard shell variety) and watching them sail along through the air, turning now to the right, and now to the left. We became interested in the mechanics of it and experimented for an hour or more. All of a sudden it came to me that it would be a good joke on the boys if I could make a baseball curve the same way.

Cummings was born in 1848 in Ware, Massachusetts, and various accounts say that he played the old Massachusetts game before moving to Brooklyn. Cummings himself did not mention this in his retelling of the curveball's origin story, but to Morris, it was a significant detail. In the 1850s, pitchers in Massachusetts were permitted to throw overhand, which made curveballs easier to throw.

"He had probably seen rudimentary curves thrown as a youngster in Massachusetts, and when he moved to Brooklyn and began playing the 'New York game,' the delivery restrictions made the pitch seem impossible," Morris wrote. "Yet the example of throwing clamshells made him think that it might be possible, and his arm strength and relentless practice enabled him to realize his ambition."

Cummings emphasized two points: his solitary persistence in perfecting the pitch despite ridicule from his friends, and the physical toll imposed by the delivery restrictions of the day. Pitchers then worked in a four-by-six-foot box, and could not lift either foot off the ground until the ball was released.

"The arm also had to be kept near the side and the delivery was made with a perpendicular swing," Cummings said, in an undated interview published after his career. "By following these instructions it was a hard strain, as the wrist and the second finger had to do all the work. I snapped the ball away from me like a whip and this caused my wrist bone to get out of place quite often. I was compelled to wear a supporter on my wrist all one season on account of this strain."

Cummings left Brooklyn for a boarding school in Fulton, New York, in 1864. He tinkered with his curveball there—"My boy friends began to laugh at me, and to throw jokes at my theory of making a ball go sideways"—and joined the Star Juniors, an amateur team in Brooklyn. From there he was recruited to the Excelsior Club as a junior member, in both age and size: he would grow to be 5 foot 9, but his weight topped out at 120 pounds.

In the curveball, though, Cummings found an equalizer. He showed that pitchers of all sizes could rely on movement and deception—not simply on power—to succeed. Soon, the notion would be ingrained as baseball fact that a pitcher with dominant stuff could humble even the brawniest hitter. Cummings began to prove this in 1867, with the Excelsiors in a game at Harvard.

"A surge of joy flooded over me that I shall never forget," he wrote in the *Baseball Magazine* piece. "I felt like shouting out that I had made a ball curve; I wanted to tell everybody; it was too good to keep to myself. But I said not a word, and saw many a batter at that game throw down his stick in disgust. Every time I was successful I could scarcely keep from dancing from pure joy. The secret was mine."

The movement could be very erratic, Cummings conceded, but in time he learned to control it, and to manipulate the umpires. When the ball started at a hitter's body, and caused him to jump before bending into the strike zone, the umpire called it a ball. Cummings adjusted by starting the pitch in the middle so he could get strikes, even though the movement carried it away.

"When it got to the batter it was too far out," he said. "Then there would be a clash between the umpire and the batter."

By age 23 Cummings was a pitcher for the New York Mutuals of the National Association. The pitching was done from 45 feet away, in that box, with a sidearm motion—and the numbers were similarly unrecognizable today. Cummings started 55 of the Mutuals' 56 games, working 497 innings and giving up 604 hits, with a 33–20 record and a 3.01 earned run average. When the National League began in 1876, Cummings pitched for the Hartford Dark Blues and went 16–8. He went 5–14 for the Cincinnati Reds in 1877, his final season.

A curious contemporary, Bobby Mathews, would go on to have more success. Mathews was even shorter than Cummings—just

5 foot 5—and as their careers overlapped in the National Association, Mathews was one of the few who could mimic Cummings's sidearm curve. Generations of pitchers would follow Mathews's example: see something interesting, study it, and make it their own.

"He watched Cummings' hands carefully, noting how he held the ball and how he let it go, and after a few weeks' careful practice in the same way could see the curve in his own delivery," explained an 1883 article from *The Philadelphia Press,* unearthed by Morris. "Then he began to use it in matches, striking men out in a way that no one but Cummings had ever done before, and in a short time he was known as one of the most effective pitchers in the field."

That was the first of three consecutive 30-win seasons by Mathews for the Philadelphia Athletics of the American Association. He did not make the Hall of Fame, but he followed Cummings as the curveball's most prominent practitioner, carrying the pitch through the sidearm era and helping to establish it as fundamental to the game.

Assuming that you believed in it at all.

———

For decades after Cummings's last pitch, many people doubted the very notion that a ball could curve. It was a staple of baseball debate that the curveball just might be an optical illusion. A favorite exercise for skeptics was to challenge a pitcher to prove his powers by bending a ball around a series of poles. This happened a lot.

"The majority of college professors really believe that the curve ball was as impossible as the transmutation of gold from potato skins," said a man named Ben Dodson, in the *Syracuse Herald* in 1910.

Dodson said he witnessed a demonstration at Harvard by Charles "Old Hoss" Radbourn, probably in the 1880s. Radbourn—whose "pitching deity; dapper gent" persona would one day make him a Twitter sensation—was an early hero of the National League. In 1884, for the Providence Grays, he was 59–12 with a 1.38 ERA and 73 complete games. The professors, safe to say, had a lot of misplaced confidence when they arranged their poles and dared Radbourn to throw curves to his catcher, Barney Gilligan.

"Radbourn, standing to the right of the pole arcade, started what appeared to be a perfectly straight delivery," Dodson said. "It turned with a beautiful inward bend and passed behind the pole just in front of Gilligan—an inshoot, and a corker. He repeated this several times. Then, standing inside the upper part of the pole-zone, he threw outshoots that went forty feet dead on a line, and swung out of the arcade."

Dodson went on to describe Radbourn's "drop balls," though not all of these pitches were curves, as we think of them today. Radbourn threw a wide array of pitches that would now be classified as curveballs, changeups, sinkers, screwballs, and so on. That day at Harvard, his charge was to prove that something besides a fastball really did exist, and Dodson, for one, considered the matter closed.

"It was a wonderful demonstration and settled the argument about curve pitching forever," he said. "And yet—because they never thought about publicity in those days—not a reporter was at hand, and the story lives only in the memories of those who saw it done."

What a pity. For some, the matter was still debatable midway into the next century, as Carl Erskine recalls. As a minor leaguer, Erskine had gotten a tip from a rival manager, Jack Onslow, who told him he was telegraphing his curveball by the way he tucked it into his hand. In Cuba before the 1948 season, Erskine taught himself a new grip and trusted it one day to preserve a shutout after a leadoff triple in the ninth. The circumstances mattered, because the team had a standing bonus of $25 for a shutout.

"My inclination was, 'Oh boy, I gotta go back to my old curve, I gotta get this shutout,'" Erskine says. "So I had a little meeting on the mound with myself, tossed the rosin bag: 'You made a commitment that you weren't gonna go back to the old curve; stick to it'—and I got the side out without that run scoring. From then on, I had good confidence in that, and the rest is history."

Erskine's history included five pennants with the Dodgers and one narrowly missed brush with infamy. On October 3, 1951, he was warming up in the bottom of the ninth inning at the Polo Grounds alongside Ralph Branca, with the pennant at stake against the Giants. Manager Charlie Dressen called to the bullpen and asked a coach, Clyde Sukeforth, which pitcher looked better.

Dressen liked the curveball; he would say of the slider, disdainfully:

"They slide in and slide out of the ballpark." But when Sukeforth reported that Erskine was bouncing his curve, Dressen chose Branca.

"People say, 'Carl, what was your best pitch in your 12 major league seasons?'" Erskine says with a laugh. "I say it was a curveball I bounced in the bullpen at the Polo Grounds. It could have been me."

Instead it was Branca who threw the fateful fastball that Bobby Thomson lashed into the left field seats—the celebrated "Shot Heard 'Round the World" that gave the Giants the pennant. We'll never know how Thomson might have handled Erskine's curve, but the Giants were stealing signs, so he might have hit that, too.

In any case, it was around this time that Erskine's pitch all but buried the tired debate about its veracity.

"TV came in around the late '40s and there was a show early on, Burgess Meredith was the emcee, called *Omnibus*," Erskine explains. "They sent a crew to Ebbets Field one day and they asked for me and Preacher Roe, who was a left-hander who threw an overhand curve, to come out early. The purpose was to film us throwing a curveball, and to prove or disprove whether a ball actually curved.

"So we got ready to go out there, and I took a new baseball and scuffed it up a little bit in order to make sure I had good bite on it. So I warmed up and the director of this film stood behind me and said, 'I'm not a baseball guy, so I don't know what I'm looking for here. Could you throw me a couple of curveballs so I could see what it is I'm trying to film?' So with this scuffed-up baseball I threw an overhand curveball and it broke big. And this director says, 'My God, is there any doubt?' So he was a novice at seeing pitches, but the first one he saw: 'Holy cow! There's no question!'

"So they put that show on, Preacher threw from the left side and I threw of course from the right side, and then they used this dotted line that was superimposed somehow on the film. And you could basically say, well, there is no doubt: yes, a rotating pitch can break out of a straight line and be a curveball."

As Erskine described the mechanics of the curveball, he spoke of using the middle finger to apply pressure to the ball, lead the wrist, and help generate tight rotation. The index finger is almost in the way, he said, which reminded him of a character he met in the "3-I" League (Iowa, Indiana, Illinois), where he played in 1946 and '47.

"One of the greatest all-time pitchers that I met when I was in the minor leagues was Mordecai Brown," Erskine says. "He lived in the Terre Haute House—that was the Phillies' affiliate—and he would come down and talk to us in the lobby, show us his hand, where he had this farm accident and it took away not only his first finger of his right hand, it even took the knuckle. So he had a hand that had three fingers—naturally, his nickname was 'Three Finger' Brown—and it gave him the ultimate best use of that second finger for the curveball, because the first finger was out of the way completely.

"He was a real gentleman, always dressed in a shirt and tie. Naturally, an old gentleman by that time, and we were just kids in the minors. But we were fascinated to talk to him, and he was anxious to show us his hand, tell us how he learned to pitch without the first finger, or even the first knuckle. It gave him the ultimate advantage if you want to throw that curveball with lots of tight rotation. The second finger became his first finger. So he must have had a wicked curveball."

Indeed he did, and his story captivated fans. Mordecai was five years old, helping his brother cut food for horses at their uncle's farm in Nyesville, Indiana, when his right hand slipped into the feed chopper. The accident mangled every finger, and a doctor amputated the index finger below the second joint. A few weeks later, his hand still in a splint, Mordecai and his sister were playing with a pet rabbit, trying to make it swim in a tub. Mordecai lost his balance and smashed his hand on the bottom of the tub, breaking six bones.

It was a brutally painful, almost slapstick way to form the perfectly gnarled curveball hand. Nobody could mimic Brown's curveball.

"When Brown holds the ball in that chicken's foot of a hand and throws it out over that stump, the sphere is given a peculiar twist," wrote the Chicago *Inter Ocean* in 1910, at the height of Brown's fame with the Cubs. "It behaves something like a spitter. It goes singing up to the plate, straight as a drawn string, then just as the batter strikes at it, it darts down like a snake to its hole."

On his way to the Hall of Fame, Brown went 49–15 with a 1.44 ERA across the 1907 and 1908 seasons. He won all three of his World Series games in those years, allowing no earned runs over 20 innings to lead the Cubs to consecutive championships. He died in 1948, shortly after he would have met the young Carl Erskine. In 2003, Bill James and

Rob Neyer ranked Brown's curveball as the second best in the history of the game. The best, they said, belonged to Sandy Koufax.

———

In January 2014, I was chairman of the New York chapter of the Baseball Writers' Association of America. In this role, I emceed and helped plan our annual awards dinner. Clayton Kershaw and Max Scherzer would be receiving their Cy Young Awards, and I sat them on the dais on either side of Koufax, who was there to present for Kershaw. I thought all three would enjoy one another's company. Sitting just to Kershaw's right, by the lectern, I noticed throughout the evening how engaged the young pitchers were with Koufax, how easily they chatted. For Scherzer, it was a master class on the curveball.

"My God, could you imagine a better person in life to ever talk to about throwing a curveball?" Scherzer told me a year later, at spring training with the Nationals in Viera, Florida. "I literally sat there on my iPhone just writing down notes: 'How are you doing this, what do you do on that?' There's definitely some principles I still think about from that conversation, what you want to do with the shape, how you want to spin the ball, the mental approach to it. Those were really good conversations."

Scherzer had learned the curveball midway through the 2012 season with the Detroit Tigers. His pitching coach, Jeff Jones, drilled Scherzer on throwing his signature slider slower and slower and slower until it morphed into a curve, which is just what Scherzer needed against left-handers. His power slider broke toward them, dropping into their "nitro zone," he said, with speed too close to his fastball. A slower option, with more of a vertical drop, could be effective against hitters from both sides.

This is a big reason many organizations implore their prospects to master the curve before the slider. It is a pitch that no hitter—even perhaps the greatest ever—wants to see.

"Ted Williams used to call once a month and we would chat about the team," said Dan Duquette, the former Red Sox general manager. "So the day after I traded Aaron Sele, Ted calls me up. He goes, 'OK, hot shot, why in the hell are you trading the best curveballer in the

American League?' I said, 'Well, he didn't want to pitch in Boston.' He goes, 'I don't give a damn, he's got a good curveball! Let me tell you something: that curveball can get out a left-hand hitter just as well as it can get out a right-hand hitter! Now don't be trading those guys when you get 'em!'"

Williams spent his whole career with the Red Sox and never faced Koufax, a career Dodger. Their primes did not overlap, anyway. In 1960, when Williams retired, Koufax went 8–13 with a 3.91 ERA and 100 walks. It was his sixth season of mediocrity. The next six would be some of the greatest in the history of baseball.

In those six seasons, Koufax went 129–47 with a 2.19 ERA. He won five ERA titles, four strikeout titles, three Cy Young Awards, and two World Series MVP awards. He was unquestionably aided by the tall mound at Dodger Stadium, where his career ERA was 1.37, two runs better than it was everywhere else. He reigned from that perch till his very last strikeout in the 1966 World Series.

"I go up there and Koufax throws me the first high fastball: *shooo*," the hitter, Hall of Fame pitcher Jim Palmer, says now. "Then he throws me the curveball and it looks the same—*the same!*—and John Roseboro catches it on the ground. And I'm going, *this* is Sandy Koufax."

Palmer's at-bat happened right after the second fly ball in a row that center fielder Willie Davis lost in the sun. Those errors cost Koufax the game and he never pitched again, retiring at age 30 with an arthritic left arm, a decade before medical advancements could have saved his career. The memory of his curveball is seared in the minds of his helpless foes.

"It sounded like a little tornado, *bzzzzz*," Orlando Cepeda told Jane Leavy, Koufax's biographer. "So fast and noisy, it scared you."

Koufax has giant hands, and when he opened his glove wide from the stretch, savvy hitters knew he was gripping his curveball. Usually, it didn't even matter. Koufax understood biomechanics decades before the industry, and knew how to propel his body to the plate with maximum efficiency and force. The curveball, he told a rookie teammate in his final season, is not very complicated.

"He said it's an elbow pitch, and you come up over the top and pull down hard on the front of the ball, like you would on a fastball, where you pull down hard on the back of the ball," Don Sutton says. "On the curveball you're doing the same thing but you're just pulling down hard on the front of the ball."

Koufax's wisdom on the curveball echoed the words of Henry Roper, an old minor leaguer who was Sutton's sixth-grade teacher in Molino, Florida. Sutton had started Little League just the year before, as a shortstop, but decided to be a pitcher because they seemed to have the most fun. He brought his glove to school every day and played catch with Mr. Roper. He never once took a mound without a curveball, and the pitch never bothered his arm.

"I think it's one of the worst-taught pitches in baseball, because we're teaching people to get out front and pull the window shade and turn the doorknob," Sutton says. "Those are all great phrases, but you're doing it with an empty hand. The simplest way I was taught was the curveball is a karate chop with a ball in your hand. So load up at a 90-degree angle with your upper arm and your lower arm and throw the karate chop, and the ball will come out spinning."

Sutton would go on to pitch for 23 seasons, finishing with 324 victories, including a club-record 233 for the Dodgers. He is in the Hall of Fame, like Bert Blyleven, who learned the curve, indirectly, from Koufax. Born in Holland, Blyleven moved to California as a boy, and his father took him to a Dodger game to see Koufax face Juan Marichal. Even from the upper deck, Blyleven could see the vicious drop on the Koufax curve. It captivated him, and he would listen with his father to Vin Scully calling games on radio.

"I used to keep score just when Koufax and Drysdale pitched, because I liked writing down the strikeouts," Blyleven says.

He liked collecting them, too. Blyleven practiced his curveball against a wall, visualizing it breaking the way Scully described, making sure his thumb was on top of the ball on release, to impart that last bit of hellacious spin. At 19 he was in the majors with the Twins, and when he retired at 41, he had 3,701 strikeouts, trailing only Nolan Ryan and Steve Carlton. The career leader in strikeouts by a hitter, Reggie Jackson, fanned 49 times against Blyleven, by far his most frequent tormentor.

"You didn't hit it," Jackson says of the Blyleven curve. "He had to hang it to hit it. The quickness of the break, the speed of the pitch, the velocity, whatever the term—the break was big and it was hard. It was electric."

There is no shame in saying this for Jackson. Even the best hitters, with the biggest egos, can be helpless to handle a pitch from the gods. Just ask Mike Schmidt, the best third baseman in major league history, about Ryan's curveball.

"Well, I could hit Nolan's fastball," Schmidt says. "I couldn't hit his curveball in a million years for a base hit. And over the years, in probably 40 or 50 at-bats from him, I probably saw 100 curveballs—hanging, snapping off the table for strikes, in the dirt—*whoom, whoom,* they're everywhere, and I don't think I ever swung at one, because it was starting behind your head, you know."

Schmidt rose from his seat in the lobby of the Phillies' training complex in Clearwater, Florida. He assumed his familiar right-handed stance, and flinched at the imaginary Ryan curve.

"I was always doing this," he says, then adds he was still astonished at breaking up a Ryan no-hitter in the ninth inning by actually hitting that dastardly curve. "I don't know why it happened or how it happened, but: curveball, hit it up the middle. Maybe one of the few curveballs I hit up the middle my whole life. So his curveball to me was the most intimidating pitch to have to deal with *at all.* From a right-hander's standpoint, it was ridiculous. *Ridiculous.*"

Ryan developed a changeup near the end of his career. But for much of his first 20 seasons, he threw only the fastball and curve. Like Koufax with the wide glove, Ryan telegraphed his curveball by grunting when he threw a fastball. If he didn't grunt, the curve was coming. Hitters had no time to react, anyway.

Ryan found stardom after his December 1971 trade from the Mets to the Angels. The biggest reason was the Angels' pitching coach, Tom Morgan, who smoothed his mechanics, allowing him to stay on top with his curveball.

"In my delivery I was a rusher, because when I got in trouble I tried to throw harder," Ryan says. "So what you do is you just develop a pattern of rushing your delivery and not allowing your arm to catch up with your body. That's not how you throw harder or a sharper curveball. So understanding what I had to do from a mechanical standpoint, and then being able to implement that consistently, my curveball got better as my delivery improved."

For an extraordinarily hard thrower, like Koufax, Ryan, or Dwight Gooden, the curveball can be the ideal complement. Alan Ashby, who caught Ryan in Houston and struggled to hit Gooden, said it was almost impossible to be ready for two vastly different pitches that started from the same spot.

"They had that curveball that came out of the same, almost eye-high location all the time," Ashby said. "It's always that in-between that kills us mediocre hitters. You couldn't hit the fastball because they had that curveball, and you couldn't hit the curveball because they had that fastball."

Roy Halladay reached the majors with a knuckle-curve, and nearly threw a no-hitter with it in his second career start, in 1998. Back in the minors after that, he learned a more traditional curveball from Chris Carpenter, and found he could control it better: throw it softer for a strike, or pull it harder to finish in the dirt.

"I could throw a fastball for a strike in any count, whether I was cutting it or sinking it, and then I was able to throw a curveball in any count, whether it be 3–2, 3–0, 3–1," he said. "If I could throw it in any count knowing it was gonna be for a strike, that played so much into a hitter's head, knowing they can't sit on any pitch, ever, 100 percent convinced it's gonna be a fastball."

Al Leiter, a power lefty known for hard fastballs and cutters, decided he had to apply this principle to have a chance in Game 7 of the 1997 World Series for the Marlins. He watched video of David Wells and Andy Pettitte, other lefties who had attacked the powerful Indians lineup. Leiter determined that his very first pitch would have to be a curveball, reasoning that he would disrupt the Indians' timing by startling them with something soft.

He got the pitch over, and Omar Vizquel took it for a strike. Leiter pitched well, the Marlins won, and two years later, with the Mets in a tiebreaker for the National League Wild Card at Cincinnati, he did it again with a shutout.

"You have all these guys speeding up, looking for 90 to 93 inside, and here I'm throwing a 78-mile-an-hour slow curveball that wraps around the back side of the plate, getting called strike one," Leiter says.

"And now it's like, 'Oh shit, you've got 78 that wraps around the back door, outer half, and I still gotta look inside because you're gonna bust me in and break my bat?' When I had that combination, those are the games I was nailing it."

———————

No pitch elicits more colorful comparisons for the way it is thrown than the curveball. There is the karate chop, as Don Sutton says. "Like a gun," says A. J. Burnett, who learned his knuckle-curve—he always called it his hook—from his grandpa. A pitching coach, Gil Patterson, compares the motion to arm wrestling. When Barry Zito threw his curve, Patterson says, "If the catcher didn't catch it, you felt like it would boomerang and come back to you." Adam Wainwright, the curveball master for the St. Louis Cardinals, uses a nickname for the pitch, Uncle Charlie, in his Twitter handle.

"It's like you're hammering—or fishing, casting a line," Mike Mussina says. "That's what you're doing."

Bob Tewksbury, a control artist of the 1990s, would practice as a boy with a tennis ball can, flipping it end-over-end so the rotation mimicked a 12-6 curveball. Drew Storen, the former closer for the Nationals, used a hockey puck for the same purpose. Tom Gordon's father taught his son the curveball by placing a bucket six to eight feet behind a seven-foot fence. Gordon would stand about six feet from the fence, make a backwards C with his fingers, rotate his thumb upward, and dump curves into the bucket, over and over. He practiced so much he killed the tree he used as a rubber.

"I had to plant another one," Gordon says.

With the Royals in 1989, Gordon finished second in AL Rookie of the Year voting to Gregg Olson, another right-handed curveball master. Olson, a closer for the Orioles, would work on his form by spinning a paper cup—smoothly, longways, not end-over-end. If it didn't wobble, it had the right spin.

Olson played for the Dodgers at the end of his career, long after his All-Star prime, when he rendered helpless some of the game's best left-handed hitters (Ken Griffey Jr., Don Mattingly, and Rafael Palmeiro combined to go 3-for-33 off him). Olson would set his grip by locking his fingertip around a seam. Koufax, he said, showed him a better way.

"His hands were enormous compared to mine," Olson says. "He would take his middle finger and slide it down along the seam that he wanted. And then he would shove the finger against that seam so the side of the finger is now flush up against the seam. If you grab a baseball and do that, the baseball is just dying to spin out of your hand. So I did that my last couple of years—that's what I teach kids now—and it's an amazing difference if you just grab that baseball. I wish I would have had that early on. That would have been hours of amusement."

When Floyd Bannister pitched for the Rangers, his son, Brian, liked to stand behind the pitchers while they threw in the bullpen, to see the movement from their point of view. Brian Bannister grew up to pitch for the Mets and the Royals, and later joined the Red Sox as a pitching consultant and coach, equally versed in the science of the craft and the mind-set of the craftsmen. To Bannister, the curveball is unlike anything else in pitching.

"The curveball is unique," he says. "It's its own special pitch, because the break comes from the spin. With the slider, the changeup, the splitter—the break comes from gravity. You're dealing with a unique pitch with the curveball, because the rate of topspin is what makes it go down, and go down faster than gravity."

The slider, he explains, is a game between how hard a pitcher can throw it while also maximizing the pull of gravity. The curveball is all spin, right through to the pitcher's finish.

"On the curveball, you're actually trying to tuck the arm and decrease the radius of the arc, which increases the spin—whereas on the slider, you maintain a full arm length and a full follow-through and all the spin is created by the wrist and fingertips," Bannister says. "Two totally different approaches, which is why some guys throw sliders better and some guys throw curveballs better and why most guys struggle to throw both. Somebody like Clayton Kershaw is very rare, to throw elite versions of both."

The curveball can start as something else before finding its true identity. Mike Mussina taught himself a curveball that Olson, his future Baltimore teammate, said nobody else could ever throw.

"When I was a kid, I couldn't throw a curveball," Mussina says. "I mean, everybody's teaching you how to throw curveballs, get ahold of it like this and whatever, and I'd throw it and it just wouldn't do anything. It was like: 'That can't be what I see on television. That's crap.'

"So I started messing around, and I'm throwing knuckleballs—and I could throw a knuckleball, but the ball would spin too much. And so I figured: 'Wait a minute, what if I can do that on purpose? Can I fire my fingers out hard enough that I can make the ball do that on purpose—like, fast?' And I just kept working at it, working at it, working at it, working at it, and that's how I held a curveball for most of college—flick my fingers out and the ball would come out with topspin. Now, it wasn't biting and nasty, but it was good."

It was good enough to take to the majors, with the Orioles in 1991, but it was not the curveball Mussina used for most of his career. That was one he learned at Stanford from a teammate, Lee Plemel, who tucked his curveball into his palm and held his index finger up, resting it lightly on top—the spike curveball. That grip felt comfortable instantly, and Mussina could vary its speed and shape much more than he could with his old one. It worked from different arm angles, too.

"It's like any technological advancement," Mussina says, pointing to his smartphone. "Why would I talk on a rotary phone when I could talk on this now? It's the same thing, my own evolution. I found something better."

Mussina, at various times, could find any kind of pitch. He faced Wade Boggs so many times that he once flipped him a knuckleball, just to mix things up. Midway through another game, Mussina called catcher John Flaherty to the mound and told him what to signal for the splitter. Flaherty reminded Mussina he didn't have a splitter; "Today I do," Mussina replied.

Mussina won 20 games in 2008, bringing his career total to 270. If he had gotten much closer to 300 wins, he reasoned, he would have had to go for it. As a 40-year-old father of three, he didn't want to pitch three more seasons—but he could have, because his will matched his talent. Mussina was capable of invention, and hungry enough to constantly pursue it.

"I don't know if I was completely lucky, but it's just not that easy to do that kind of stuff, apparently," he says. "And it took me a little while to figure that out, but once I did, that's how I was able to play. It wasn't because I threw 96. It was because I could keep learning, I could keep adjusting, and I had a large—not large—but a pretty good selection of ways to pitch. I didn't just have to be throwing as hard as I could, plus a curveball. I could be a thumber, I could sink the ball, I could throw 75 percent sinkers instead of 75 percent four-seamers."

A thumber?

"A thumber's just like a guy who throws a lot of junk, that you might as well throw with your thumb, as hard as you're throwing it," he says, smiling. "Instead of throwing it, you're just kind of flipping it, junking it. That's what a thumber is—a junkball pitcher."

Every junkballer has a curve. When the fastball goes, a slow, looping curveball, with impeccable command, sound mechanics, and a durable body, can keep a pitcher going for a long time.

"I saved my best fastball for 20 percent of the time and the other 80 was just nibbling and changing speeds," says Frank Tanana, describing how he survived after injuries zapped his heat. "So when I threw my 80 or 85, it seemed like 95, because the other stuff was so crappy—or so slow, I should say. It's just an art, and I was very blessed."

Steve Stone could describe himself the same way, for different reasons. Stone was 33 years old in 1980, when he went 25–7 for the Orioles. He wears a custom-made ring with "Cy Young" surrounding a diamond on the face, commemorating his award for the achievement. Stone won largely by throwing as many curveballs as he could—seven out of 10 pitches, most days. His trick was to vary his curves at three speeds, depending on where he held the ball and how he applied finger pressure. Maybe all those curveballs hurt his longevity, he says; he lasted just one more season, a casualty of elbow pain.

But the recognition from his big year led directly to a long and successful career as a broadcaster. And maybe the curveball didn't ruin his arm at all.

"I had also completed my twelfth year of pro ball," Stone says. "And this might have eluded you, but I'm not the size of C. C. Sabathia. So I think being a relatively smaller pitcher at 5'9"—or 5'9" and a quarter; I swelled up during the season—my arm only had so many pitches in it."

———

Gregg Olson also blew out, and when he describes his best curveballs as coming from "a violent turn of the elbow," injuries sound inevitable. Actually, Olson says, a mechanical change was responsible; his drop-and-drive, hip-twisting motion looked peculiar but worked for him, and his arm reacted badly when the Orioles forced him to learn a slide step. His favorite pitch is blameless.

"When you come through and your hand's facing your face and you're pulling down in front, I believe that is fine for your arm," Olson says. "My curveball was thrown correctly and it was protected with my body."

Adam Wainwright's most famous curveball was the called third strike to the Mets' Carlos Beltran that ended Game 7 of the 2006 NLCS. (He would also end that fall's World Series with a strikeout, against Detroit's Brandon Inge, but that was on a slider.) Looking back, Wainwright says, the Beltran pitch was a product of youthful swagger; ahead in the count, 0–2, it was crazy to throw a strike to such a dangerous hitter.

But the pitch was just that good, and would remain so for many years. In 2013, two years after Tommy John surgery, Wainwright threw a staggering 276⅔ innings, including the postseason. A year later, he won 20 games. Wainwright's brother, Trey, who is seven years older, showed him a curveball grip at age 10. The pitch felt perfectly natural. "Back then there was no talk of age limits to throw curveballs, which I believe plays into people hurting their arms by not throwing it till later in life," Wainwright says. "Everybody's parents think it's bad for them to throw curveballs, but we have a higher rate of Tommy John [surgeries] than ever, and everybody's throwing harder than ever. So people are building arm strength, building arm strength, building arm strength, and then they say, 'All right, you're in high school now, you're throwing 90, now we can work on a curveball.' So what you're doing is you're taking an arm that's fully developed and strong and throwing bullets, and then all of a sudden you're entering a totally new movement at max speed rather than bringing along a properly thrown curveball. A curveball's much less strain on your arm than a slider is. A slider is a variation of the fastball, and you kind of have a wrist twinge. It's just not as good on your elbow."

Curveball enthusiasts say this all the time: the slider is more dangerous, and the curveball, *when taught properly,* is just fine. Teaching it, though, is the problem. There are far more young pitchers than there are coaches qualified to teach a safe curveball.

"I tell kids and I tell parents: throwing a curveball will not hurt your arm if you throw it properly, but the problem is that most people don't throw it properly," Nolan Ryan says. "So they have to learn to throw it properly. If you do that, it won't hurt your arm any more than a fastball. Everything's the same, it's just your hand position on the ball. So with kids, it's a touchy thing to get 'em to understand what they have to do and what they shouldn't do. It's not something you learn overnight, either."

What do kids do when they throw the curveball improperly?

"They try to put spin on the ball by putting pressure on the elbow, which is not where you get it," Ryan continues. "You get the spin on the ball, it's in your hand and your wrist."

Jon Lester, the veteran left-hander who won titles with the Red Sox and Cubs, says the curveball itself is not a problem. The danger, he says, is that kids often struggle to repeat the proper mechanics.

"People always ask, 'How old can I be when I start throwing curveballs?'" Lester says, shrugging his shoulders. "Throw 'em when you're two years old. That's not the problem. The problem is your mechanics. The problem is you have a 12-year-old, he can't repeat his arm slot. That's the torque on the elbow. That's the problem with throwing a curveball when you're younger: you can't repeat. You're not strong enough."

When a pitcher throws a curveball properly, the arm protects itself by tucking itself in, toward the glove-side rib cage, as it follows through. A slider puts more pressure on the elbow because it requires full extension. Blyleven dismisses the notion that curveballs cause injury—"A myth," he says. "A slider will hurt your arm more"—and Mussina echoes him. Mussina never had arm surgery and says that whenever something felt off, the fastball caused him more discomfort than the curve.

"Anytime that I had a sore elbow or anything like that, I never, ever, ever felt like it was my curveball that did it," he says. "Never. It was never really in a place that seemed like my curveball would be the reason."

Mussina lives in the shadow of Williamsport, Pennsylvania, home of the Little League World Series, and has served on the Little League International board of directors. Every August, there's a mild outcry when folks watch 12-year-olds spinning curveballs in Williamsport on ESPN. Yet Mussina doesn't rail against the dangers of the pitch, and neither does Dr. Glenn Fleisig, who studied the issue with his colleagues by tracking the progress of 481 youth pitchers for a decade. Their report, issued in 2011, found no relationship between throwing curveballs before age 13 and serious arm injury after.

"What was a strong indicator was pitching too much," Fleisig says. "So the kids who pitched year-round baseball in high school and these travel teams, they get hurt whether or not they're the ones who throw the curveballs."

For pitchers of all ages, Fleisig says, the fastball and curveball exert similar amounts of stress on elbows and shoulders; the curveball, in fact, was found to have 5 to 10 percent less stress on the shoulder, though that was deemed statistically insignificant. (The study did find "significantly less elbow and shoulder torque and force" from the changeup.)

If kids who throw curveballs get hurt more often, Fleisig says, don't blame the pitch.

"The kids who threw curveballs at the younger age were also the ones with the pushy parents," he says, "and also the ones who played year-round."

Need more testimony? Here's Tom House, the former reliever and pitching coach: "The curveball, which everybody thought was the worst pitch on the arm, is actually the easiest pitch on the arm, because if it's thrown properly, it's the strength position, and it's the slowest velocity. When you're karate-chopping a brick, you're not doing it with your palm, you're doing it with the side of your hand, just like you throw a curveball. If you twist when you do it, that's where all the issues in the elbow come in."

Curveball hysteria is misguided. There is just no evidence that, *with proper technique,* curveballs are bad for developing arms. And it's not just recent science. Here's Bob Shaw, a longtime pitcher and coach, in his 1972 pitching manual:

"At what age should a youngster start throwing a curve ball?" Shaw wrote. "In my experience, most of the good curve-ball pitchers have started young. You can injure your arm at any age if you do not throw the curve correctly. Age is not a factor."

———————

You see it all the time in the clubhouse, or if you watch the relievers while they're sitting in the bullpen. They'll flip balls to themselves, like a lifeguard lazily whirling her whistle around her fingers while staring out at the water, just to pass the time. In this case, though, there's a purpose: spin. It's not the same kind of spin, exactly, but the more idle time you spend flicking that ball, exercising the wrist and fingers on the muscle memory of a curveball, the better.

"You've got free time, you're just sitting around during a game," Mike Montgomery says. "Why not grab a ball, grip it how you would, and just spin it?"

Hitters would rather you didn't. One of the best, Mike Piazza, learned this at a young age as a bat boy for the Dodgers. Someone asked Bill Madlock, the veteran third baseman, how to hit a curveball. "Don't miss the fastball!" Madlock replied. By then he had won four batting titles.

"It's just harder to hit," says Mark Teixeira, who slugged 409 home runs. "Drop a ball from a 20-foot ladder and have me try to hit it, going straight down. Even for the best hitters in the world, that's gonna be tough to do. Now, give me a 100-mph fastball—straight, in the zone—I'll hit it every time. I may not get a hit, but I'm gonna hit it. But if you do it the other way, that's what a curveball does. A good curveball with a lot of break, it's not necessarily that I don't recognize it, but it's moving so much that it's tougher to square up."

A few decades ago, some worried that the slider would all but wipe out the curveball, because it is easier to throw and easier to get called in the strike zone. Candy Cummings found a way to work around that problem; a century later, it persisted.

"The strike zone was bigger in my day," says Carl Erskine, who pitched from 1948 to 1959. "Just under the letters used to be a called strike; now if it's above the belt, it's a ball. So the strike zone has been compressed, and that's caused pitchers to adapt more to breaking pitches that are smaller. It's hard to get the big curveball a called strike sometimes, because it starts above the strike zone and breaks down into it. Sometimes the umpire sees it too high."

Al Jackson, a stalwart lefty of the early Mets, later became a coach with the Red Sox. In 1977, he lamented to *The Boston Globe*'s Bob Ryan: "Pitchers have become so slider crazy that the curve is fast becoming a dying art."

Yet the slider never came close to eliminating the curveball. Ryan and Blyleven overlapped with Mussina and Olson, who overlapped with Zito and Wainwright, and so on. Now, as pitchers dominate with high, hard stuff as never before, it is more and more critical to have the contrast of a tumbling curveball.

"Guys are throwing so hard, if they can throw a slower pitch, it's too big a speed variance to cover," Wainwright says. "If you're throwing fastball/slider, everything's hard, so a hitter can gear up for basically one tempo, one speed. Whereas if you've gotta worry about hard/slow, it's very tough."

John Smoltz, a power version of Mussina, loved the curveball. When Smoltz had his hard stuff going, as he usually did, the curve would give him a free strike. Hitters prepared for a fastball or slider, and when Smoltz tossed a curveball instead, they'd be so surprised at the different shape and speed that they'd lock up and watch it drop in the zone. Smoltz calls the curveball a forgotten art and is glad to see it coming back through stars like Kershaw and Madison Bumgarner. There's really no excuse for a curveball—at least the kind to steal a strike—to be missing from a pitcher's tool belt.

"When I was first coming up, you'd see the big 12-6 curveball, with Matt Morris and Darryl Kile for the Cardinals," says David Ross, who caught in the majors for 15 seasons, through 2016. "I think that's starting to come back. It's just evolution. When guys are throwing so hard now, you have to commit a little bit sooner as a hitter, and you're way out in front. It's one of those things where the fastball's so hard, so the 12-6 starts at your head and drops in for a strike, or it starts where the fastball does and it's more of a chase pitch."

Ross ended his career riding off the field in Cleveland on the shoulders of his Cubs teammates, after Montgomery's final curveball won Game 7 of the World Series. That concluded a season in which major league pitchers threw 7,732 more curveballs than they had in 2015, according to Statcast data from MLB.com. The average curveball was also spinning more, at 2,462 rpm, up from 2,302. In 2017, pitchers threw curveballs with 10.6 percent of all pitches, a 15-season high.

There are get-me-over curveballs to dump in the zone for called strikes, and curveballs in the dirt to bait a free swinger. But more and more, Montgomery is convinced, pitchers are throwing true curveballs: pitches in the zone, meant to induce swinging strikes. It is simple evolution, with the information flowing from the front office to the field. The data tells decision makers what to seek, so now they seek curveballs with high spin rates.

Mussina rolls his eyes at all this. He practically spits out the term: "Spin rate. That's the dumbest thing I've ever heard." What he means is that spin rate for a curveball matters only as much as the radar gun reading for a fastball. It doesn't mean the pitch is any good; not even close, actually. A great pitch that cannot be commanded is not, in fact, a great pitch. As hitters say about a bad curveball: "You hang it, we bang it."

Yet as the curveball's essential raw ingredient, spin rate is important to know. Organizations use those figures to tell them, empirically, which of their prospects might have a major league pitch. A nondescript pitcher with a high spin rate now gets chances once reserved only for those with a mid-90s fastball: *Hey, there just might be something here.*

Collin McHugh had made it through high school, college, and four years of pro ball without ever hearing of spin rate. A former eighteenth-round draft choice, he was 24 years old and pitching in the Arizona Fall League in 2011 when a coach circulated a thick packet of detailed statistics. McHugh found his name near the top of the list for rpm on his curveball.

"It was right up there with Verlander and Kershaw and Felix, some of these guys with really good curveballs," McHugh says. "To see myself in that echelon with any one thing that I did, it gave me confidence. It gave me at least some kind of reference to say, 'I'm not just some other Double-A guy somewhere. There's something that I do exceptionally well, and I want to try to capitalize on it.'"

The next year McHugh was in the majors. He bounced from the

Mets to the Rockies, and while his statistics were bad, the fast-spinning curveball still made him a prospect. The Astros signed him off waivers, and in 2015 he went 19–7 to help them reach the playoffs.

The Mets lost McHugh, but they held on to Seth Lugo, a thirty-fourth-round draft pick with a curve he had first honed, as a boy, with the tennis-ball-can drill. Lugo's first minor league manager, Frank Fultz, took one look at the pitch and told him it would someday lift him to the majors. Five years later, with injuries ravaging the Mets' rotation, Lugo earned a promotion and sparkled down the stretch. His curveball had the best spin rate in the league.

That August 30, in the sixth inning of a win over Miami, Lugo let loose a curve at 3,498 rpm, the highest recorded in the first two years of Statcast. Lugo was ahead in the count to Xavier Scruggs, 1–2, and wanted the pitch below the zone. Scruggs, who swung over the ball as it plunged hard and late, knew right away he had seen something extraordinary.

"Guys will swing and miss all the time, but you know when it's a different swing and miss," Scruggs says. "That ball didn't go anywhere near where I thought it was going."

Eleven days later, the Dodgers' Rich Hill toyed with the Marlins for seven perfect innings. Hill threw curveballs with 57 percent of his pitches, the crowning example of the freedom he felt the year before, when the Red Sox signed him from the independent Long Island Ducks. Working with Bannister, Hill learned different ways to shape his curveball, and trusted Bannister's advice to throw it much more often than any other pitcher in the game. Hill pitched well for Boston, then signed a 2016 contract with Oakland for $6 million.

Traded to the Dodgers, Hill sliced curveballs through the National League, ending with six shutout innings against the Cubs in the playoffs. That December, the Dodgers brought him back with a three-year, $48 million contract—a jackpot, at last, after 15 pro seasons, a deal that would soon lead Hill to the World Series. He wept at the news conference announcing it.

"I think that's life, right?" Hill said, reflecting on the rocky path brought to riches by perseverance and a killer curve. "You're going to be thrown a lot of different curveballs."

THE
KNUCKLEBALL

Grabbing the Wing of a Butterfly

The old knuckleballer grips his favorite pitch with three fingernails. Most pitchers use two, but for him that makes the pitch wobbly, impossible to control. Jim Bouton uses his ring finger, too. This is the grip he displayed for the nation four decades ago on the set of *The Tonight Show,* and the grip he showed me in his backyard a couple of years ago, high up in the Berkshires near Great Barrington, Massachusetts.

Bouton was 78 then, yet he was still throwing a couple of times a week. He built a cinder-block backstop in a sunlit corner of the yard, and hit the strike zone most of the time. His hat did not fall off anymore, as it did for the Yankees, back when he threw hard and beat St. Louis twice in the 1964 World Series. We played catch for 15 minutes, and his knuckler hit my glove every time. Mine hit his, too; the three-finger grip was the closest I'd ever come to controlling this most peculiar pitch.

If we were really on our games, though, we'd have let loose a few wild pitches. The best knuckleballs often zig and zag away from the mitt, sending their catchers scrambling. But if Bouton's knuckler can't quite dance like it did for the Seattle Pilots, it remains his pitch—slower now, but authentically his.

It was good for Jim to have company, said his wife, Paula Kurman, who has a doctorate in interpersonal communications from Columbia. They have been married since 1982 and have lived in the Berkshires for more than 20 years, among the foxes and black bears, surrounded by pine trees. A cloud might roll by, straight through the screened-in porch, and there are no other homes in sight. Their children are grown and live elsewhere.

Bouton had a stroke on August 15, 2012. They know the date because it was the fifteenth anniversary of the death of Bouton's daughter, Laurie, in a car accident. Bouton's body was largely unaffected. But his mind, the one whose pointed and poignant observations produced the classic *Ball Four* in 1970, will never be the same. He has a brain disease: cerebral amyloid angiopathy, a form of dementia. He struggles with numerical concepts. Processing questions can be frustrating. Writing is too complicated to organize and enjoy. Life is filled with unforeseen gaps in understanding.

"Sometimes we'll have conversations and it's like it's 10 years ago," Kurman said. "Things are flowing along. And then you step in this pothole and you didn't know it was there."

He still remembers a lot of old baseball stories, many in precise detail from years of retelling. He is gentle and funny and kind, as ever. And when I mention that I always keep my baseball glove in the trunk of my car, he eagerly scurries to find his own: a brown, well-worn Louisville Slugger marked with his old number, 56, in thick black pen. Let's play catch.

There are no potholes in the yard, only green grass and pine trees and sunshine. It remains for Jim Bouton as he once wrote: he can still grip a baseball, and baseball still grips him. The knuckleball endures.

———

Baseball people like to say that your worst day at the ballpark is better than your best day at the office. It reminds them that the baseball life is really not too bad. Yes, it's stressful, with relentless travel and meager pay in the minors. But somebody wins every day, you're outdoors a lot, and deep down you recognize that, of all the industries out there, you're lucky to work in the baseball one.

Maybe for that reason, I've found that most people in baseball tend to be . . . pretty nice. And of all the subsets of folks in the game, knuckleball pitchers might be the nicest. They are also part of the smallest group, which helps explain it. Almost all knuckleballers were rejected by the game before they could last very long. They earned their living by grabbing the wing of a butterfly and then, somehow, steering it close enough to the strike zone, again and again, to baffle the best hitters in the world.

"Most of our careers were headed in a different direction, and out of desperation, we all found the knuckleball," says Tim Wakefield, who won 200 games with it. "So I think the knuckleball itself has humbled most of us to a point where we're grateful that we still have a job and we're still able to compete."

"Compete" is the word Charlie Hough uses to explain his reason for throwing it. Hough was a decent pitcher in Class A for the Dodgers, but after six months in the Army reserves, his shoulder hurt when he tried to pitch again. With average stuff to begin with, Hough guessed that his future would be working at the Hialeah Race Track, two blocks from his home in Florida.

Then a scout named Goldie Holt showed him how to throw a knuckleball. Hough gave it a try.

"If you want to compete, you compete," he says. "You find something."

That something, for Hough and just a few dozen others in baseball's long history, is a pitch as quirky as its name. Pitchers once threw it with their knuckles actually pressed against the ball, and the knuckles are still prominent in the visual presentation. But the pitch is really thrown with the fingertips—"positioned between the thumb, index and middle fingers," as Wakefield wrote in his book with Tony Massarotti, "as if it were a credit card being held up for display."

The whole concept of the knuckleball is to be fundamentally different from every other pitch. With almost everything else, pitchers want to increase spin for greater velocity or a more deceptive break. They manipulate the ball to serve their will, to send it to a specific spot. If executed properly, the pitch will obey.

Because knuckleballers want no spin at all, they don't engage the same muscles as conventional pitchers. If a robot could pitch, it would throw like a knuckleballer, like one mechanical piece instead of a flexible acrobat stressing multiple leverage points to impart spin. The physical dangers of repeated throws at maximum effort do not apply for these craftsmen. Theirs is the safest pitch of all, but the trade-off is severe: it is also the hardest to master, and to trust.

Simply put, the trick is to use the seams to deflect the air and move the ball erratically, like an airplane flying into turbulence. A University of Iowa study, cited by the author Martin Quigley, described the aerodynamics like this: "When the ball leaves the pitcher's hand, it runs head on into a 'wall' of air. This air pushes at the front of the ball and pulls at the back. The air also tends to 'pile up' on the seams and rough surfaces. The forces holding the ball back build up so fast that the ball slows down suddenly and drops unusually fast . . . usually a short distance in front of the plate, and causes the batter to swing 'where it was, not where it is.'"

This results from what is known, in science, as the Bernoulli Effect, which states that the pressure within a flowing fluid (including a gas, such as air) is less than the pressure surrounding it. An object that is not spinning—or just barely spinning—will move toward an area of less pressure. As Robert K. Adair, PhD, wrote in *The Physics of Baseball,* the seams on a ball create chaos: "If the ball is thrown with very little rotation, asymmetric stitch configurations can be generated that lead to large imbalances of forces and extraordinary excursions in trajectory."

Then we have the unofficial explanation, from the batter's box, by the longtime outfielder Bobby Murcer. Trying to hit Phil Niekro, Murcer memorably said, was "like trying to eat Jell-O with chopsticks."

A good knuckleball will leave you laughing and stupefied, like a comedian who also does magic tricks; Satchel Paige called his the "bat-dodger." The pitch has a deep and rich history in the game, yet remains so uncommon that it is often an object of ridicule.

Sometimes the teasing is playful: in Wakefield's heyday with the Boston Red Sox, catcher Mike Macfarlane would cry "Freak show!" in the clubhouse before games. Sometimes, it is not so much teasing as a deep dislike, for practical reasons. Joe McCarthy, the Hall of Fame Yankees manager, groused that when a knuckleball breaks, the catcher misses it, and when it doesn't, the batter crushes it. He had little use for pitchers who did not throw hard.

"Any time you've got a soft ball pitcher," McCarthy would say, "then you've got a .500 pitcher."

Hough was .500 personified, with a career record of 216–216. Nobody else with that many victories has precisely the same number of losses. Then again, nobody else has made 400 appearances as both a starter and reliever, and few others have spent a quarter century on major league mounds.

Hough is a very nice guy, too. Bobby Valentine, who was teammates with Hough in Los Angeles, managed him in Texas, and hired him as a coach in New York, called him one of the best baseball men in the world. But Hough was not simply happy to be there. Nice does not mean pushover. Floating knuckleballs for a living takes a special kind of athletic bravery.

"I think you need a *huge* ego," Hough says. "You need to believe that you're the best pitcher in the world when you're in there. When they put down '1' for Nolan Ryan, he threw it 100 miles an hour. When they put down '1' for me, I threw what I felt like was a pitch they couldn't hit."

Adrenaline is the enemy. If you overthrow a knuckleball, it spins— and if it spins, you're in trouble. Trusting it defies logic, but doing so is essential. The pitchers who throw it do not frustrate easily. They need to stay calm so their pitch will behave. Low-key, happy-go-lucky people—with the guts to bring Silly String to a battlefield—just might have a chance.

The knuckleball is, at once, the most frustrating and fascinating pitch in baseball. It is also relatable, much more than any other pitch, to the fan in the stands. No one sees a turbocharged fastball or jack-knife curve and thinks: "Yep, I could do that." Yet anyone can look at a dancing knuckleball and say, "You know what? Maybe."

Bouton's knuckleball was like a character of its own in *Ball Four,* his famous diary of the 1969 season. Like Bouton, the pitch was a nonconformist struggling for respect in the game. It had intrigued Bouton as a boy, when he rooted for Hoyt Wilhelm and the New York Giants. He learned the grip from a cereal box that told the story of a knuckleballer named Dutch Leonard.

"It was like a magic thing," Bouton told me, several years ago. "You didn't need to be big. You didn't need to be strong. The idea was to throw a ball with perfection, really. And once you've thrown a success-ful knuckleball, you become entranced by it. If you've hit somebody in the chest with a knuckleball, you'll never forget it."

When something leaves us awestruck, we usually can't do it or wouldn't want to try—a mural on a church ceiling, a rousing guitar solo at a concert, a chainsaw-juggling act at a circus. Yet a fluttering knuckleball at a ballgame seems to be within our grasp. That is part of its appeal, and a reason it stands out as one of the more colorful patches on the baseball quilt.

But the premise that anyone can become a knuckleballer? Well . . . it's dead wrong. There are many reasons the pitch always flirts with extinction, but the most fundamental is this: it's really, really hard to throw. Fastball pitchers are born; knuckleballer pitchers are painstakingly self-made.

"People watch us throw and they say, 'Oh that's easy,'" Wakefield says. "Throwing it 65 or 70 miles an hour, anybody could do that. But in reality, it's really hard. And to be able to throw it for strikes consistently, that's the big thing. I mean, every middle infielder had a good knuckleball—but can they get on the mound and throw it to a hitter with a game on the line?"

Indeed, plenty of position players fool around with knuckleballs while playing catch—Mickey Mantle and Cal Ripken Jr. were well known for it, and R. A. Dickey, who won the 2012 National League Cy Young Award, says a different teammate would find him every year to show off his version.

But pitching from the slope of a mound makes it harder to keep the palm behind the ball, and changes everything. And even if a pitcher has the patience and the temperament for it, the knuckleball still requires the same kind of extraordinary athleticism as any other pitch—that is, the ability to repeat sound mechanics. This delivery is just engineered differently, for a much different kind of result.

"From your shoulder down you're all stiffed up, everything's locked in, there's no flip of your wrist," says Phil Niekro, the greatest knuckler of all. "In baseball—curveball, slider—it's all what you do with your wrist and the movement of the ball, the spin of the ball. Here, you want to throw something that's not gonna do anything at all, and you figure: 'What the hell, it's not doing nothing, but it'll do more than any other pitch you throw up there.'"

By doing nothing, the pitch with no spin can do anything.

———

Could it be that the first pitcher famous for the knuckleball, the last-chance weapon of the friendly warrior, was a notorious scoundrel? History knows Eddie Cicotte best as one of the eight Chicago White Sox banned for life for conspiring with gamblers to throw the 1919 World Series. Cicotte sent the signal by hitting the Cincinnati leadoff man in the back in the opener.

By then, Cicotte was well known as a master of the knuckleball, which he threw about 75 percent of the time. His nickname, after all, was Knuckles, and he threw the pitch—at first—by resting his knuckles on top of the ball. Cicotte had played with Nap Rucker (another early knuckleballer) in the minors in 1905, but would cite a 1906 minor league teammate, Ed Summers, with developing the pitch in its modern form.

Lew Moren, who pitched a few years for the Pirates and Phillies, would unveil his knuckler in the National League at roughly the same time as Cicotte and Summers in the American League. The knuckleball showed up in their 1908 stats: Cicotte led the league in wild pitches, Summers in hit batters. That July, Summers explained the difference in their grips to *Baseball Magazine:*

"I watched Eddie Cicotte, who first used it, and followed him. He rested the ball on his knuckles, but I couldn't see the value of that, because I couldn't control it, and one can put but little speed on it. . . . I found by holding the ball with my finger tips and steadying it with my thumb alone, I could get a peculiar break to it and send it to the batters with considerable speed and good control."

Summers said the pitch was not a knuckleball, and he was right, in the literal sense. But the pitch he threw is the one that would carry that name through the ages. In 1908, *Sporting Life* used the term "finger nail curve" to describe a pitch by Ralph Savidge of the Reds. The ball made no revolutions and moved erratically, but actually, Savidge would say, he did not really use his nails to throw it.

"I never know what's going to happen after the ball leaves my hand," he told the same publication in 1909. "Sometimes it breaks upward and sometimes it drops and it is just as liable to break to either the right or left."

Savidge would make just five appearances in the majors, and while the knuckleball appeared sporadically—a Phillies pitcher, Tom Seaton, won 27 games with it in 1913—it faced the first of many death scares with the banishment of Cicotte after the 1920 season. Fortunately for the knuckleball's survival, something else was banned after that season: the spitball.

When Eddie Rommel reached the majors with the A's in 1920, he brought a knuckler taught to him by a semipro first baseman, Cutter Drury, who had suggested it as a spitball alternative. In time, Rommel noticed that the softer he threw it, the more it would move. He led the majors in victories in 1922, with 27, and even flummoxed the Browns' George Sisler, who hit .420 that season.

"If it made a one-way hop, the batter would be able to set himself and familiarize himself with the break," Sisler said, as quoted by Rob Neyer. "But that's just where Rommel's success comes in. It goes down one time and the next will take an upward break. I believe I hit more infield flies against Rommel than any other pitcher in the league."

Rommel went 171–119 in all, but his ending was proof that even knuckleballers have physical limits, and arms that can be destroyed by abuse. As Neyer described, Sunday baseball was illegal in Philadelphia in 1932. So that July 10, in the middle of a 10-game home stand, the A's made a one-day trip to Cleveland. Times were good for the A's, who had won the last three AL pennants, but owner-manager Connie Mack still tried to save on train fare by bringing along only two pitchers. Lew Krausse worked the first inning, and Rommel—who had also worked the prior two days—*pitched the next seventeen.* He gave up 14 runs, a major-league-record 29 hits, and never won another game. Finished at 35, he would fashion a second act as an umpire for 24 years.

With Rommel's success, a pattern was setting in—one prominent knuckleballer gives way to another, with a few more flitting on and off the scene. Jesse Haines and Freddie Fitzsimmons overlapped Rommel, with better careers, but they threw the pitch off the knuckles, not the fingertips, and Haines (a Hall of Famer) sometimes used it just a dozen times a game. The 1945 Washington Senators had four knuckleballers in their rotation and nearly snagged a pennant, but just one—Dutch Leonard—had a winning career record. The others had little success outside the war years.

Gene Bearden, a 22-year-old minor leaguer who had already bounced through three organizations, found himself aboard the USS

Helena in the South Pacific in July 1943. Bearden was in the engine room when a Japanese destroyer struck his ship with a torpedo. As Bearden climbed a ladder to escape, another torpedo strike sent him crashing to the floor, unconscious, with a mangled knee and a severe gash to his head.

"Somebody pulled me out," Bearden would tell the Cleveland *Plain Dealer*. "They told me later it was an officer. I don't know how he did it. The ship went down in about 17 minutes. All I know is that I came to in the water some time later."

About 200 men died in the attack, but Bearden was rescued by an American destroyer after two days on a raft. At a Navy hospital in Florida, he had an aluminum plate inserted in his head and an aluminum cap and screw in his crushed kneecap. He took seven months to walk again and spent all of 1944 in the hospital.

Doctors told him to forget baseball, but Bearden returned anyway. He could not raise his right leg very high off the ground, and could not use a full windup. But he had no limp, and he won—15 games for the Yankees at Class A in 1945, then 15 more the next season in the Pacific Coast League for Casey Stengel.

Stengel had managed Leonard with the Dodgers, and noticed Bearden working on a self-taught knuckleball in spring training. He encouraged Bearden to use it, and a catcher, Bill Raimondi, called it often and handled it well. Traded to Cleveland before the 1947 season, Bearden was a rookie sensation in 1948, going 20–7 and clinching the pennant in a playoff at Fenway Park.

Most pitchers feared throwing inside at Fenway, where Red Sox hitters could pull pitches for homers down the short foul lines. Yet Bearden, with the moxie that runs so strong in the knuckleball family, worked inside anyway, surprising the Red Sox and going the distance in a five-hitter. A week later—after shutting out the Braves in Game 3 of the World Series—Bearden was back on a different mound in Boston, closing out the Indians' last championship in Game 6.

Bearden headed for Hollywood and appeared in two movies—*And Baby Makes Three* and *The Monty Stratton Story*—but his stardom quickly faded. He pinched a sciatic nerve in his leg the next spring, and his control, shaky in the best of times, deserted him. Batters hunted fastballs, and as Ed McAuley wrote in the *Cleveland News*, "Gene's fastball never was more than an invitation to an extra-base hit." After stints with four more teams, Bearden was out of the game just five years after his World Series triumph.

———————

Only two pitchers have gotten to the Hall of Fame with fingertip knuckleballs—not counting Wade Boggs, a third baseman who knuckled through a scoreless inning for the Yankees in 1997 and reprised the act for Tampa Bay two years later, just before retiring.

Cooperstown's first true fingertip knuckleballer was Hoyt Wilhelm, who made his major league debut the year he turned 30 and pitched until the month he turned 50. Voters needed eight ballots before electing Wilhelm in 1985. The next inductee was Phil Niekro, who earned a staggering 208 victories *after turning 35*. He made it on his fifth try, in 1997.

For both men, persistence was everything.

"My first year in professional baseball, in 1959, I was pitching in Kearney, Nebraska, and I remember meeting Phil Niekro," Bouton once told me. "I was sitting in the bleachers before a game and I see this skinny, crew-cut kid in the outfield, and he's throwing the knuckleball. I could see, even from a distance, that ball was moving. So I walked over and introduced myself and told him I throw a knuckleball, too. I said, 'What do you throw besides the knuckleball?' And he said, 'Nothing, just the knuckleball.'

"We had a nice chat and I thought to myself, 'Phil Niekro, that poor son of a bitch. He's never gonna make it because he's only got one pitch—and I, Jim Bouton, I'm on my way to the big leagues because I have all these pitches.' And then when I was in the big leagues, after my 20-win season, I remembered him and thought, 'Oh that poor kid, he's still in the minor leagues and I don't know how he hangs on because I'm on my way to the Hall of Fame.' Well, guess what? That poor kid, limited to one pitch—he's in the Hall of Fame now. It's a good reminder for me of the tortoise and the hare."

Niekro would make 716 career starts, fifth on the career list, yet 102 of his first 103 appearances came from the bullpen. In the 1950s and most of the '60s, that was usually where knuckleballers went—and Wilhelm was the model.

In Wilhelm's teen years in North Carolina, Leonard was rising to stardom in Washington. Wilhelm, who did not throw hard, noticed a photograph of Leonard's knuckleball grip in the Charlotte newspaper. He practiced with a tennis ball and found that the feel came naturally.

That experience convinced Wilhelm that the knuckleball could not be taught. Though he would spend many post-playing years as a coach, he believed that if you did not throw the pitch as a kid, you could never pick it up as a man. Though countless examples contradict this, Wilhelm was firm: you either have it or you don't.

"Nobody has ever asked me to teach them, but even if they did, I wouldn't," Wilhelm told *The Atlanta Journal* in 1973. "It's an unorthodox pitch. You have to have a knack to throw it to start with."

Wilhelm favored a fastball/slider/changeup mix for young pitchers, but if he happened to see his old pitch, he loved it. Coaching the Yankees' rookie leaguers in 1991, he insisted that a promising lefty from Texas keep throwing his knuckler, even though the other instructors wanted him to stop.

"He was just a crusty old dude," Andy Pettitte would say, many years later. "I loved him to death. I'd come back and say, 'Hoyt, dad-gum it, why did I do this?' or, 'Why didn't I do that?' And he'd say, 'Pettitte, just keep turning 'em to the right,' meaning when they get to first base, turn them to the right, back to their dugout. That's all he would say: 'Pettitte, just keep turning 'em to the right.'"

The other coaches persuaded Pettitte to scrap his knuckleball, but late in his career he would joke that he just might revive it as a last resort. He stayed strong to the end and never did, and besides, Pettitte said, the pitch would have gone stale by then. The knuckleball needs constant nurturing, as his old coach believed and proved.

Wilhelm was the first pitcher to appear in 1,000 games. He twice led his league in earned run average and no-hit the Yankees for Baltimore in 1958—incredibly, through 2017, it remained the last complete game no-hitter against them. Ted Williams ranked Wilhelm with Bob Feller, Bob Lemon, Eddie Lopat, and Whitey Ford among the five toughest pitchers he faced.

"Wilhelm had a sure-strike knuckler, then a real good knuckler, then with two strikes, a real bastard of a knuckler, dancing in your face," Williams wrote in his autobiography. "The closest thing to an unhittable ball I ever saw."

You might think teams would hold on to a pitcher with that kind of weapon, especially in the era before free agency. By any measure, Wilhelm was an elite and versatile performer, and his pitch made him almost ageless. Yet teams never seemed to trust him very long. Over 21 years, Wilhelm spent time with nine teams—not counting the Royals, who took him in the expansion draft and traded him—but never stayed more than six years in one place.

Even if he chafed at teaching his signature pitch, Wilhelm helped its spread by encouraging Wilbur Wood, a journeyman left-hander who had bounced between the minors and majors for seven seasons before joining the White Sox in 1967. As a boy, Wood had learned to throw a pitch off the fingertips that imparted no rotation. His father taught it to him and called it a palmball, which typically means changeup. Wood did not think much about terminology; he just liked having a pitch to stifle the big kids on the sandlots of Boston.

Wood reached the majors at 19 but struggled to stick. His fastball, he says, in a thick and endearing accent, was "a few yahds too short," so batters could wait for his curveball and crush it. With Chicago, Wood decided to revive his father's pitch, and Wilhelm, his new teammate, eagerly approved.

"That's when I just said, 'What the hell, I gotta make a change,' and that's when I made the change, really, to go 100 percent with the knuckleball," Wood says. "His biggest thing was: 'If you're going to do it, you've got to stay with it and you've got to throw it. It's great to throw a curveball, fastball, slider, whatever else it may be, but you're either gonna make or break with the knuckleball.' Hearing those words, it's a pretty easy decision, isn't it?"

For the next several years—until a line drive shattered his kneecap—Wood was a sensation. He led the league in appearances three years in a row. Then he became a starter and ripped off four straight seasons with at least 20 victories and 300 innings pitched. Just two others—Fergie Jenkins and Robin Roberts—had done that since the 1930s, and no one has done it since. Across a five-year period, Wood made

199 of 224 starts on fewer than four days' rest. His 1972 workload (376⅔ innings) is the most by any pitcher since 1919. Staggering facts, all, and only one part of Wood's legend is typically overstated: he did start both games of a doubleheader, in 1973, but it was a disaster. He got 13 outs, gave up 13 runs, and lost twice.

In any case, Wilhelm had proven in his own career that trusting the knuckleball meant everything. In 1969, when he saved the NL West division clincher for the Braves, Wilhelm was 47 and his catcher, Bob Didier, was 20. Facing a dangerous hitter, Alex Johnson, Wilhelm fell behind, 3–0, and Didier twice flashed the fastball sign. Both times, Wilhelm shook him off. Didier trotted to the mound.

"Wilhelm says, 'What the fuck are you doing? The only thing you know about pitching is it's hard to hit! Get your ass behind the plate right now!'" Didier recalls. "So I turned around, 3–0 knuckleball, 3–1 knuckleball, 3–2 ground ball to short, we're Western Division champions. After the game [sportswriter] Furman Bisher came up to me and said, 'Bob, you really showed me something the way you settled Wilhelm down in that big situation.' Yeah, I really settled him down all right; he was chewing my ass out!"

The winner that day was Niekro, completing his first 20-win season. He was 30 by then, but the skinny, one-pitch kid who had earned Jim Bouton's pity was well on his way. He had never doubted his knuckleball because he had never thrown anything else. It was his father, Phil Sr., who used the pitch in desperation.

Phil Niekro Sr. worked in the coal mines and pitched as a teenager; somewhere, Phil says, he has news clippings of his father striking out 17 or 18 in a game with his fastball. One cold spring day, Phil Sr. was called in to pitch without having warmed up. He blew out his arm and turned to the knuckleball, taught to him by an old minor league catcher named Nick McKay. Phil Sr. passed the pitch on to his daughter, Phyllis, and then to his son, Phil; Phyllis, her brother would say later, handled his knuckler better than some major league catchers.

Joe Niekro, younger than Phil by five years, struggled to learn it as quickly; his hands were too small. Joe had enough other pitches to fashion a decent major league career, then found stardom for the Astros when he came home to the knuckler in his mid-30s. But Phil never strayed.

"Me and my buddy John Havlicek"—the NBA Hall of Famer—
"would get the bat and choose sides and that's when I would throw it,
to get all the girls and boys out in that little town of Lansing, Ohio,"
Phil Niekro recalls. "So I was throwing it all the time. I didn't know
there were knuckleball pitchers in the big leagues. I didn't even know
what a knuckleball was. It was just something I had fun with, playing
catch with my dad."

Phil used the knuckler to make the Bridgeport High School varsity
team as a freshman, and he signed with the Milwaukee Braves at
age 19. He would spend two decades perfecting the pitch for the
franchise, from 1964 through 1983. By the time he finished, with a
one-game cameo for the Braves in 1987, he had thrown 5,404 innings;
only Cy Young, Pud Galvin, and Walter Johnson threw more. Niekro
never apologized for his pitch.

"He has as much confidence in the knuckleball's effectiveness as
Aroldis Chapman does throwing 106," R. A. Dickey says. "It blows you
away, the mentality he must have possessed as a competitor."

For his 300th victory, as a Yankee on the final day of the regular
season in 1985, Phil tried something new. He waited until the final
out to throw a knuckleball.

He had failed in four attempts at 300. On the fourth try, on
September 30 in New York, he carried in his back pocket a note from
Phil Sr. that said: "Win—I'll Be Happy." Phil Sr. wrote it because he
could not talk; Phil and Joe, by then a Yankee teammate, had visited
him in the hospital the day before, in Wheeling, West Virginia. Phil
Sr. was on a breathing tube, his health failing.

Phil's last chance came on October 6 in Toronto. His hard stuff, such
as it was, seemed strong in the bullpen, and he figured that fastballs
might confuse the tired Blue Jays, who had won their first division title
the day before. Knucklers had not worked lately, anyway, and Niekro
liked the idea of proving he could win without them. It worked in the
first inning, and he kept on going through eight.

Joe came out to warm up Phil before the ninth. With two outs, a
runner on second, and Phil's old Braves teammate, Jeff Burroughs,
coming to bat, manager Billy Martin sent Joe to the mound for a conference. The brothers agreed that Phil should throw a knuckler, at last,
for their dad. George Steinbrenner had arranged for the Yankees' TV

feed to be played through the phone to the hospital, so their mother, Henrietta, could give play-by-play to Phil Sr. The final knuckleball dipped down and away, and Burroughs swung over it to end the game. The brothers took the ball to the hospital the next day.

"He had a smile on his face," Phil says. "I walked up and gave him that ball and said, 'This is yours as much as mine,' and put my Yankee hat on him. The doc came in and said, 'He's been up all night waiting for you guys to get here.' So we stayed the next few days, and in a couple of weeks he was home. I got to pitch another couple of years, Joe got traded to Minnesota and got to the World Series, and I think that's what he wanted to see in his lifetime: both his boys, one got to the World Series, the other won 300 games and then 18 more. Because he was struggling for about two years there, and then after Joe and I both retired, he passed. But that's why he was hanging on."

———

When knuckleballers meet, they bond instantly. They are all Jedi knights, possessors of a shadowy power few can understand or believe. The old recognize it in the young.

"I grew up a Dodger fan in Northern California," Tom Candiotti says. "I can't remember the exact year, but my older brother takes me to a Giants game, and the Dodgers are coming out before BP, stretching. Charlie Hough comes out to left field and I'm down the line there at Candlestick with my glove. And he goes, 'Here!'—and he throws me a knuckleball. So I throw one back to him like that, and he goes, 'Hey, kid, that's not bad!' He throws me another one, I throw it back. So we played catch for about five minutes with me in the stands, just throwing a knuckleball, and I go, 'That was cool, I played catch with that number 49 guy out there!'"

Candiotti would grow up to wear 49, too, like Hough and Wakefield, a tribute to the retirement age of the great Wilhelm. His was a typically wild backstory—an undrafted college pitcher with a nothing fastball, Candiotti tagged along on a summer trip with a buddy who was trying out for the independent Victoria (British Columbia) Mussels. Candiotti brought his fishing pole, not his baseball glove, but a scout recognized him, told him to hop on a mound, and signed him for

$400 Canadian a month. The money did not go far. "I'm probably still wanted for dining and dashing up there," Candiotti says.

The Royals soon signed Candiotti, lost him in the minor league draft, and before long, without ever having pitched in major league spring training, Candiotti was on a big league mound for the Brewers. He told his catcher, Ted Simmons, that he threw an occasional knuckler, and tried one as a goof for his last warm-up pitch. Simmons startled Candiotti by calling it for his very first pitch in the majors. It sailed for ball one of a four-pitch walk.

The knuckleball was Candiotti's destiny, but he didn't see it. The Brewers implored him to work on his knuckleball, but Candiotti resisted. The knuckleball was just for fun, a gimmick he had learned from his dad, and he was proud of his fastball and curve, even if they screamed Triple-A. Then he signed with Cleveland as a minor league free agent and a new teammate, soon to be 47, changed everything.

Phil Niekro, back for more after that 300th win, played catch with Candiotti every day, comparing knuckleballs. Candiotti threw his as hard as he could, imagining a dastardly knuckler that would fool the hitter and the catcher and peg the umpire in the chest. Niekro told him to settle down, throw it softer, in the zone. You want them to hit it, he said.

Oh, and one more thing: you shouldn't throw anything else.

"I said I still had a curveball!" Candiotti says. "He goes, 'Trust me, this is what's gonna keep you in the big leagues for a long time. Keep working on it and developing it.' He was my own pitching coach. He'd sit next to me on the bench when I started. The other pitching coaches, they don't know what to say to you."

Coaches can try. The good ones will study a knuckleballer's mechanics and learn the proper checkpoints in his delivery. But unless you have thrown it, knuckleballers say, you just cannot relate. They tell each other to be their own coach, to know their pitch intimately. That is why they enjoy talking about it—with each other, with conventional pitchers, with writers. They have to immerse themselves in the culture of the knuckleball to even have a chance. R. A. Dickey would take a ball around with him in his car, steering with his left hand, practicing grips with his right.

Rare is the knuckleballer who has not talked shop with the others

Steve Carlton warms up near the first base dugout at Veterans Stadium. His peerless slider helped make him the first pitcher to win four Cy Young Awards—and the last to work 300 innings in a season, in 1980.

Bob Gibson started nine World Series games, completing eight and going 7–2 with a 1.89 ERA. He set a single-game strikeout record in the 1968 opener, with 17.

A perfect game flipped Rand[...] Johnson's famous scowl into a smi[...] in 2004. Eddie Perez, who struc[...] out to end it, insists the final fastba[...] rose.

That's eight—*count 'em, eight!*—baseballs in the mighty right hand of J. R. Richard, whose overpowering fastball and slider still inspire awe in those who faced him.

Brad Lidge, whose topspinning slider baffled hitters because it never had a telltale red dot, strikes out Eric Hinske to win the 2008 World Series for the Phillies.

"My favorite pitch," Cy Young said, "was a whistler right under the chin."

Carl Mays closed out the World Series for the Red Sox in 1918. Two years later, with the Yankees, his errant fastball killed the Indians' Ray Chapman.

Walter Johnson, greeting President Calvin Coolidge at Griffith Stadium in Washington, D.C., "was so great that he almost belongs in his own Hall of Fame," said Bob Feller.

Two of baseball's greatest power pitchers, Bob Feller (left) and Satchel Paige, were teammates on the Indians' 1948 championship team.

With the Angels in 1973, Nolan Ryan set the single-season strikeout record (383) while going 21–16 with a 2.87 ERA and 26 complete games, including two no-hitters.

Madison Bumgarner embraces Buster Posey after baiting Salvador Perez with a high fastball for the final out of the 2014 World Series in Kansas City.

Many claimed to have invented the curveball, but only Candy Cummings gets credit on a Cooperstown plaque: "Pitched first curve ball in baseball history," it reads.

Sandy Koufax (left) and Jim Palmer shake hands before Game 2 of the 1966 World Series. Palmer, age twenty, threw a shutout. Koufax, age thirty, never pitched again.

Mike Mussina—shown as a Yankee at Camden Yards, his old home with the Orioles—
earned 270 victories with an ever-evolving array of weapons.

The Cardinals' Adam Wainwright learned his signature curveball from his older brother at age ten.

The Cubs' Mike Montgomery charges across the mound in joy after his curveball won Game 7 of the 2016 World Series in Cleveland. Yes, he got his glove back.

in their small fraternity. Phil and Joe Niekro helped Wakefield. Hough helped Dickey. Candiotti helped Steven Wright. They all have a piece of each other's success.

"I always thought if each organization gave up two of their good athletes that aren't gonna make it and see if they can make knuckleball pitchers out of them, me and Charlie Hough and Tim Wakefield can open a knuckleball school," Phil says. "We'll send these guys to it, evaluate them, work with them for a couple of months and report back to the organization: hey, he has a shot or he doesn't have a shot."

It can be done. When the Brewers decided that a prospect named Steve Sparks had no future as a conventional pitcher, they told him to learn a knuckleball. Sparks had never tried it before, and as his first resource he scoured his childhood baseball cards, purchased with the money from his *Tulsa World* paper route as a teen. Sparks studied the grips of Hough and the Niekros, learning to minimize drag on the ball by making sure no fingers touched the seams. Before reporting to winter ball in 1992, Sparks met with Candiotti at the Astrodome, where Candiotti's Dodgers were finishing the season. He peppered him with six pages of questions, and learned to lock his wrist by turning it inward slightly, keeping it from rolling over and imparting spin.

Sparks would pitch nine seasons in the majors, weathering the American League in the steroid era. He was not Tim Wakefield, but he was a reasonable facsimile. As his career wound down, in 2004, Sparks put the knuckleball brotherhood above another payday.

"My agent told me the Yankees wanted me to throw to them, to prepare for their playoffs with [Wakefield's] Red Sox," Sparks says. "He told me they said, 'Name your price.' I'd probably get a nice hotel and $10,000 if I wanted, I didn't even know. But I just told them I'd rather not. Tim was a friend and it just didn't feel right."

The benefits of having a knuckleballer are clear enough: at worst he can absorb innings in blowouts, save the other relievers, and make a spot start now and then. But opportunities are scarce, and most teams are too timid to try. The Red Sox invested eight seasons in the development of Charlie Zink—a knuckleballer from the baseball powerhouse Savannah College of Arts and Design—but gave him just one big league start, in 2008. Zink allowed eight runs.

In 2016, the Rays hoped to take advantage of the humidity of their climate-controlled dome by cultivating low-cost knuckleballers. Their pitching coordinator, Charlie Haeger, had thrown the knuckler briefly in the majors, and they gathered a few prospects, including former position players, to try the pitch. In the end, they gave seven September relief outings to Eddie Gamboa.

"A lot of organizations will shy from it because they don't have anybody to instruct or they're not familiar with it," Haeger says. "It's that uniqueness that people are maybe a little scared of at times."

In 2013, MLB Network hired Wakefield to coach five former college quarterbacks in a reality show called *The Next Knuckler*. Most of the contestants, Wakefield says, had no feel for the pitch, no chance at all. Josh Booty, who had played briefly in the majors as an infielder, won the contest, signed with the Diamondbacks, and never made it out of spring training.

"I've probably worked with 12 guys," Dickey says. "I've seen one that might have a chance. *Might*. It takes a complete surrender to doing what is necessary to cultivate the pitch, and a lot of guys don't have that. Most guys have some entitlement, like: 'I shouldn't have to go on the back field at the minor league complex and grind it out against Gulf Coast Leaguers.' It's hard, because most guys come to this pitch when they're older, and they've had somewhat of a career as something else. It's a real struggle, having to start all over again from the ground up."

The success stories are the exception. The miracle is that anyone at all can throw the pitch consistently. Most pitchers like it when the wind blows in, to reduce the chances of home runs. Knuckleballers hate it, because more wind behind the pitch can cause it to whoosh away from the catcher or dive into the dirt. Most pitchers, unless they're scuffing the ball, have no reason to fret about the length of their fingernails. Knuckleballers depend on it.

Joe Niekro got a 10-game suspension in 1987 when, during a game in Anaheim, he emptied his pockets for umpires and an emery board and sandpaper flew out. He tried to explain that of course he had those products—he needs to groom his nails on the bench between innings. Did they really think he could dig them out of his pocket and deface baseballs in the middle of the field?

"Put yourself out there on the mound with 30,000 people, six TV cameras, and four umpires around you, and you've got an emery board in your back pocket," Phil Niekro says, still bothered by his brother's punishment decades later.

"Explain to me how you're gonna take that emery board out of your back pocket and doctor the ball up, when everybody's watching. You can't do it. As soon as he threw the emery board out of his back pocket, the umpire threw him out of the game. If I was out there, they would've had to handcuff me. Until you show me something on camera that I'm using an emery board in my back pocket to take it out on the mound and scuff up the ball, you've got nothing, because you can't do it. And if you did they would sure as hell see it."

The grip on a knuckleball is naturally unstable. The fingers and the nails must be strong enough to lock the ball in place as the pitcher whips his arm through the air. Use of the seams can vary from pitcher to pitcher, but the general rule is to leave them alone. Engaging the seams leads to friction, which leads to tumbling, which leads to trouble.

The knuckleballer should have a short stride, the better to stay behind the ball and send it on its wobbly path. He should follow through down the center of his body, almost as if hitting himself in the protective cup, because finishing over either leg could cause that dreaded spin. (A benefit of this is that knuckleballers tend to finish in a strong fielding position; Niekro won five Gold Gloves and Dickey won one.)

Hough urged Dickey to keep his mechanics compact by imagining he was pitching through a doorframe. Once he's through it, Dickey says, he visualizes a vertical shoebox at the top of the zone and tries to put the pitch there. When he was at his best, in 2012, Dickey led the league in strikeouts by throwing a flat knuckler that stayed high; hitters expected it to fall and swung under it. He remained an effective starter thereafter, but that same strikeout pitch largely abandoned him. It bothered Dickey because he wanted to be trustworthy, to fight the notion that his pitch was not.

"A conventional pitcher gives up 10 runs in a game? 'Ah, it was one of those days,'" Dickey says. "If I give up 10 runs in a game? 'I told you so.' That's the difference. And that's across the board with guys in those offices, all across baseball."

One reason for the lack of trust, though, is that no other starter takes the mound with just one option. If another starter is struggling with one pitch, he tends to have at least two others. And while pitchers from the 1930s and '40s may have incorporated the knuckleball into a wider repertoire, today's knucklers don't.

It is all or nothing—the Niekro doctrine—and it is not all up to the pitcher, either.

———————

The best advice for catching a knuckleball might have come from Mike Sandlock, who played for the Braves and the Dodgers from 1942 to 1946. He slipped back to the minors after that, and might have stayed there if not for his success with Johnny Lindell, a converted outfielder whose knuckler earned them both a promotion to the Pittsburgh Pirates in 1953. It did not go well: Lindell led the league in walks and wild pitches, and Sandlock in passed balls. Neither ever played in the majors again.

"A knuckleball is like a dame," Sandlock once said. "If you reach for it, you're licked. You've got to wait until it reaches for you."

John Flaherty played 14 years in the majors and was used to weird events; in his debut, for Boston in 1992, he caught an eight-inning, no-hit loss by Matt Young. Back with the Red Sox in spring training of 2006, Flaherty was asked to replace Doug Mirabelli, who had been traded after serving as Wakefield's personal catcher. Flaherty got a knuckleball glove from Wilson, caught some soft deliveries from Wakefield in the bullpen, and didn't think much of it.

Then Wakefield took the mound for batting practice and told Flaherty he would mix in some hard knucklers, too.

"That kind of threw me off, because when he's throwing them soft, you can kind of wait and let the ball catch you, so to speak, instead of you trying to catch the ball," Flaherty said. "But when he started throwing them harder, then it's like, 'Oh shit, I don't know where this is going.' It was almost like it could be a hard slider, it could be a hard split going down, it could be a screwball. It kind of got in my head a little bit.

"And then when we got into a game, he walked the first batter, Luis Castillo, who could run. And I said, 'Wait, I haven't even thought about throwing a runner out.' So that was a whole other level. I turned to

Tim Timmons, the home plate umpire, and I said, 'You're working the last game I'm ever gonna catch.' In the first inning. He said, 'No, no, you're gonna get it.' I said, 'I don't want to get it. That's the problem. I don't want to do this.' And I caught him for another inning, it went pretty well, caught three more innings and then said all the right things to the media, how I'm gonna get it, I'm gonna work at it, it's gonna be fine.

"Then I walked into [manager Terry] Francona's office the next morning: 'Gone, time to go.' Best decision I ever made."

In truth, Flaherty said, he was already wavering on how much he still wanted to play. But the knuckleball confirmed his feeling. He tried to imagine himself in the cauldron of Yankee Stadium, with a runner on third and a knuckleball darting somewhere near his regular catcher's mitt (the oversized pillow, he said, had been uncomfortable). The effort it would take to roll with that knuckleball, and endure the embarrassment, was just not worth it.

With Flaherty gone, the Red Sox turned to Josh Bard—and watched in horror as he committed 10 passed balls in April, seemingly well on his way to the modern record of 35 by the Rangers' Geno Petralli, when he caught Hough in 1987. In hindsight, Bard says, he was the wrong man for the job. He was long-levered, big for a catcher at 6 foot 3, and liked to extend his glove to reach for pitches. The concept of letting the ball travel went against Bard's instincts, and he constantly felt he was letting down the team.

"It was the only thing in my life that the harder I tried at it, the worse I got," Bard says. "You felt a ton of tension, and the only way to deal with it was to almost not care about it. That's not really in my DNA." He smiled: "I was more of a chaser than I was a catcher."

With nowhere else to turn, and Wakefield set to face the Yankees on May 1, the Red Sox panicked, trading Bard and a young pitcher to San Diego to reacquire Mirabelli. They whisked him from the airport to Fenway Park, Mirabelli changing into his uniform in the back of a police cruiser careening through the tight city streets. The Red Sox stalled, delaying the first pitch by eight minutes, and Mirabelli left his protective cup behind in the car. But he made it in time to guide Wakefield through seven strong innings of a Red Sox victory.

A decade later, another Boston knuckleballer, Steven Wright, would emerge as an All-Star. His primary catcher in the first half, Ryan Hanigan, sat across the locker room from Wright one day, the skin on his bruised lower legs the color of old bananas. Nothing felt natural about catching a knuckleball, Hanigan said. A catcher wants to snag other breaking balls—except for the high curveball—before they dart out of the zone. Letting the knuckler get deep was testing him, and Hanigan was only barely passing. Wright had given him a choice of six or seven gloves, none of them a good fit. The job wiped him out mentally, too.

"There's so many innings in a year, you've got to relax as a catcher," Hanigan said. "But there's no relaxing. You have to catch it in an action stance. You have to be up on your legs, engaging your muscles, not what you'd call sitting back. He's a lot more taxing for me than anybody else, by far."

Even a two-strike count can bring a well-founded sense of dread for a catcher. Consider the plight of the Rangers' Orlando Mercado, working with Hough on June 16, 1986. Hough took a no-hit shutout into the bottom of the ninth inning in Anaheim, but lost it on an error and a single. That happens. Later that inning, though, Hough lost the game on a *strikeout.* A third-strike knuckler bounced away from Mercado for a passed ball, and Hough was too stunned to cover the plate. Wally Joyner, who had reached second on another passed ball, dashed home from there to end the game.

In the archives of Baseball-Reference.com, this was the first game ever to end on a strikeout–passed ball—and the knuckleball just had to be the culprit. Robert K. Adair, the physicist, concluded that hitting the knuckleball squarely is essentially an accident, and suggested a strategy of striking out and hoping for a passed ball. Bob Didier agrees.

"When I managed in the minor leagues, I told my team the best way to hit a knuckleball pitcher is get two strikes, swing, and start running," Didier says. "Because the catcher probably ain't gonna catch it."

Didier had never played above Class A when he reported to spring training with Atlanta in 1969. That March the Braves traded their starting catcher, Joe Torre, and another catcher got hurt. Didier was young, but he had a few hits—and somehow, despite no prior experience with the knuckleball, he could handle Phil Niekro. He made the team.

"You know how you block a ball in the dirt and you put your body in front of the ball? I did that with the ball in the air," Didier says. "I tried to center my body behind my glove and if I missed it with my glove, it caught my body and it would kind of stay in front of me. I would have 10 or 12 balls a game when Niekro was pitching that missed my glove and hit my chest at 60 or 65 miles an hour. Keep your body behind your glove and hopefully behind the ball, and use whatever you could—legs, stomach, chest, shoulder—to just keep it in front."

That first season, Didier led the majors in passed balls, with 27. The toughest pitches, he said, were the ones from Niekro that would swoop over his left shoulder. Then the Braves traded for Wilhelm, and Didier battled the corkscrew action of his softer knuckleballs.

"After a game, I felt like I'd caught a doubleheader or a 15-inning game or something," Didier says. "I was just worn out, fighting that. I can't think of another word, other than *fighting* a knuckleball."

Pitchers can help in that fight. Sparks created a prototype for a knuckleball catcher's glove—the Pro Sparks model, by Rawlings—with reduced weight in the padded area and special attention to the curved webbing, to keep balls from escaping on tag plays. And with so little margin for error in the running game, knuckleballers tend to work especially hard on their pickoff moves.

But the pitch still makes for a different kind of day for everyone. A game of incredible speed is suddenly played in slow motion. Some hitters would rather avoid it altogether. Their typical theory on trying to hit it? See it low, let it go; see it high, let it fly.

"You have to wait as long as possible—and then explode," said Jesse Barfield, who had four homers off Hough but was 3-for-25 against the Niekros. "If you've played Slo-Pitch Softball, you know what I'm talking about. So you treat it almost like that. Wait, wait, wait—and then explode."

You look like a fool if you miss, but the explosions can live forever. Reggie Jackson's third home run in Game 6 of the 1977 World Series came off a knuckler from Hough. Barry Bonds's record seventy-third homer in 2001 came off a Dennis Springer knuckleball. Aaron Boone, who had been 1-for-10 off Wakefield, belted his knuckler for the pennant-winning homer in Game 7 of the 2003 AL Championship Series.

A year later, though, facing elimination in Game 5 of the ALCS, Wakefield tiptoed through shutout innings in the twelfth, thirteenth, and fourteenth, surviving two passed balls and beating the Yankees. He would start the opener of the World Series when the Red Sox won their first title since 1918.

"The challenge is that you need to know going in there's gonna be walks, there's gonna be stolen bases, and there's gonna be passed balls," Francona says. "As a manager, if you can't handle that, you have a chance to miss out on a really good pitcher. So I kind of learned early: take your hands, put them under your butt and sit on them, and stay out of the way. And you'd look up and Wake would be pitching into the seventh or eighth inning."

Most managers cannot afford to do that; few pitchers can throw a knuckleball like Tim Wakefield or will ever come close. College and high school coaches want to win, not give away games as an aspiring knuckleballer learns his quirky craft. A low minor league setting is the best laboratory, but even there, teams tend to see more potential in the waves of hard-throwing prospects they draft every year.

But the pitch will survive, because the aggravation is worth it—and deep down, baseball people like it. When Sparks pitched, umpires routinely tossed him knucklers when they gave him a new ball. (John Shulock and Greg Kosc had especially good ones.) Conventional pitchers might not need the knuckleball, but they envy it just the same. Says Chuck Finley, the longtime Angels lefty, "Every starting pitcher would love to go out there for just one game and throw nothing but knuckleballs."

And for all its unpredictability, throwing the knuckleball takes the kind of toughness widely admired by the smartest people in the game.

"I've got a lot of respect for Wake because he goes out on the mound and fights," Pedro Martinez said in Wakefield's book. "If he doesn't have a good knuckleball, he ain't got shit. But he fights."

When all else fails a pitcher—when the gun runs out of bullets and the blade on the sword turns dull—he can always try a slingshot.

Why not? There's really nothing to lose. It probably won't work, and he probably won't understand it, anyway.

"You could throw two knuckleballs that look the same, have no spin coming out, but they do two different things," Steven Wright says. "One might move all over the place and one might not do anything. Like, how does that happen?"

Wright laughed. He was riding the knuckleball to an All-Star season, and even he was completely baffled.

"That's the beauty of it, man," he says. "When it's working, it's fun as hell. When it's not working, you just chuck and duck."

THE
SPLITTER

Through the Trapdoor

I was 12 years old the first time I visited the Hall of Fame. I remember noticing the tag on the inside of George Brett's hat: 7¼. This astonished me. I wore fitted hats all the time back then, and my head size was 7⅜. I had a bigger head than George Brett.

This had no practical application, of course. All it really meant was that, if George Brett and I ever found ourselves at one of those hat stores in the mall, and we both wanted to buy the same hat, we would never have to fight for the last one—an unlikely scenario, for sure, but at 12 it sort of mattered. My head was already bigger than the head of a grown-up baseball superstar. How about *that*!

This feeling came to me again, almost 30 years later, when talking with Dennis Eckersley about the split-finger fastball. Eckersley's Hall of Fame career spanned the era of the split-finger craze: from the mid-1970s, when the pitch was still evolving from its forkball roots, through the late 1990s, when injury fears dimmed its popularity. Eckersley had thrived with precision command of a fastball and slider, but never mastered a changeup. A right-hander, Eckersley yearned for a pitch that would dive straight down, or down and away from left-handers. He just did not have the fingers for it.

"You know how some guys carry around softballs so they can split their fingers?" he said. "I actually had the doctor make a cast for me. I strapped it on, and I'd have my two fingers in there for a while. I'd drive around with that cast on in the off-season. That's how sick I was!"

Sometimes, Eckersley said, the pitch would work for him in the bullpen. But it was never consistent enough to use in the ninth inning, when there's no room for error, and remains a fanciful wish, a superpower beyond his reach. If only he could have split his fingers like . . . *me?*

In the course of our talk, I held my index and middle fingers in front of me, like a flat peace sign, the way a pitcher would before straddling the commissioner's signature on either side of a baseball's seams. Eckersley howled.

"That's a major split!" he cried. "I can't do that!" Brian Anderson, Eckersley's broadcast partner that day and the brother of a former major league pitcher, stood nearby. He split his fingers, too. "This is as far as I can go," Anderson said. His spread was much narrower than mine. "You don't want to hurt something there," Eckersley told me, admiringly. But it didn't hurt at all.

I felt a little like George Costanza on *Seinfeld,* when he learns he would be a perfect hand model. Really, these hands? Was the great Dennis Eckersley—an A+ source on this kind of thing—actually telling me my fingers were better equipped to throw the split-finger fastball than his?

Well, yes and no. Eckersley is enthusiastic about a lot of topics. I've also shaken hands with enough major leaguers to know that my fingers—while apparently quite flexible—are pretty stubby next to theirs. And nearly everyone I've talked to about the splitter says long fingers are essential, locking the pitch in place to keep it from flying away.

Functionally, then, my better-than-Eckersley finger spread is useless. Just as my big head would not help me hit .390 like George Brett, my freakish fingers would not help me harness the magic of Bullet Joe Bush, Shigeru Sugishita, Elroy Face, or Bruce Sutter.

When it comes to that final name, especially, I am not alone. Of the millions of people who have ever thrown a baseball, Sutter stands alone as the master of the split-finger. Few pitches in the game's history are as synonymous with one man as the splitter is with Sutter. Like Mariano Rivera would do with the cut fastball, Sutter took an existing pitch, modified it, and inspired a generation of imitators.

But while others could at least mimic Rivera's method of throwing the cutter, Sutter was almost a singular phenomenon in the history of his pitch.

"Nobody could throw it the way he threw it," says Roger Craig, the coach most synonymous with the splitter. "I could never learn to throw that, or teach that. Bruce Sutter's really the one."

————————

History assigns a prominent place to Craig for the sudden rise—and sharp demise—of the split-finger fastball in its modern form. He deserves the acclaim, but context is important. Before Roger Craig, there was Fred Martin. He taught the pitch to Sutter, and the two of them showed it to Craig. Without Martin, the splitter would never have taken off the way it did.

Because of Martin, there is a plaque in Cooperstown for Sutter, with the split-finger fastball mentioned in the very first line. Because of Martin, there is a dream home for Sutter on Red Top Mountain in Georgia, with a Cy Young Award displayed in the man cave. One day in 2016, Sutter was repairing a broken drawer and found a black-and-white photo of Martin, some four decades old, holding up a baseball with his right hand. Wearing a Cubs uniform as the sun splashes his craggy face, Martin looks not at the camera but at his creation: the grip he taught Sutter, with the index and middle fingers stretching to hold the ball on either side of the seams, like prongs supporting the diamond of an engagement ring.

For Sutter, the pitch was just as precious and far more valuable. Without it, he never would have pitched above Class A. Sutter learned it in 1973, when his future was bleak. His manager that season, Walt Dixon, wrote this in a report to his bosses: "Bruce Sutter will make the major leagues when a communist regime is ready to take over this country."

Martin was not the kind of guy who dealt in sarcasm. And Sutter was not the kind of pitcher who gave up easily—on baseball, anyway. He had dropped out of Old Dominion because he wanted more time to play ball. He went back home to Pennsylvania and worked at a printing shop in Lancaster, where a local meatpacker sponsored a semipro team called Hippey's Raiders. The draft was over, but a Cubs scout, Ralph DiLullo, noticed Sutter's enormous hands. He gave the kid the last $500 from his annual bonus budget.

"When I saw those hands," DiLullo told writer Gerry Fraley years later, "I said to myself, 'Wow, that kid can do something with those hands.'"

Back then, nobody linked long fingers with the splitter, because Sutter hadn't thrown it yet. Martin had, as a kind of changeup, but nobody really noticed. As a 31-year-old Cardinals rookie in 1946, Martin jumped to the Mexican League and thrived for parts of two seasons. But he was barred for a year upon his return and spent almost all of the 1950s in the minors. He managed for a year in the Cubs' chain and then became a coach—in the majors for a while, but mostly in the minors, where he met Sutter.

Sutter had tried to learn a slider in 1972, but it hurt his elbow after just two pro games. Back home that winter, he paid a doctor to reroute a pinched nerve in his elbow; knowing he was expendable, Sutter planned not to tell the Cubs. He confessed the next spring, when the Cubs nearly cut him, and his gumption saved his job. The Cubs kept Sutter more for his will than his talent, and assigned him to play for Dixon in Quincy, Illinois, where he was the mop-up man in blowouts. "You might as well have a D on your hat," Dixon told him one day, "because you're in for the duration."

Like most organizations then, the Cubs had one pitching coach for the entire minor league system. Theirs was Martin. He would visit the affiliates every month and show the pitchers several ways to throw each pitch. They would work on the pitches until his next visit, experimenting with grips in hopes of unlocking something worthy of the majors.

"He showed us all how to throw the split-finger," says Sutter, who quickly realized he had an edge. All his life, Sutter had thrown breaking pitches by applying pressure with his index finger instead of his middle finger. It was counterintuitive, and it wasn't much help on the curve or the slider, but it felt right. With the splitter, Sutter found a pitch that was meant to be thrown like a fastball, but required a dominant index finger to generate its straight-down—or down-and-away-from-a-lefty—movement. Sutter did not split his fingers very far apart or wedge the ball too deep between them, as he would have if throwing the slower forkball. With his thumb positioned to the side, Sutter squirted the ball through, imparting it with a devastating tumble. Sutter said he made one small adjustment the first day Martin showed him, moving his index finger just a bit off the left seam, and never changed it again.

"I'd like to tell you I had to work at it," Sutter says, "but it broke right away."

It did take Sutter time to control the pitch, to learn when to make it do what. His overall performance at Quincy was ordinary—10 hits per nine innings and a 4.13 ERA—and fellow farmhands wondered if he would have a roster spot in 1974. Luckily, he had an advocate.

"He wouldn't have made it out of spring training had it not been for Fred Martin," says Mike Krukow, a teammate who would also go on to a long career. "He said, 'Give this guy a chance.' But then Bruce broke camp, and they were only gonna give him until June when the new draft came in. If he didn't show anything by then . . . well, he tore it up. It was amazing."

As he got to know Sutter, Krukow was not surprised. Whatever Sutter did—shooting baskets, playing pool, throwing darts—his fine motor skills were incredible. He was perfectly suited for this quirky new pitch, the only man Krukow ever saw who could manipulate it with such precision, commanding the pitch to the left or the right, into or out of the strike zone, depending on the pressure he applied to his index finger.

"He brought that pitch into baseball in such an impactful way that if you didn't try it, you were an idiot," Krukow says.

Sutter was in the majors for good by 1976, and Martin was his confidant, building a bond with positive reinforcement and a trust forged over dinners at his Phoenix home in spring training. As his wife cooked, Martin would open scrapbooks and spin stories, with the toughness of a coal miner's son but the softness of a favorite uncle. He spoke often of his years in Mexico, and being blackballed, and shared the nuances of the craft: how to deal with rain, or a hot hitter, or a bad umpire. He promised his pitchers they would never allow three homers in a row—because after two, they should drill the third guy.

"He was from Oklahoma, and he was always real suntanned, looked like his skin was dried out," Sutter says. "Looked like one of those Old

West cowboys, always had the cigarette hanging out of his mouth. It was just different times."

In the Hall of Fame, Sutter represents the Cardinals. He played four seasons in St. Louis, led the league in saves three times there, and closed down Game 7 of the 1982 World Series by striking out Milwaukee's Gorman Thomas—with a high fastball, actually. But his greatest years were really his five with the Cubs. Sutter had more saves, a better ERA, and a better strikeout rate with Chicago, where he won his Cy Young Award in 1979.

His pitch was a revelation. Sutter was the closer—or fireman, as the job was known then—by the end of his rookie season. Joe Coleman, a veteran forkballer, set up for Sutter and was amazed by how different their seemingly similar pitches behaved. Coleman's forkball hardly spun at all, dropping almost like a knuckleball. But Sutter's splitter, Coleman said, spun like a helicopter. Pete Rose said flatly that the pitch was impossible to hit.

"I had never seen a pitch like that, ever—nor had anybody, because his was thrown with incredible vertical variance," says Ted Simmons, who faced and caught Sutter. "So visually it's starting at your forehead and you say it's high and then *vvoomp,* right in the middle. Then he throws it right in the middle and, *bang,* you go after it like a fastball and when you start to swing it dives vertically, and the ball's in the dirt."

When Sutter threw his best splitters, he never even saw them drop; his head would bob precisely as the pitch fell through the trapdoor. If he kept his head up to watch it, it meant he was not finishing his delivery and getting the proper whip at the end. When he struggled in those early years, he would ask the Cubs to fly in Martin for a few days. Sutter needed the reassurance of a calm mentor, and trusted him implicitly.

"You're gonna get a lot of help when you're struggling, and if you don't have someone you trust, you're gonna get confused and change something else," he says. "That's what you always have to worry about. With Fred's personality, he knew what to say around me to get me relaxed. He knew hollering at me is not gonna work. Bullshitting me is not gonna work. You had to tell me something that I believe that'd work. He had that knack."

One of Martin's visits was in San Diego, on a Cubs road trip. As

Sutter got loose in the bullpen for an early mound session, Roger Craig, then managing the Padres, asked Martin about the split. They went to the bullpen and Sutter showed Craig the grip. Sutter's pressure points made that precise pitch unique to him, Craig thought. But the up-close look greatly intrigued him: *this was a fast forkball that tumbled.*

Martin would not live long enough to see where Craig would take the pitch. As Sutter embarked on his Cy Young season, Martin, 63, was dying of cancer. The Cubs played only day games at Wrigley Field then, and Sutter and some teammates would visit Martin in the hospital after they played. Sutter was there when Martin died on June 11, 1979.

"We were kids; we just thought he was sick," Sutter says, softly. "We didn't think he was going to die."

"In a way, it hurts you more than when you lost an actual relative, because of what he meant to us," Krukow says. "I mean, he was our guy. You had that feeling of emptiness and loneliness."

Sutter would find another mentor in Mike Roarke, a different Cubs minor league instructor who would later coach him in St. Louis. Sutter would leave the Cardinals for a six-year contract with the Braves in 1985, but by 1988 he was finished. He had a pinched nerve in his shoulder, and when he came back too soon from arthroscopic surgery, he tore his rotator cuff. His special pitch went with it, forever.

"I never threw it again, really, where I could throw it right," Sutter says. "No, I couldn't. You had to get your arm in position. You had to get your arm up quick, and I couldn't do that anymore. I lost those muscles in my back, part of the rotator cuff, those muscles were pinched off by that nerve again at the end, so I never could get my arm in position to throw it the right way."

Does he miss it?

"It's one of those things—you don't miss the pain," Sutter says. "I mean, I was in a lot of pain when I left. In fact, I started keeping balls, I think, when I was at 290 saves. I didn't know which one was gonna be my last one, because, man, I was hurt. But I got through it, I got to 300 and that was the last pitch I ever threw."

His last pitch was a fastball, alas, for a swinging third strike past Roberto Alomar. Sutter joined Rollie Fingers and Goose Gossage as the only pitchers with 300 saves, and made it to Cooperstown in 2006.

In his speech, he said he would never have reached the majors without learning Fred Martin's pitch. The pitch did not change how the game was played, Sutter told the crowd, but it represented a new way to get hitters out. Everyone who uses it, he said, owes Martin a measure of thanks, because he taught it first.

"I know he has a crowd around him right now," Sutter said, "and he's showing someone how to hold the split-finger."

———————

The splitter, as taught by Martin, applied by Sutter, and imitated by pitchers ever since, stands on its own as a pitch. But it sprang from a diverse lineage, with traces of the changeup, the knuckleball, and the sinker running through its yarn. Buck O'Neil, the Negro Leagues legend and the first black coach in the majors, thought the splitter was a myth—it moved so viciously, he said in Joe Posnanski's *The Soul of Baseball*, it must have been a *spitter*.

The splitter is sometimes referred to as a forkball, because a pitcher splits his index and middle fingers into a V to throw both pitches. But if there's open space at the bottom of the V, it's the faster-moving splitter. If the bottom of the V is flush against the ball—that is, tucked farther back in the hand—it's the slower-moving, nearly spin-less forkball.

"Fred knew it was different than the forkball," Sutter says. "Actually when I first got called up and I went to Pittsburgh, I met Elroy Face, and Elroy showed me how he held his. He said it was more like a knuckleball. His was slower and it didn't spin a lot, where mine had a lot of spin. Mine had a backup spin, like a backup slider. It had a dot, but it was going in the opposite way. The slider's breaking right to left. My ball would break left to right most of the time."

After that final out in 1982, Keith Hernandez was the first to embrace Sutter and catcher Darrell Porter, rushing over from first base to start the celebration. Mostly, though, Hernandez and Sutter were rivals—and Hernandez owned him, going 15-for-35 with seven walks. He said he tried to think of Sutter as just another sinkerballer.

The pitch does sink, and the differences can be subtle. In 2015, closer Jeurys Familia helped the Mets to the World Series with an arsenal of sinkers and splitters to go with a slider. Familia said he simply threw the splitter like the sinker, but spread his fingers a bit more. Just as the sinker would, the splitter helped Familia against lefties in particular.

"His splitter's like 96 and it sinks a foot," catcher Travis d'Arnaud explains. "His two-seamer's like 99 and it sinks half a foot."

Familia's velocity was extreme—"He's a freak," says Oakland reliever Blake Treinen, whose own freakish 100-mile-an-hour sinker once made him an answer on *Jeopardy!*—but d'Arnaud's sketch holds up: a splitter is indeed slower than a sinker, and drops more. It is not as slow as a changeup, but like a changeup, it is slower than a fastball and tends to drop away from the opposite-hand hitter . . . unless it doesn't.

"The split was somewhat unpredictable at first," says Chuck Finley, a 200-game winner, mostly for the Angels in the 1990s. "Sometimes it worked as a cutter, and then as a screwball. I don't believe, at the time, a lot of lefties were even throwing one."

Finley is indeed one of the few left-handers associated with the splitter, an oddity that makes it a little like the knuckleball, which is also thrown almost exclusively by right-handers. Because lefties are harder to find, they tend to get more chances to stick, and rarely must resort to a last-chance trick like the knuckler or splitter. Lefty relievers invariably need a breaking ball that moves away from a lefty hitter; once they have that to go with a fastball, there's usually little need for a third pitch.

If they do try one, it's usually a changeup. If that doesn't work, the splitter can be another option.

"The only reason I throw it is because I can't throw a changeup," says Chasen Shreve, a left-handed Yankees reliever. "I tried for years and I couldn't do it, so my college pitching coach said, 'Try this'—and the first one I threw was just ridiculously good."

Finley, too, learned the splitter only after exhausting all attempts at a changeup. He was suited for it because he threw from a high angle, which a pitcher must do with the splitter so his fingers get on top and yank it down. (Mark McGwire faced Finley more than any other pitcher, and hated it. "He was *nasty*," says McGwire, who hit .188 against him. "He was 6-6 and straight over the top, so he was actually even taller. Nasty.")

Many masters of the split-finger turned to the pitch for the same reason as Finley and Shreve. Ron Darling's hands were too big for the changeup. John Smoltz threw his changeup too hard. Dan Haren could never turn over his wrist comfortably, and begged the Cardinals to let him throw his old high school splitter in the minors.

"They said as long as you don't abuse it, you can throw it," Haren said. "I started throwing it quite a bit—low-A, high-A—and I got to the big leagues quick."

Haren stayed for 13 seasons and made three All-Star teams. By the end, in 2015, he guessed that there were so few pitchers who threw the split-finger, he could probably name them all. Even fewer threw the forkball, which is harder to control because of the way it almost knuckles as it drops. It also requires even longer fingers, which can be a problem. As a young catcher in St. Louis, Todd Zeile would call for forkballs from Jose DeLeon, who threw them in a way that made his thumb bleed when he scratched it after release.

"The fingernail on the index finger of his throwing hand was always a little bit longer and sharper because his hands were so big, and he tried to dig into the side of the ball to get a little extra traction," Zeile says. "And then when he'd follow through—if you think of following through like holding a peace sign—he'd snap his wrist, and his index finger would snap down and cut the side of his thumb.

"After three or four innings, it was almost inevitable. They put New-Skin and stuff over it, but they could never put a bandage on it because it wasn't allowed. So if he lasted long enough and if his forkball was effective, he'd be bleeding at some point past the fifth. What you used to be able to see, when he was having effective games, is he'd dab his thumb on the right side of his pant leg and have a blood spot. People thought it was coming from his leg, but it was coming from the cut on his thumb."

Finger strength is central to the forkball's best-known origin story. The first pitcher known to throw it was Bert Hall, for a Class B team in Tacoma on September 18, 1908. The local paper, the *Daily Tribune,* referred to it as a "fork ball," and *The Seattle Times* described its motion as wiggling, writing that it "beats all the spit-ball and knuckle ball combinations to death." Hall apparently learned the pitch from the team's player-manager, Mike Lynch, who had experimented with it but found that it tired his fingers. Hall, who had worked as a plumber and had a strong wrist, was more effective with it and briefly reached the majors, with the Phillies in 1911. He pitched in just seven games, returned to Tacoma, and took his funky new pitch back with him.

The forkball needed a more successful pitcher than Hall to market it, and Bullet Joe Bush could have been the guy. After winning championships with the 1913 A's and the 1918 Red Sox, Bush hurt his arm and could no longer throw curveballs. With a diminished fastball in 1920, he needed a new pitch to survive. A furious Ty Cobb insisted it was a spitball, but umpires found no wet spot. Bush—who would star for the Yankees' first championship team, in 1923—had actually found a forkball, but would not divulge his secret until years later.

"It was while I was experimenting on different deliveries that I placed the ball between my index and middle fingers, resting the bottom of the sphere on my thumb, and threw it," Bush told *The Saturday Evening Post* in 1929, as quoted by Rob Neyer and Bill James. "I discovered that the ball took a funny hop. I tried it again, moving my thumb to the inside of the ball. It took another peculiar hop as it passed over the plate. I repeated the same thing a number of times, moving my thumb in different positions under the ball and noticed that it broke over the pan in all sorts of strange ways."

Bush said he worked on the pitch so much that his fingers and thumb would get sore—even though his hand was large. "A pitcher with a small hand would have great difficulty controlling this pitch," said Bush, who claimed to be the pitch's inventor and the first to call it the forkball.

Yet Bush proved to be an unwilling publicity agent. By keeping quiet about his pitch until retirement, Bush kept a competitive advantage but prevented its spread. It was not until the 1940s that another pitcher would be widely known for the forkball: Tiny Bonham, who used it to help the Yankees win two World Series. His time in the Bronx overlapped with Joe Page, a lefty reliever who closed out the championships of 1947 and 1949.

That was just about it for Page, who struggled the next season but made it back for a few games with the Pirates in 1954. That spring he met a right-hander named Elroy Face, who had been hit hard as a rookie the year before, when he threw only a fastball and curve.

Branch Rickey, the legendary executive, told Face he was sending him to a minor league team in New Orleans, with instructions to learn an off-speed pitch. Face noticed that the forkball seemed to be working for Page, so he tried it.

"It took half the season to stretch the fingers to get the ball back in there," Face says. "At night my fingers used to ache a little bit from trying to throw it, trying to get it spread out."

Once he did, Face says, he never lost the feel. Like so many practitioners, Face had big hands, which he used in his post-baseball job as a carpenter at Mayview State Hospital in Pennsylvania. Retired at 88, he said in 2016 that he could still comfortably grip his pitch the way he did as a premier reliever. His highlight was an 18–1 season in 1959, followed by a World Series title with Pittsburgh the next year. He holds the Pirates' record for games pitched, with 802.

Page appeared just seven times for the Pirates, and not very effectively. His pitch, it turned out, was not the same one Face had admired in the spring of '54. When the men compared grips years later, Face noticed that while his fingers touched only leather, one of Page's always touched a seam.

In practice, Face says, his forkball served the same purpose as a changeup. He aimed for the middle of the plate, down, and let the ball sink whichever direction it wanted. Deception was everything.

"It worked as a good changeup with the same motion," Face says. "If they were looking for that, I could throw the fastball by 'em. And if they were looking for the fastball, they were out in front."

Face would teach his changeup/forkball to a contemporary, Lindy McDaniel, who would last 21 seasons in the majors. But the pitch, he remembers, was not in the arsenal of another National Leaguer of the era: Roger Craig, a righty who won big with the Dodgers (two championships), lost big with the Mets (46 defeats in two years), and became the most vocal acolyte and influential teacher the pitch has ever known.

"He got all the credit for the pitch," Face says. "But I don't think he ever threw the forkball."

Roger Craig didn't teach the forkball, either. He has always, *always* emphasized that the split-finger fastball is a different pitch, and still makes sure to include the word *fastball* in its name; if pitchers think fastball while throwing it, they will do so with fastball arm speed and deceive the hitter. But, yes—Craig threw many pitches, and the forkball was not among them.

"I had a pretty good fastball, a good curveball and slider, and I threw kind of a straight change, palmball type pitch," Craig says. Then he tore his rotator cuff—in the final game ever played by the Brooklyn Dodgers, on the road in Philadelphia in 1957—and everything changed. Unable to rely on pure stuff, Craig lasted nine more seasons, mainly by commanding a sinker. His experiences would serve him well.

Craig was the first pitching coach for the Padres, in 1969, before a stint with the Astros in the mid-1970s. It was there, he said, that he first began experimenting with the pitch that would become the splitter. Craig's meeting with Martin and Sutter came when he returned to San Diego later in the decade, around the time he was also running a baseball school.

"I'd have kids 17, 18 years old, starting to put some pop on the ball, and they were looking for a changeup pitch," Craig says. "Actually, they were not looking for it. When you see you can throw hard enough, that's all you want to throw."

Yet sooner or later, Craig knew, those kids would *need* to learn an off-speed pitch. And if they tried on their own, he feared, they would hurt themselves. Craig wanted to show them something safe, and the split-finger fastball required no manipulation of the wrist. It was just a fastball with a wider grip.

Craig became pitching coach for the Tigers in 1980 and taught the pitch to Milt Wilcox the next season. Wilcox was throwing it in the bullpen one day in Oakland in 1982, with Jack Morris watching. Morris was a star by then, but his slider had started to flatten and he needed an out pitch. In his previous start, in Anaheim, he had been torched for six runs without a strikeout. Wilcox showed Morris his grip.

"So I'm getting loose and I throw about 20, and *nothing*," Morris says. "I was about ready to quit and he goes, 'Put your thumb on the side this time, make sure you get your hand out in front, pull through out here.' So I threw about three more and the fourth one was just—*whomp,* straight down. And immediately I go, 'Holy shit, this is like cheating. If I get this down, there ain't nobody alive gonna hit it.' And two starts later I was throwing it in games."

Morris would go on to win more games than any other pitcher in the 1980s, and reach the Hall of Fame in 2018. Robin Yount, who rarely struck out, whiffed more times off Morris than any other pitcher, and said the splitter made Morris a star.

"That pitch alone took him to greatness," Yount says. "It was one of those pitches I never could recognize, because it always looked like a fastball to me. I swung at plenty of bouncing split-fingers from that guy. Most good hitters can recognize pitches early; you see the ball leave the pitcher's hand and can realize what the pitch is by the rotation. And a split-finger just didn't have the look of anything else.

"Now, in saying that, a lot of guys tried to throw them, but only a handful could really throw them well."

Many in that handful learned under Craig. The 1984 Tigers rolled to a championship, going 7–1 in the postseason with all of their starters—Morris, Wilcox, and Dan Petry—throwing the split-finger fastball. The pitch itself became a star.

"Most people believe Babe Ruth was the greatest baseball player ever—I wonder if he could have hit the split-finger fastball." Morris said after beating the Padres in Game 4 of the World Series, for his second complete game victory. "Ty Cobb? I've seen his swing. I know he couldn't hit it!"

Craig temporarily retired after the World Series, but his pitch had helped win a championship, and everyone wants to imitate a winner. A year before Buddy Ryan's "46" defense made him a celebrity coach with the Chicago Bears, the split-finger gave Craig the same status. He was not shy about explaining it, and even wrote a book chronicling the 1984 season.

In it, Craig explains that Wilcox threw the pitch on his fingertips, while Morris—who refers to it today as a forkball, not a split-finger fastball—tucked it back in his palm. He instructs readers not to grip the ball too deeply.

"The important thing is to assume a grip which feels comfortable and allows you to throw strikes," Craig wrote. "You can concentrate on the thumb once you feel comfortable gripping the ball with your middle and index fingers. Try to manipulate the thumb by imparting a little pressure upon release of the ball. This will give the pitch a tumbling effect. You also can curl the fingertips of your middle and index fingers, especially the index finger. That friction will give the pitch even more of a tumbling effect."

The tumble was essential, and so baffling that perhaps only a five-time batting champion with 20-12 vision could make it seem easy to hit. Wade Boggs had more at-bats off Morris and Dave Stewart than any other pitchers in his Hall of Fame career. He hit .363 off them.

"I could see the tumble, and if it started out up, it was gonna be a strike, but if they threw it down in the zone it was gonna tumble out of the zone," Boggs said. "So that was the thing. But when my eyes started to go bad, I couldn't see the tumble anymore."

That made Boggs like most hitters, who struggled to identify just what they were seeing. Was it a fastball, or maybe a changeup, and where did that drop come from? The effect was so devastating, and so well-chronicled, that at one point George Steinbrenner offered Craig and his wife an all-expenses-paid trip to Hawaii if Craig would tutor the Yankees' pitching coach. Craig declined.

In September 1985, on their way to the only 100-loss season in franchise history, the Giants hired Craig as manager. Attendance at his first game was 2,668. The important stuff happened beforehand, anyway.

"The first day I took all our pitchers down to the bullpen and I told them I'm not gonna push this on anybody, I'm gonna show everybody how to throw it and if you can learn to throw it, good, it could help the ball club," Craig says. "Anyway, I asked one pitcher who said he'd never thrown it before and it was Mark Davis. I said, 'OK, I'm gonna use you as my example.' So I got him on the mound and instead of having him throw a fastball with the seams, the two-seamer, I opened his fingers about an eighth of an inch. I said, 'Throw another fastball,' and I kept opening his fingers on every pitch until he had it out about, oh, three-quarters of an inch or something, and from then on he couldn't throw the ball as hard, but it would go down a little bit."

Two years later, with San Diego, Davis made the All-Star team. The next year he won the NL Cy Young Award. By then the Giants had become a winner, with a division title in 1987 and a pennant in 1989. And the splitter, as they would say years later, had gone viral.

Even at the time, it stood out as a quintessential '80s fad. In *The New Yorker,* Roger Angell likened the splitter to the Rubik's Cube. In *Sports Illustrated,* Ron Fimrite compared Craig's faith in the pitch to "the way Cap Weinberger believes in Star Wars—as the ultimate defense weapon." Hands across America—big hands, anyway—were letting those splitters fly. Heck, even the era's best *hitter*, Tony Gwynn, showed off his splitter grip for his 1986 Topps baseball card.

"I think it is the pitch of the future," Angels closer Donnie Moore told the *Los Angeles Times* in April 1986. "I think it's going to be a pitch like the slider was. Now almost everybody throws a little slider. I think in years to come, it's going to be *the* pitch."

Moore, once a Cubs farmhand, had learned the splitter from Fred Martin. His pitching coach in the Braves' system, the great Johnny Sain, encouraged him to trust it. Yet while the pitch made Moore an All-Star, he hung it at the worst moment, to Boston's Dave Henderson when the Angels were one strike away from the 1986 World Series. Henderson golfed it over the left field fence for a homer and the Red Sox soon claimed the pennant. Moore questioned his pitch selection after the game: "Maybe if I had tried to blow it past him, we'd be drinking champagne right now," he said.

(Moore's life unraveled in the years to follow. In 1989 he shot his wife, who survived, and then shot himself to death—an act of madness that almost certainly had much more to do with a history of domestic violence than with an errant split-finger fastball.)

Usually, the splitter was responsible for moments of glory. Red Sox lefty Bruce Hurst learned it from Craig before a game in 1984, and used it to beat the Mets twice in the 1986 World Series. The Blue Jays made the playoffs four times, and won their first World Series, with Tom Henke and his splitter locking down the ninth. Stewart's forkball helped him to four consecutive 20-win seasons and the MVP award in the 1989 World Series for Oakland—against Craig's team.

The Giants could not blame Craig for teaching Stewart the pitch. Stewart learned his forkball by modifying a splitter grip Sandy Koufax had shown him with the Dodgers at spring training in 1982.

"Sandy had really helped me with my mechanics when I was younger, and he told me, 'Hey, look, I want you to split your fingers a little bit and that should give you more downward movement on the ball,'" Stewart says. "I started experimenting a little more, and the split-finger that Sandy had pretty much taught me to throw, I changed it into a fork."

But it took a while. Traded the next year to Texas, Stewart shelved the pitch at the insistence of manager Doug Rader. His career sputtered and he drifted to the Phillies, who released him in May 1986. Signed by his hometown A's two weeks later, Stewart finally unleashed the forkball in Tony La Russa's first game as their manager, on ABC's *Monday Night Baseball* in Boston that July. Roger Clemens was 14–1 at the time, but Stewart beat him—the first of his eight victories over Clemens, without a loss, after joining the A's.

Oakland's championship rotation included two other starters, Mike Moore and Bob Welch, who threw Stewart's pitch. That was how it spread, from one master to others, alluring to both failing and thriving pitchers.

Mike Scott was failing: through the 1984 season he was 29–44 with a 4.45 ERA for the Mets and the Astros. With Craig temporarily retired, the Houston general manager, Al Rosen, asked him to tutor Scott for a few days. Scott entered Craig's San Diego baseball school as a washout, and left as an ace.

"The first couple, three days, he says, 'I just can't,'" Craig says. "He didn't have a good breaking ball but he had that good, live fastball and he said, 'I can't get it.' I said, 'You're getting it, you're getting it, just give it a couple more days.' He came up with one of the best in baseball."

Scott quickly became Craig's most celebrated protégé, and he thanked him with a division-clinching no-hitter in 1986—against the Giants. Historically Scott belongs more to the family of (alleged) scuffballers, but his influence on the splitter could be felt long after his last game in 1991.

Scott taught the splitter to Clemens at a golf event after the 1986 season, when both pitchers won the Cy Young Award. Clemens did not use it for a while; he was winning big with a slider as the main complement to his fastball. But by the late 1980s and early '90s

Clemens had turned to the pitch he called "Mr. Splitty"—and won five of his record seven Cy Young Awards after doing so.

"It's a devastating pitch to have," Clemens says. "It's game-changing. It's a huge out pitch if you need it. I consider it to be a violent pitch, even though it's not violent on your arm the way I throw it. I don't hook a seam."

In a game of 110 pitches, Clemens guessed, he would throw 20 or 30 splits. But hitters always thought he threw more, he said, because that was the third-strike pitch they would see on the highlights. To Clemens, the key to the pitch's deception was its presentation out of the hand.

"They see your fat wrist," he says. "When you throw breaking balls, you've got a thin wrist. But you see fat wrist on heater and split."

Naturally, learning a splitter did not work for everyone. Of all his pupils, Craig said the one with the best split was a right-hander named Randy O'Neal, who spent seven undistinguished seasons with five teams and lacked a respectable fastball to go with it. Other pitchers simply didn't have the hand for it. When Steve Carlton joined the Giants in 1986, Craig could not impart his new trick.

"Steve Carlton had real small hands for a big guy, and he just could not get his fingers spread apart," Craig said. "He used to sit during the game and have the trainers tape his fingers apart on a baseball and keep it in there the whole game trying to stretch it out. But he never really could get it. You have to have a little bit better than average-sized hand to throw a good one."

Mostly, though, the enduring memory of the Giants' staff under Craig is a procession of pitchers with dive-bombing splitters. When Craig arrived, the Giants' best reliever was a right-hander named Scott Garrelts, who had actually learned the splitter the year before, in winter ball. In Craig, he had a mentor who could refine it and the license to use it as often as he wanted.

Garrelts wanted to use it a lot. In 1984 he had a 5.65 ERA, but armed with the splitter in '85, the same hitters who owned him seemed helpless. He made the All-Star team and threw the split at 90 miles an hour. Tony Gwynn called Garrelts's splitter the best he ever saw; when Garrelts was at his sharpest, from 1985 to 1987, he held Gwynn to one hit in 18 at-bats.

"The thing with how Roger taught it is, obviously, split the fingers—but then it was more, you'd snap your wrist out, more like a fastball," Garrelts says. "The way I was throwing it, it was good and bad. I was really pronating—like, *really* hard. And the good thing was I had a lot of movement, a lot of downward movement, a lot of movement away also. The bad thing was: it's not so good on your arm. But there's that risk-reward. Those '85, '86, '87 seasons, especially being in the bullpen, I could throw really, really hard but I could definitely tell it was hard on my elbow."

Garrelts also threw his slurvy breaking ball in a way that stressed his elbow, which would eventually require Tommy John surgery. When he recovered from that, his shoulder gave out. Garrelts never threw a major league pitch in his 30s, but by then he had won an ERA title, started twice in the World Series, and spent parts of 10 years in the majors. He did what he had to do.

"If you need that pitch, you'd better throw it, because you don't want to look back 15 years from now and think, 'Maybe I should have thrown it,'" Garrelts says. "That's the decision everybody's got to make."

———

Bobby Valentine managed in Japan in 1995. At the end of the next season, he began a long stint managing the Mets. When Valentine returned to Japan as a manager in 2004, he recognized something that had largely disappeared from the American game: the splitter.

"It was a noticeable difference, because they just never discontinued the process," Valentine says. "We were similar in the '80s and early '90s, a similar amount of guys throwing it, I'll bet. And then we stopped, and they continued."

Major league teams overreacted, Valentine said, when split-finger maestros like Garrelts, Scott, and Sutter got hurt. The panic never spread overseas, Valentine says, partly because the mind-set behind the splitter was deeply embedded in Japanese baseball culture. It is the perfect substitute for the changeup.

"The reason the Japanese throw it as opposed to a straight changeup is because they don't think you should throw a slower pitch without movement," Valentine says. "It's just part of the pitching vernacular:

slower pitches move, faster pitches are straight; it's just the way the Japanese baseball brain works. They'll use a split, some form of a split, because they know it's a very similar arm stroke and the only thing that's different is the placement on the ball, which will propel the ball forward and also relieve the force behind the ball, so therefore you can't throw it as fast as your arm speed would dictate."

Hideki Matsui, who left Japan to join the Yankees in 2003, said his biggest adjustment as a hitter was facing so many changeups; the pitch was indeed rarely thrown in Japan, but nearly everyone threw a splitter. Japanese pitchers who preceded Matsui to the majors—Hideo Nomo, Shigetoshi Hasegwa, Kazuhiro Sasaki—brought the split with them. So did others who followed, like Hiroki Kuroda, Junichi Tazawa, and Koji Uehara.

"I used to only throw sliders and I wanted to expand my repertoire, and that's how I started throwing the pitch," says Uehara, the former Boston closer, whose splitter struck out St. Louis's Matt Carpenter for the final out of the 2013 World Series. Uehara's inspiration?

"With me it's Hideo Nomo," he says. "And with older generations there was a player called Shigeru Sugishita. I've only heard of him; I've never seen him throw. But he was supposed to have a really devastating splitter."

Sugishita threw his last pitch in 1961, long before Uehara was born. Known as the God of Forkballs, he was a three-time winner of the Sawamura Award as Japan's best pitcher. In 1954, for the Chunichi Dragons, he was also the Central League's MVP, going 32–12 with a 1.39 ERA across a staggering 395⅓ innings. Then he was MVP of the Japan Series. A god, indeed.

Sugishita turned 91 in 2016, when my friend Gaku Tashiro of Sankei Sports asked him a few questions for this book. Sugishita said that he learned the forkball at Meiji University in 1948, after first trying a knuckleball as an off-speed pitch. A coach noticed he had longer fingers than most pitchers and suggested the forkball, then thrown by only a few U.S. pitchers.

He took to the pitch instantly. The next year, Sugishita was pitching for the Dragons, and in 1950 he led his league in strikeouts. Nobody else, he said, was throwing the forkball.

"My advantage was that my two fingers are able to open widely," he told Tashiro, explaining that he got about three feet of vertical drop on the pitch. "It was helpful to grip the ball and to throw it with no spin. Sometimes the catcher could not catch my forkball because it was breaking too much."

Sugishita's forkball inspired the next generation of Japanese pitchers. By the mid-1970s, kids who had grown up in the 1950s were using the pitch in force. Helping their effort was that, for many years, the Japanese baseball was slightly smaller than the one used in MLB, making it a bit easier to throw for a split.

"Oh yeah, everybody threw it in Japan," says Clyde Wright, who pitched three years for the Yomiuri Giants after his major league career ended in 1975. "Young kids coming out of high school, all of 'em threw it. Everybody threw it. You get two strikes on you, you knew you were gonna get some kind of split-finger."

Ty Van Burkleo, a future major league hitting coach who played in Japan from 1988 to 1991, said: "It got to the point where, 3–1, I'm sitting forkball. If they threw me a fastball, I was like, 'Challenge me!'"

Tazawa, a future top setup man in the majors, was born in 1986 and said that in his youth, nearly every Japanese pitcher threw a split. Things changed, he said, after Nomo joined the Dodgers in 1995. Interest in Major League Baseball exploded, and with easier access to the American game, young pitchers started learning changeups, two-seamers, and so on.

American hitters, though, were confounded by the splitter, and have largely continued to flail away at it. While no Japanese pitcher has won a Cy Young Award, several have been dominant relievers or slotted comfortably into the front of winning rotations. Nomo started the All-Star Game as a rookie—he struck out Kenny Lofton and Edgar Martinez on splitters in the first inning—and went on to pitch two no-hitters.

The pitch's decline in popularity in the United States makes it less familiar to hitters.

"I don't think American and Latin kids see it anymore, because nobody teaches it," says Brian Bannister. "It's very, very rare, because of the perceived health risk, that a kid is willing to put his career on the line, not even knowing if it's true or not. And so it's not taught, therefore the hitters never see it; they don't get opportunity to practice against it. So in Japan, where it's taught more prevalently—it's taught like a changeup and everybody throws one—a lot of those pitchers have come over and had a ton of success because it's a lost pitch."

What is largely lost here is still ingrained in the Japanese game. Americans who sign there are generally told that they must learn the pitch. When Chris Leroux joined the Yakult Swallows in 2013, he could not throw the split without pain. He altered his arm angle and was bombed in five starts. But his teammate Tony Barnette, a career minor leaguer in the U.S., had a different experience.

"I had tinkered with it in junior college and even a couple of times in the minor leagues, but it was never really a pitch I took seriously," Barnette says. "Then I went over there and they kind of hammered it home. My pitching coaches said, 'Let's try the split, let's try the split.' They kept introducing it. Ended up being the right decision."

Barnette spent six years in Japan, finishing with 41 saves in 2015. At 32, with a sharp splitter but no major league experience, he signed a two-year, $3.5 million contract with the Texas Rangers. His ERA as a rookie was 2.09, and he appeared in every playoff game.

The splitter didn't hurt his arm, and even if it did, Barnette said, he would still throw it.

"Some people say the split causes Tommy John—now all of a sudden nobody's throwing splits, and guess what, they're still having Tommy Johns," Barnette says. "It's not a science. I don't think it has any more pressure than any other pitches I throw. It feels pretty comfortable, it feels pretty natural—and at this point in my career, what do I care? It's getting late in the game. I'm gonna use what I got, how much I've got, until I don't got it no more."

———

To prove the point that the splitter must be dangerous, pitchers often suggest that you spread your index and middle fingers as wide as possible.

"You'll get this incredible tenseness in your forearm, just physically spreading your fingers," says Ron Darling, who still could not resist throwing a lot of splitters in his prime with the Mets. "I consider it, in the short run, an incredible pitch. In the long run, I think it thwarted the length of my career."

Mike Mussina is also suspicious of the splitter, because of how tightly the pitcher must grip the sides of the ball. Then again, Mussina said, his hand is not really big enough to throw the pitch, and he rarely did. When his Yankee teammate Andy Pettitte tried to throw splitters in early 2002, the pitch hurt his elbow and led Pettitte down a dark road: in his recovery, he has admitted, he briefly resorted to human growth hormone.

When John Burkett pitched in Triple-A for the Giants, his pitching coach suggested he use a splitter to get Craig's attention and earn a promotion. The plan worked, but in time the pitch caused a grinding sensation in his elbow; once, Burkett said, his hand actually throbbed on the mound from a forearm spasm. Ken Hill, later Burkett's teammate in Texas, also felt a strain from the pitch and was rarely effective after age 32. Hill could not say for sure that the splitter caused his trouble, but it sure sounds painful.

"I'd get to a certain pitch count, my arm would be on fire," Hill says. "Right in the elbow."

Then there are cases like Chuck Finley, who logged more than 3,000 innings and said his hand was so big that gripping the splitter did not stress his fingers at all. Finley's wrist and elbow stayed loose and the pitch never hurt his arm. Nor did it bother Curt Schilling, who lasted through age 40 and was at his best in October, still strong after long seasons. Schilling used the splitter to become the only pitcher ever with more than 3,000 strikeouts and fewer than 750 walks. Don't tell him the pitch is dangerous.

"I think it's one of the easiest pitches in the world on your arm, because you don't change anything," Schilling says. "You don't manipulate the ball with a split, you just split your fingers. It literally is what it sounds like—you throw your fastball and split your fingers. I don't have to curl my wrist, I don't have to spin the ball. My elbow doesn't do anything other than what I do on my fastball for the most part. It's the easiest pitch to learn, easiest pitch to teach, and in my mind one of the easiest pitches to throw."

Clemens, Morris, and Stewart also had long careers. Jack McDowell, the 1993 AL Cy Young Award winner for the White Sox, was done at 33, but he has cited a surgical error that caused nerve damage. Sutter's pinched nerve, he said, came from a birth defect. Scott, who was finished at 35, refused to blame the splitter.

"I know it's one of the theories out there, but I guarantee you that it didn't shorten my career," he told ESPN in 2003. "People were having arm problems with it, which I really have a hard time believing because it's basically a fastball with the fingers split on the baseball. It's no different from throwing a fastball."

Craig draws a distinction between the pitch he taught and the forkball that preceded it.

"I never had a guy go all the way down," Craig says, referring to a ball pushed back in the palm. "That's like the forkball, and how many fork-ball pitchers do you remember? Elroy Face, Lindy McDaniel—they put it so deep they put some pressure on your arm. But the split-finger, if you throw it right, the way I taught it, you might hurt your arm—but you might hurt your arm throwing a rock."

Dr. Glenn Fleisig said there was no scientific data to cast the splitter as inherently dangerous. Yes, it might cause pain for some pitchers, but that doesn't mean the risk is universal. Sometimes, a splitter might only seem to cause an injury.

"Maybe it was the amount of pitching, total," Fleisig says, "and it just showed up on the splitter."

The industry doesn't want to take a chance. In 2017 only three of the 58 pitchers who qualified for the ERA title threw a split even 10 percent of the time: Masahiro Tanaka, Kevin Gausman, and Ricky Nolasco. Of the other 55 starters, according to FanGraphs, only three tried a splitter even once.

Yankees pitching coach Larry Rothschild says coaches would rather emphasize a changeup than a splitter, since the pitches work similarly. Even so, he could not say for sure that the splitter was any riskier than a hard slider—and besides, he added, fastballs might cause the most arm tension, anyway. Late in 2016, one of Rothschild's starters, Nathan Eovaldi, was found to need a second Tommy John surgery. Eovaldi threw splitters with 23 percent of his pitches, but said he had no plans to stop doing so when he returned.

A generation earlier, Bryan Harvey said the same thing. A two-time

All-Star closer with a devastating splitter, Harvey would wrap his fingers around a softball in the clubhouse; he did not have big hands but was determined to make the most of what he had. In May 1994, before Harvey returned from an elbow injury with the Marlins, Gordon Edes asked him if the pitch caused the pain.

"All I know is that I'm going to keep throwing it," Harvey said. He was 30 years old and would pitch just five more games in his career.

In an industry forever trying to solve the riddle of pitching injuries, stories like that stand out. The split-finger fastball is like a breed of dog that bites a few famous people. Word gets around and people avoid the breed altogether. There are plenty of other dogs to choose from.

Garrelts, who coaches kids in Shreveport, Louisiana, says people tend to ask him the same two questions about his career: Did you throw a no-hitter, and did you pitch in the World Series? He laughs and says he lost a no-hitter with two outs in the ninth and lost two starts in the World Series.

What about the pitch that made him famous for a while, the unhittable pitch that swept through his generation?

"Nobody's asked anything about the splitter," Garrelts says. "Nobody."

THE
SCREWBALL

The Sasquatch of Baseball

The final line on Christy Mathewson's Hall of Fame plaque is the most concise, exquisite bit of prose in the museum: "MATTY WAS MASTER OF THEM ALL." It is presented as a quotation, though the source is lost to time, if there ever was one. Perhaps it was just accepted gospel about Mathewson, the only member of the Hall's first class in 1936 who never lived to see the building. Mathewson was exposed to poison gas as an Army captain in France during World War I and spent the last years of his life fighting tuberculosis. It was a sad ending to a towering life that needed no embellishment. Mathewson really was the master.

No pitcher in baseball history has as many wins as Mathewson (373) with an earned run average so low (2.13). Only one man with even 250 wins (Lefty Grove, with 300) had a better winning percentage than Mathewson's .665. He led his league in strikeout-to-walk ratio nine times and threw three shutouts for the Giants in the 1905 World Series. More than that, though, Mathewson had a *story:* at a time when many ballplayers were mostly hard-bitten, poorly educated ruffians, Mathewson was a dignified, Christian gentleman from Factoryville, Pennsylvania, where, as a boy, he honed his famous control by throwing a ball—three inches wide—through a four-inch hole in the door of his father's barn. Mathewson went on to Bucknell, where he played sports but also sang in the glee club and belonged to the campus literary society. He was a man of letters beyond his many Ks; at the height of his fame, in 1912, Mathewson wrote a book that gave a detailed look at what happens on the field and why.

He called it *Pitching in a Pinch*—and what he did in that spot was throw his famous fadeaway, the pitch now known as the screwball.

"Many persons have asked me why I do not use my 'fade-away' oftener when it is so effective, and the only answer is that every time I throw the 'fade-away,' it takes so much out of my arm," he wrote. "It is a very hard ball to deliver. Pitching it ten or twelve times in a game kills my arm, so I save it for the pinches."

Mathewson, a right-hander, continued: "Many fans do not know what this ball really is. It is a slow curve pitched with the motion of a fast ball. But most curve balls break away from a right-handed batter a little. The fade-away breaks toward him."

In two paragraphs Mathewson defined the pitch forever, describing its effect on the pitcher and the hitter. He also added just enough mystery to cloud exactly what this pitch really is. Using a fastball motion to disguise a slower pitch—one that moves into the same-hand hitter—is also fundamental to the changeup. But a changeup is not shaped like a curveball, and generally is not tough on the arm. So if the pitch is not a changeup or a curve, it's something else. In the decades after Mathewson, it would be called the screwball, an oddity now all but extinct.

For years, the pitch was considered to be Mathewson's alone. In 1934, a former teammate, Red Murray, told the *Brooklyn Eagle* that the fadeaway was so hard to learn, and put such strain on the pitcher's wrist, that Mathewson was "the only man ever to master" it. Murray said Mathewson's inspiration had come from umpiring freshman games at Bucknell and wondering if he could make a curveball spin in reverse. Maybe so, but Mathewson himself cited an early teammate, Dave Williams, with giving him the idea for the fadeaway in 1898. Williams could not control the pitch well—he would make just three appearances in the majors, for the team now known as the Red Sox in 1902—but he showed Mathewson how to throw it.

"I was trying to work my way through college by pitching for a team in a little Pennsylvania mountain town called Honesdale," Mathewson told the Chicago *Inter Ocean* in 1910. "One day I saw a left-handed amateur throwing the ball with that peculiar reverse twist. I thought it might help me, so I learned it, but I worked at it steadily for five years before I got it perfected."

Mathewson, who referred to Williams by name in other sources, went on to distinguish his pitch from that of Virgil "Ned" Garvin, a turn-of-the-century journeyman who pitched for six teams in seven seasons.

"All the sporting books credit old Virgil Garvin with being the inventor of the fade-away," he said. "Well, maybe he was, but [Williams] had never heard of Virgil Garvin in all his life. He simply stumbled onto it by chance just as I had stumbled onto him."

When Mathewson joined the Giants in 1900, at age 19, he showed off his pitches for George Davis, the shortstop and manager, in practice. Davis immediately rejected the roundhouse curve, a pitch Mathewson called his pride and joy. Mathewson tried a tighter curve—a drop ball—which impressed Davis, who asked if he had anything else.

"I've a sort of freak ball that I never use in a game," Mathewson said. It was his fadeaway, which he hadn't even named and could rarely control. But he broke off a beauty to Davis, who swung and missed by a foot. Eyes bulging, Davis asked for another, and missed that one, too.

"That's a *good* one!" Davis declared, as recalled by Mathewson for *St. Nicholas* magazine in 1912. "That's all right! It's a slow in-curve to a right-handed batter. A change of pace with a curve ball. A regular fallaway or fadeaway. That's a good ball!"

Other Giants were similarly amazed, and Davis told Mathewson to practice the pitch diligently so he could control it for the future. He would pitch just six times that season, with more walks than strikeouts, but soon began a captivating magic act on the mound: a no-hitter in 1901, a 30-win season in 1903, those record three World Series shutouts in 1905, and so on. All along, Mathewson eagerly shared the secrets of his fadeaway: turning over his hand, snapping his wrist away from his body—it was all there, in print or in person, waiting to be imitated.

"Many times I have tried to teach other pitchers in the Big League—even men on opposing clubs—how to throw this ball," he said. "But none have ever mastered it."

A richer origin story than the Dave Williams version involves Rube Foster, a Hall of Famer best known for organizing the Negro National League in 1920. Foster was a top pitcher before that, and John McGraw, as Giants manager, is said to have recruited him to help his pitchers. A legend persists that Foster then taught Mathewson the fadeaway, though the evidence clearly contradicts this. Even so, the fact that Foster also threw it, with great success, supports Rob Neyer's theory that nobody really knows who used it first. John Clarkson and Tim Keefe were well known for changing speeds in the 1880s, like another ace of that time, Mickey Welch, who said late in life that he recognized Mathewson's fadeaway as the same pitch he had used.

"Just about anybody could have invented it," Neyer wrote. "Once everybody realized that you could make a baseball curve *that* way by twisting your wrist *this* way, it wouldn't have taken a genius to realize that reversing the process should be possible, the result being what we might call—and what might actually have been called—a 'reverse curve.'"

"Reverse curve" is the most accurate shorthand for screwball, a baseball term that long ago crossed over into everyday life. In the 1930s, the prime of the great Giant lefty Carl Hubbell, "screwball" came to describe a specific genre of Hollywood comedies: battle of the sexes, often with a woman's madcap antics upending a stuffy man's world. In his book about Depression-era films, Andrew Bergman wrote that "screwball comedy," like Hubbell's famous pitch, was "unconventional, went in different directions and behaved in unexpected ways."

By that description, the knuckleball would fit better. But screwball just *sounds* right, as it does when describing a personality type: eccentric at best, deranged at worst. If someone is known as a screwball, he's not a reliable guy, and it's not a reliable pitch, either. The definition has become self-fulfilling: it's so bizarre and deemed such a health risk that pitchers use alternatives—the changeup, mostly—to achieve the same result. The pitch has all but vanished from the majors over the last three decades, so much so that the Hall of Fame slugger Jim Thome, who played 22 seasons, said he had *heard* of the pitch, but never *seen* it. The screwball, in that way, is the Sasquatch of baseball: believed to exist but with no credible evidence from many experts.

The record does show that Thome batted once against a Reds left-hander named Daniel Ray Herrera, grounding out in 2009. Herrera made 131 appearances from 2008 to 2011, and without the screwball, he would have made none. He used it because he could not throw a changeup, and it distinguished him just enough to give him his modest career.

Herrera's quirky profile fit the pitch: he is 5 foot 6, and at the time of his debut, no pitcher had been shorter in more than 50 years. He is also the only major leaguer ever to attend Permian High School in Odessa, Texas, best known as the featured football program in *Friday Night Lights*.

"When I was in high school, they actually tore down the outfield fence so they could have spring football practice," Herrera says. "So our center field and right field would be just dirt pits from the guys rustlin' around on the ground out there."

In college, at New Mexico, Herrera found that his changeup moved sideways, almost like a sinker, without the downward fade he needed. He tried pronating his wrist more deliberately, and found that the more he did it, the more over-the-top spin he imparted on the ball. Herrera snapped down with his wrist, just as he would for a curveball, but in the opposite direction. His command was shaky, but he knew a good weapon when he saw it: this new pitch had curveball spin but ran away from a right-hander. The oddity alone made it valuable.

"When I started throwing it, everyone kept calling it a changeup, a changeup," he says. "And in the back of my head I kept saying: 'A changeup doesn't move like this; a changeup doesn't spin like this.' I actually didn't classify it as a screwball when I started throwing it. I just knew it was something different, and hopefully I could work with it in the future."

It took 1,345 picks and 45 rounds in the 2006 draft, but Herrera was finally chosen by the Rangers. Within two years he was pitching in the majors for the Reds, relieving Aaron Harang—who is 13 inches taller—against a stacked Phillies lineup. In his first inning, he struck out a power-hitting lefty (Ryan Howard) and a power-hitting righty

(Pat Burrell). Jamie Moyer, the ageless Philadelphia left-hander, sought out Herrera before the next day's game.

"You have to show me how to throw that pitch," Moyer cried, before Herrera could even say hello. "I need to revive my career!"

Herrera was stunned. Here he was, with one game in the majors, and a veteran of two decades had noticed him, just because of the screwball. It would be a recurring theme in Herrera's brief career. Pitchers would regularly ask him for guidance, but none could repeat what he did. They usually weren't flexible enough to get their arm over their head, as Herrera did. And if they could, they couldn't throw anything else from that slot.

"Daniel really had to clear his head to get into that position," says Bryan Price, who coached Herrera with the Reds. "It's hard to throw other pitches of similar quality from such a dramatic position, because the head has to clear to get on top of the ball to such a degree. From what I've seen, from the guys I've had who've thrown screwballs, it would be very difficult to have quality secondary pitches—meaning fastball command or a breaking ball—off that pitch."

Some pitchers, like Mike Norris, are born to throw the screwball. Don't think so? Go grab a household item, like a ketchup bottle or a paper cup. Chances are you pick it up with your palm turned in, toward you. Norris says he always did this the opposite way, with his palm turned away from his body. His mother, Lulu, worried he would drop the milk when he lifted it from the kitchen table. Norris never did.

As an amateur, Norris was practicing one day at Balboa Park in San Francisco when he noticed an unmistakable figure off in the distance: Juan Marichal, the star Giants righty with the impossibly high leg kick and nasty screwball. Norris did not ask for an autograph, but for his screwball grip. Marichal obliged, and in 1980 Norris went 22–9 and nearly won the Cy Young Award. His trick was a screwball thrown at three speeds, with such deception that his manager, Billy Martin, called it a dry spitter.

"Mine was an optical illusion," Norris says. "So with the arm speed, it looked like a fastball, then the seams started turning over, going the other way, and it looked like it just stopped in midair. It moved about two feet, and I could throw it from one side of the plate to the other. So this is why they'd have difficulty hitting it, because they're throwing their hands at it and it's not there yet. Now it's starting to go down, and the velocity as it goes down is incredible. It's even harder going down than it is going away."

With Norris's screwball drifting and dropping away from them, left-handers hit just .185 off him in 1980. Yet Norris's description of the pitch, and the way he threw it—the further back in his palm, the slower it was—again evokes the changeup. The pitches are close cousins, often mistaken for twins. The Reds once had two lefties, Tom Browning and John Franco, who threw a pitch with the same action. But Franco's came from a circle-change grip, so his was called a changeup. Browning used a two-seam grip, pulling his thumb down to impart the slashing movement away from a righty. His was called a screwball but served the same purpose, and helped him pitch a perfect game in 1988.

"My fastball was probably major league average, if that, although some guys may say it was never that," Browning says. "But [my screwball] complemented it so much that it allowed my fastball to look better, look firmer, because they had to stay back a little bit in case I came with the changeup—or the screwball."

Warren Spahn, whose 363 wins are the most ever by a lefty, basically carved out a second prime—in his late 30s and early 40s—by perfecting an off-speed pitch that flummoxed right-handed hitters. The pitch was widely known as a screwball, and that's what Joe Torre, his catcher at the end, also calls it.

But here's Roger Angell describing Spahn teaching the pitch in spring training in 1987. Angell calls it a sinker-screwball, but it accurately describes a circle change: "His left thumb and forefinger were making a circle, with the three other fingers pointing up, exactly as if he were flashing the 'O.K.' sign to someone nearby. The ball was tucked comfortably up against the circle, without being held by it, and the other fingers stayed up and apart, keeping only a loose grip on the pill. Thrown that way, he said, the ball departed naturally off the inside, or little-finger side, of the middle finger, and would then sink and break to the left as it crossed the plate."

Spahn's late-career dominance was nearly unprecedented; he is the only pitcher in the last century with two 20-win seasons after turning 40. He missed three years to military service in his early 20s, saving wear on his arm at a critical age. His father, Ed, a wallpaper sales-man, emphasized momentum in his son's delivery, transferring weight from back to front with an exaggerated leg kick that Spahn believed protected his arm.

"Dad had a theory about pitching," Spahn told *The Washington Post* in 1955. "He used to say if you learned to throw properly you could pitch forever without hurting your arm. He was right, too."

If it was, indeed, a screwball that Spahn threw, it certainly didn't hurt him. And while the screwball's most notorious victim is thought to be Carl Hubbell, consider that Hubbell's arm trouble might have been caused by piling up four seasons in a row with at least 300 innings—and besides, he did pitch past his fortieth birthday and go down as an all-time great.

"I've heard about how he inverted his arm in a weird way, and when I was younger I thought, 'Well, I'm gonna play for 10 or 15 years, and then what if my arm does that?'" Herrera says. "I always kind of looked at the angle of it, but nothing has ever changed. My arm hasn't twisted inward like that. So maybe it is a legend, who knows? But I think I'd make that sacrifice—and then just write upside down with my left arm."

———

Ah, the inverted arm of Carl Hubbell. You might think Hubbell's staggering success would be a powerful selling point for the screwball. For a decade (1929–38) he had 195 wins, a 2.81 ERA (best in the majors), and two Most Valuable Player awards. He dominated the Senators in the 1933 World Series, allowing no earned runs across 20 innings, and the next summer he used the screwball to strike out five Hall of Famers in a row at the All-Star Game: Babe Ruth, Lou Gehrig, Jimmie Foxx, Al Simmons, and Joe Cronin.

Alas, physical deformity trumps all that. Hubbell, nicknamed "Meal Ticket" for the Depression-era Giants, blamed his own meal ticket for the way his arm bent awkwardly at his side, turned out to the left as if in perpetual follow-through on a screwball. Jim Murray—who once wrote that Hubbell "looks as if he put it on in the dark"—shared this anecdote in the *Los Angeles Times* after Hubbell's death in 1988:

The screwball was not really a pitch, it was an affliction. I met Hubbell only once. He was in his late 60s but still the gaunt, spare, Gary Cooperish character I remembered as a kid. I gave him a ride to the airport on his way to scout some phenom in Northern California for the Giants.

"Tell me," I asked him, "was that screwball that hard a pitch to throw? Hard on the arm?" Hubbell laughed. And rolled up his sleeve. He showed me a left arm you could have opened wine with. It should have had a cork on the end of it. I whistled. Why did he risk it? Hubbell laughed again. "In those Depression days, you would have let them twist your neck for a living. An arm was nothing."

The screwball gave Hubbell a career—and like Mathewson, he was inspired by another pitcher with just a sliver of time in the majors. Claude "Lefty" Thomas appeared in seven games for Washington in 1916, but otherwise spent 18 pro seasons in the minors. Near the end of his wandering, with the Des Moines Demons of the Class A Western League in 1925, he caught the attention of Hubbell, then with the Oklahoma City Indians and just starting his career.

In an interview in his clip file at the Hall of Fame, Hubbell mentions that Thomas made pitching seem so easy. Others could throw harder, but Thomas just flipped sinkers down and away to right-handers for harmless ground balls. Hubbell decided to pitch the same way.

"I must have had the right kind of instincts to pick him," Hubbell said. "It's like learning to walk: monkey see, monkey do. I picked the right monkey."

As he worked on the sinker, Hubbell found he could get more spin when he turned the pitch over with his wrist at the end. This was the screwball, christened as such by the Oklahoma City catcher Earl Wolgamot. As Hubbell told *The New York Times'* George Vecsey in 1984, Wolgamot caught the pitch in warm-ups one day and called it "the screwiest thing I ever saw."

Hubbell said he could tell right away the pitch was unnatural—"my elbow had to fly up just as I turned it loose"—and, apparently, so could the Tigers. At spring training with Detroit in 1925, coach George McBride forbade him from using it, insisting it would ruin his arm.

Ty Cobb, then Detroit's manager, may have ordered McBride to say this, though Hubbell said he never actually spoke to Cobb, who was gone when the Tigers released Hubbell in 1928, without ever letting him pitch in an exhibition game.

Hubbell moved on to the Beaumont Exporters of the Texas League. He decided the only way to distinguish himself was to use the screwball, whether it hurt him or not. That June Beaumont played in Houston, site of the Democratic convention, and a delegate named Dick Kinsella took in the game. Hubbell pitched a four-hitter, impressing Kinsella, a scout for the Giants and a friend of McGraw, who was still their manager.

According to author Frank Graham, Kinsella called McGraw and told him of his discovery. He warned McGraw that Cobb had rejected Hubbell because the screwball might damage his arm, but McGraw laughed it off. He had managed Mathewson, after all.

"That's a joke," McGraw said. "When Matty was pitching it, they called it a fadeaway and it never hurt his arm. If there isn't anything wrong with him, I'd like to know more about him."

Kinsella agreed to follow Hubbell around for a while, leaving the convention for a more promising prospect than the Democrats' nominee, Governor Alfred E. Smith of New York. Smith would lose in a landslide to Herbert Hoover that November, but Kinsella secured the contract of a pitcher who would win prodigiously, long after Hoover left office.

Hubbell was the National League's MVP in 1936, guiding the Giants to the World Series with a 26–6 record and a major-league-best 2.31 ERA. The screwball was a big part of his mystique.

"I've tried never to let pitching success turn my head; but it has twisted my arm," Hubbell wrote the next spring in a story for *This Week* magazine. "This left 'salary wing' of mine hangs from my shoulder strangely, with the palm facing out and backward. Because of this strange twist, I can throw a screwball with ease. The screwball, a reverse curve which breaks, in my case, away from a right-handed batter instead of toward him, as a southpaw's natural hook does, has ruined many pitchers' arms. However, although it has 'swiveled' my arm at the elbow, it never hurts."

Alas, by the next summer, just after his 200th career victory, Hubbell could no longer raise his arm to his shoulder without elbow pain. A doctor in Memphis removed bone chips and a calcium deposit on the joint, and Hubbell believed he knew the reason.

Before the 1940 season, he told an interviewer that the ban on spitballs—by then nearly two decades old—had forced pitchers to "invent freak deliveries" to do their jobs. The balls they were using, meanwhile, were slick and shiny, because umpires quickly discarded any ball that might be scuffed. Hubbell insisted it was murder on that salary wing:

"These unorthodox pitches result in a great strain on the arm. Take my screwball, for instance—the peculiar twist I must give it if I hope to fool anybody with it is the reason for those splintered bones I had in my elbow."

Hubbell remained a useful pitcher in his final four seasons, finishing 253–154 in a remarkable career that made him an inner-circle Hall of Famer. Even so, Hubbell was never interested in passing down the screwball; a teammate who tried it, Cliff Melton, was also bothered by elbow pain. The hazards to Hubbell were ever present in that mangled throwing arm, at once the best and worst advertisement the screwball ever had.

―――――――

The screwball had its moments after Hubbell's dazzling prime. The Cardinals' Harry Brecheen beat the Red Sox three times in the 1946 World Series. Luis Tiant—the father of the future Boston ace— finished his career in Cuba, where he threw one of the best screwballs the island has ever seen. Verdell "Lefty" Mathis, a star in the Negro American League in the 1940s, used screwballs to thwart one of the game's great sluggers, Josh Gibson. Mathis loved facing lineups stacked with right-handed hitters—including Gibson, whose Cooperstown plaque says he hit nearly 800 homers.

"I always used the screwball on Gibson, low and away," Mathis told the author John Holway. "He never hit a home run off me."

In popular lore, though, the screwball still belonged to Hubbell. In

Players' Choice, the 1987 book that polled hundreds of ex-players on various topics, Hubbell got about four times as many votes for best screwball as any other pitcher. Still, there were prominent pitchers who featured it in their arsenal, including Juan Marichal, who was yet another Giants Hall of Famer.

Marichal had first been intrigued by the screwball at Class A in 1959, knowing that Ruben Gomez had thrived with it in the majors. He asked Andy Gilbert, his manager in Springfield, Massachusetts, how to throw it, learning that the pitcher must break his wrist the opposite way as he does for a curveball. For Marichal, though, there was a handicap: he could not throw the screwball sidearm, as he did for his other pitches. He had to throw it overhand.

That would be a challenge, but as a right-hander, Marichal believed he had to try it. Candlestick Park opened in 1960 and favored left-handed hitters, meaning he would need a pitch that broke away from them. He picked it up quickly, and in 1962 began a string of eight All-Star seasons in which he averaged more than 21 wins per year. Even those who hit him well, like Joe Torre, admired Marichal's wide repertoire.

"He would throw you a fastball, a curveball, a screwball; he had a big curveball and he threw a slider—and then he threw everything [sidearm] too, except the screwball," Torre says. "I tried not to look at his delivery because he had that big leg kick and he threw basically stiff-arm. But he was remarkable, because with the wild windup and the big leg kick, his control was better than anybody else's. He could throw the ball over a rosin bag, I guarantee it."

Marichal's most famous game was his marathon duel with Spahn at Candlestick in 1963. Marichal twirled 16 shutout innings and Spahn 15, until Willie Mays bashed a hanging screwball for a game-ending home run. Marichal would pitch 12 more seasons, finishing 101 games above .500, though a championship eluded him; he made just one appearance in the World Series.

That was in 1962, when Ralph Terry played the hero for the Yankees. Four years later, Terry was barely hanging on, trying to learn a knuckleball at the instructional league for the Mets. There he met a plucky young lefty named Frank Edwin "Tug" McGraw, who had lost 16 of his 20 major league decisions. Terry went golfing with McGraw, and passed on a tip that would one day help two franchises win their first World Series.

McGraw had a clean, overhand delivery, and Terry thought the screwball would be a good fit. He had learned it from Spud Chandler, the 1943 AL Most Valuable Player for the Yankees, who had once coached Terry with the Kansas City A's. Terry remembered how Marlin Stuart, an otherwise ordinary righty in the 1950s, had humbled the great Ted Williams with screwballs. Williams generally owned Terry (career average: .455), but on June 20, 1958, Terry retired him three times in a row with screwballs.

"That's a good pitch," Williams told Terry after the game. "Don't use it all the time."

That was the screwball's reputation: a valuable weapon that must be conserved, for fear of injury. And while McGraw picked up the pitch from Terry in about 10 minutes—"Man, he *had* it, just like Warren Spahn, right over the top," Terry says—he met the same kind of resistance Hubbell had found decades earlier.

A Mets coach, Sheriff Robinson, would not let McGraw use it. Yet Terry's explanation made sense to McGraw, who used the pitch in the minors and felt no soreness. As McGraw wrote in his first autobiography:

What Ralph Terry had taught me was to rotate my arm in such a way as to get opposite rotation from every other breaking pitch. When you throw the baseball over the top of your head or ear, it makes just as much sense to turn your wrist inside-out. If you put a clock in front of you, you twist the ball toward three o'clock. It turns your whole arm all the way back to your shoulder. By the time you release it you lose some velocity, but the ball breaks away from a right-handed hitter instead of toward him the way a curve does. The fastball will tail away from a right-handed hitter, and a curve will break into him. But this one broke away and destroyed his timing.

Sounds good, but the Mets were not convinced. They buried McGraw in the minors for all of 1968, then left him unprotected for three rounds of the expansion draft. He went unclaimed, and the next spring they finally relented and let him throw screwballs. McGraw instantly became an ace reliever, struck out Hank Aaron to help save a playoff game, and won a championship ring with a team forever known as the Miracle Mets.

McGraw also met Hubbell that season, at an Old-Timers' Game at Shea Stadium. They compared screwball grips and noticed they gripped the pitch differently to get the same action. McGraw held his parallel to the seams, Hubbell across them.

"We came to the conclusion that it's not so much how you hold it in your hand as how you release it," McGraw wrote. "You know, the way a guy holds the ball, against the seams or with them, is just a matter of comfort. But what counts is the thing that gives the ball its final rotation."

The screwball became integral to McGraw's persona. He was the epitome of the lovable screwball, thumping his glove on his thigh as he bounded off the mound between innings, leading an orchestra in a dramatic reading of "Casey at the Bat." In the 1970s he even authored a nationally syndicated comic strip about a team of misfit players. Appropriately, he called it *Scroogie*.

As McGraw's fastball waned, he called it his Peggy Lee—as in, "Is That All There Is?" There were variations to the fastball, and McGraw named them, too. The Bo Derek, he said, "had a nice little tail on it." The Cutty Sark sailed, the John Jameson went straight (like Irish whiskey), and the gopher ball was his Frank Sinatra pitch—as in, "Fly Me to the Moon."

The most important pitch McGraw ever threw came for the Phillies in the ninth inning of Game 6 of the 1980 World Series, with two out and the bases loaded. Police dogs circled the field at Veterans Stadium to keep the fans from rushing the turf. McGraw noticed the K-9 Corps and instantly made the connection: here he was in the ninth, needing a K.

Somehow, the silly thought relaxed McGraw. He ran the count full to the Royals' Willie Wilson, setting him up for a screwball. Wilson hesitated just long enough on his swing, flailing at the high fastball to end it.

McGraw exulted, whirling his left arm like a windmill and bouncing as he turned to third base and caught Mike Schmidt in his arms.

Seventy-five years after Mathewson's fadeaway had carried the Giants to a championship, the screwy pitch from a screwy lefty had delivered the Phillies the title.

McGraw's success highlighted the last peak era for the screwball. It had briefly made Mike Norris an ace in Oakland, and in 1984, Willie Hernandez would use it to win the AL Most Valuable Player award while leading Detroit all the way. Hernandez had learned the screwball two years earlier from Mike Cuellar, the former star lefty for the Orioles.

But the true locus for the screwball, in these years, was Dodger Stadium. In 1974, the Dodgers' Mike Marshall won the NL Cy Young Award with one of the most mind-bending seasons in major league history: a record 106 relief appearances, with more than 200 innings, while leading the Dodgers to the pennant. Seven years later, Fernando Valenzuela carried them to the championship, becoming the only pitcher ever to win the Rookie of the Year and Cy Young awards in the same season. Both men featured the screwball as their primary weapon, but had little else in common.

Marshall was a right-handed reliever from Michigan. He does not work in organized baseball and condemns its understanding of pitchers. Valenzuela was a left-handed starter from Mexico. He has broadcast the Dodgers in Spanish since 2003 and remains extraordinarily popular, at once familiar and larger than life.

The Dodgers share a spring training complex with the Chicago White Sox, whose former manager Robin Ventura said the one pitch he had always wanted to face was Valenzuela's screwball. Ventura, who grew up in California, was in junior high when Fernandomania swept through the game in 1981. He was playing in the majors a dozen years later, when Valenzuela pitched for the Orioles.

"That was the only time in my career that I went to the plate and thought, 'I'm just going to watch this—from, like, right here, I'm going to watch it, because I want to see it,'" Ventura says. "Not even a thought of hitting it. I was gonna purposely just sit and watch. He didn't throw that hard back then, but just that action of when he turned it over, it was still a good pitch."

Careers like Marshall's and Valenzuela's, marked by uniquely memorable peaks, tend to reinforce the screwball's reputation as an outlier kind of pitch. There is a reason Mathewson and Hubbell both used the word "freak" to describe it. Marshall's last manager in the majors, Joe Torre, describes him like this: "He was a freak of nature, because he threw every single day."

This is nonsense to Marshall, who has a PhD in exercise physiology from Michigan State and has devoted his life to kinesiology, the study of human movement. He threw a pitch that supposedly destroys the arm, yet endurance was his hallmark. As a rookie with Detroit in 1967, Marshall threw his slider the usual way—releasing it over the top of his index finger—and his elbow hurt so much he could not raise it to brush his teeth. His studies, supported by his use of high-speed film, showed him that the proper way to pitch—the *only* way to do so safely, he insists—was to pronate on everything. And pronation—that is, a counterclockwise turn—helps the screwball.

"When you throw the screwball, you start out with the hand facing away from you, which means you are already in a full pronated situation," Marshall says. "And you can't do anything but put spin on the ball. But the way that I throw, you come in and drive and my elbow pops up, and the powerful inward rotation gives me a very high spin velocity. I can start it over your head and it'll end up at your ankles—one of those pitches that will really bite the air molecules."

Like so many others, Marshall was initially told not to throw the screwball. His fifth organization, the Montreal Expos, finally let him throw it in 1970, and he went on to lead the majors in relief appearances for the decade. He calls the screwball "an absolute must" for any pitcher, and has spent many years as a college coach and private pitching instructor in Zephyrhills, Florida.

Yet for all the innovation in baseball lately, the sport has never turned to Marshall in any official way. His unwavering support of the screwball is just a small part of the revolution he believes he could unleash: 10 miles an hour added to everyone's fastball, and pronated breaking balls that never damage the elbow. Baseball teams are willing to innovate with their methods, but not to blow them all up.

"There's no major league team that seems to be interested in having a completely injury-free pitching motion," he says. "These traditional pitching coaches, they just get together and talk about this stupidity stuff, and nobody's interested in learning how to have the very best pitchers you could possibly get. Of course, this would change baseball. You're gonna have to move the mound back."

That's quite a thought, but it's also a fantasy—the pitching distance has been 60 feet, 6 inches since 1893, and it's not changing. Velocity is climbing, anyway, and for his part, Valenzuela laments the loss of nuance in the modern game.

"If scouts don't see 90-plus, I don't think they can sign pitchers," he says. "I can see a good pitcher in Mexico with good control, but if the velocity's not there, they say no. No velocity, no prospect for the big leagues."

Valenzuela threw a fastball and curveball when he signed with the Dodgers in 1979, at age 18. Mike Brito, the scout who signed him, visited Valenzuela that summer at Class A in Lodi, California, and decided he needed a third pitch. After the season he sent another pitcher he had signed, Dodgers reliever Bobby Castillo, to teach Valenzuela the screwball.

"We believed that his fastball was below average, so we needed a pitch to make his fastball better," Brito says. "That was the pitch that made him successful in the big leagues."

Valenzuela, it turned out, had just the right wrist for the screwball, and soon he would catapult to stardom, packing stadiums and connecting with Los Angeles fans in a way no other Dodger ever has. The Dodgers rode him hard, and in Valenzuela's first 10 seasons only one pitcher in the majors (Jack Morris) logged more innings.

That workload, not the screwball, is probably the main reason for Valenzuela's sharp decline in his 30s. Even so, his prime was so inspiring that you'd think some pitcher, with two weapons but not a third, might ask him how he threw his best pitch.

As he leaned on a fence in Arizona one spring day, signing autographs and watching the Dodgers practice, Valenzuela considered the question and shook his head.

"If somebody approached me, I'd try to help them out," he said. "Right now? Nobody."

Really? All those pitchers in camp, majors and minors, and nobody asks?

"Nobody," Valenzuela said.

————————

We see this phenomenon with the splitter, too—a pitch proven to be a devastating weapon, but now mostly hidden behind layers of yellow police tape. At least some pitchers still throw splitters, though. Almost nobody throws a screwball on purpose anymore. Most pitchers still need something that moves away from the opposite-handed hitter. But there are more options today, and the screwball is a relic.

"What you see nowadays is a modern variation of it, and it comes in the form of a Felix Hernandez or Zack Greinke changeup," says Brian Bannister. "It's the modern, power, flat-spin-axis changeup. That's how it's evolved. Instead of in your mind trying to throw a backwards curveball, in a way it's, 'Let's throw a changeup with no vertical rise,' one where the bottom just falls out—like James Shields. The ball is spinning like a helicopter, therefore it has no backspin and no vertical rise and the bottom just falls out. That to me is the modern screwball."

Jim Mecir, a right-handed reliever for Oakland and four other teams from 1995 to 2005, was the last pitcher to have a long career throwing screwballs. Mecir learned it at Eckerd College from a coach, Rich Folkers, who played for several teams in the 1970s. Mecir threw it as a classic reverse curveball, turning his fingers away from his head and pulling down, never pronating, never hurting his elbow—and always keeping his catchers on alert.

"Just like a left-handed breaking ball," says A. J. Hinch, who caught him briefly for the A's. "You'd have to remind yourself to catch it with your thumb up, because it was going to go the wrong way."

Mecir's career was a testament to ingenuity. Born with a clubfoot, he could not generate much power with his legs as he pushed off the mound. His strength came from his upper body and he threw awkwardly, with an open delivery that kept him from having a good curveball or slider. The screwball was his remedy—but he wouldn't recommend it.

"I teach pitching lessons and I would never think about—especially with liability now—'Hey, do you want to throw a screwball?'" Mecir says. "Because I don't know, myself. I just know it works for me. My mechanics were a little different and it's what I had to do."

It is not a pitch anyone seems interested in teaching, from Hubbell on down. In 2016 Fox aired a drama series called *Pitch* about a woman, played by Kylie Bunbury, who makes the majors by throwing a screwball. But fantasy did not meet reality: her on-set coach, the former Oriole Gregg Olson, has never taught a screwball to a nonactor. Too hard on the shoulder, he says.

Even as a family heirloom, the pitch often stays on the basement shelf. Clyde Wright was 1–8 for the Angels in 1969, learned a screwball from Marv Grissom in winter ball, and immediately had a dream season: 22 wins, an All-Star appearance, a no-hitter. His son, Jaret, went on to pitch in the majors, too, but Clyde never thought to teach him a screwball.

"No, no, no, no, no," Wright says. "He had the circle change. When you can throw it 97, 98 and you can get it over with the breaking ball and the changeup, you really don't need it."

Jaret Wright's career began with great promise—he nearly pitched the Indians to victory in Game 7 of the 1997 World Series—but injuries ultimately held him back, even though he never used the screwball. Clyde is not convinced the pitch is dangerous. It never hurt his elbow, he said, yet pitchers today seem to be constantly in pain.

"If they're worried about it hurting arms, then somebody's a lot dumber than I am," Wright says. "How many guys go on the DL every year in the big leagues—and not one of them throws the screwball that I've heard about."

Yet Wright, too, knows the story of Carl Hubbell and his inverted pitching arm. That example is not the reason the screwball has gone away, but it symbolizes the pitch's notorious reputation. Few people threw the screwball to begin with, and now there's almost nobody to advocate for it, let alone teach it.

"There's just too much at stake now," Bannister says. "With the money in the game, it's not worthwhile for a coach to put his own career on the line to destroy a kid's arm. Whether he would or not isn't the issue, it's just that any form of risk in pitching, as far as health is concerned, is considered taboo.

"Teams in general are always in this limbo between performance and health. You have these massive investments in money and kids, and you don't want to blow them out because you only get so many draft picks, and they're expensive. But at the same time, there's this sacrifice in performance that a lot of older pitchers used to have, because they were willing to go places with the pitches and with their arm action that most teams won't approach nowadays."

Some pitchers, like Hector Santiago and Trevor Bauer, have periodically promoted the screwball in recent years, rooting for its return. They've never really stuck with it, or stood out enough for people to pay much attention, but as teams chase every little edge, they're more and more open to shattering old perceptions. Theoretically, this could help the screwball's chance of survival.

One day in 2016, around the batting cage in Houston, Astros pitching coach Brent Strom spoke about the splitter, how it was the rage of the 1980s. "I want the next rage," said general manager Jeff Luhnow, smiling. "But we're not gonna tell you what it is."

Could it be the screwball? Strom, a contemporary of Marshall, McGraw, Jim Brewer, and other screwball masters of the 1970s, wouldn't dismiss it.

"It's the easiest pitch to throw and nobody throws it," he said. Because the arm is already pronated on a screwball, Strom explained, it's in a better position to decelerate than it is for other pitches. Think of a car slowing down as it approaches the stop sign, instead of slamming on the brakes.

That is the analogy used by Brent Honeywell Jr., a top right-hander in the Tampa Bay farm system whose background and attitude make him the screwball's best hope. Honeywell's father, Brent Sr., is Mike Marshall's cousin. Marshall coached Brent Sr. at Saint Leo University in the 1980s, and taught him the screwball. Brent Sr., who pitched briefly in the minors, passed on the pitch to Brent Jr., telling him the screwball would take him to the majors.

Honeywell is not especially close with Marshall, who disagrees strongly with any teaching not precisely aligned with his own. Specifically, he worries that the Rays will ruin Honeywell by forcing him to throw a traditional breaking ball, not the pronating version Marshall favors.

But Honeywell did work with Marshall as a teenager, and he stays limber and flexible by training with a six-pound shot put, a Marshall technique. He also has a strain of iconoclasm in the way he talks about the family pitch: when it comes to the screwball, Honeywell is a true believer. Before the Rays could even think about taking the pitch away from him, Honeywell said, he told them to forget it.

"I think there's this false thing about it that it hurts people's arms," Honeywell says. "That just scares people away. It's actually better on your arm than another pitch, because it takes the stress off the elbow, is what it does. You pronate to maximum pronation, is what people call it. I just call it turning it over. When you turn it over as far as you can turn it over, you're getting full-on pronation and it takes the stress off your elbow. It's better for your arm. It's what Mike says and what is scientifically proven."

Honeywell succumbed to Tommy John surgery in spring training 2018, but insisted the procedure was inevitable and had nothing to do with his screwball, which had dazzled his U.S. teammates at the Futures Game in 2017. The Astros' Derek Fisher called it a "dinosaur pitch," and Lewis Brinson, now with the Marlins, was awestruck.

"I don't know what it is," Brinson said, "but it started in their dugout and ended up in the strike zone."

Jim Hickey, who spent 11 seasons as Tampa Bay's pitching coach before joining the Cubs in 2018, does not call the pitch a screwball. "Remember Daisuke Matsuzaka and the 'gyroball,' how it was gonna revolutionize the game—and it was a freaking changeup," Hickey said, referring to the Japanese sensation who never quite matched his hype for the Red Sox. "Brent's more inside the ball than you would be with a conventional change, but I'm not sure you'd call it a screwball."

Honeywell is used to skeptics; teammates joke with him that his precious pitch is nothing more than a glorified changeup. He laughs off the doubts. "It's gonna be the first time they've ever seen a changeup move like that," he says.

Fair enough. The screwball is its own pitch. But this is roughly what has happened, in simplest terms: the screwball gave way to the splitter and the splitter gave way to the changeup. And all three pitches, in most cases, are different means to the same end.

With his family connection, Honeywell has a natural tie to the screwball. For others, there's little reason to reach so far back through history to find it. Even Herrera doubts it will ever return.

"You're looking for a revival of something from the old times, and I just don't think it can," he says. "I don't think guys are really, actually willing to try and develop it. Most of the guys that I've tried to show, they'll throw it a couple of times and they'll either say, 'That will hurt my elbow' or 'It's just too weird.'"

The weird pitch that hurts the elbow. In the graveyard of baseball, those words could be etched on the tombstone of the screwball, a pitch that once brought glory to so many. The fadeaway, it turns out, was the right name all along.

THE
SINKER

The Furthest Strike from the Hitter's Eyes

The sinker used to be baseball's most sensible pitch. Its allure was efficiency, not force. Throw it low for ground balls, conserve pitches, last deeper in games.

"All you had to do was take it off the plane that the hitter was starting his swing at," says Steve Rogers, a five-time All-Star for the Montreal Expos. "Just take it off the plane *that much,* in the last 10 feet, and it's a soft ground ball."

A sinker is really just a fastball, usually thrown with the index and middle fingers aligned with the seams at their narrowest point, the hand slightly pronated at the finish. It is also called a two-seamer because, thrown this way, only two seams bite the air for each revolution.

Yet it is not really a fastball in the way we tend to think of that pitch. You would not test your arm strength at a carnival booth by throwing a sinking fastball. You'd slap your fingers across the seams and fire it as hard and as straight as you could. With that kind of fastball, four seams backspin each time through the air, defying gravity just a bit longer.

"If you throw it 96, 97 miles per hour, the ball gets to home plate before the spin has a chance to make it sink," Tommy John says. "But the metrics people don't want that. They want speed, speed, speed."

They might not be wrong. If we started the sport all over again, untethered to tradition, we might structure it the way many analysts now prefer: pitchers throw fastballs up and curveballs down (the north-south approach, as they say) for short bursts, then turn the game over to another pitcher, and another, and another, all throwing hard. With a deep supply of power arms today, why bother conserving pitches? And if you've trained all your life to throw hard, why sacrifice speed for sink?

"It's a harder sell, because there's a lot of glory in throwing the ball hard," says Dave Duncan, one of the most successful pitching coaches in history, mostly for the A's and the Cardinals. "If you throw 98, 100 miles an hour, you get a lot of attention. How are you gonna get signed as an amateur? You think they're out there signing 90-mile-an-hour guys? No, they're not signing them. You know why? Because scouts see a guy that throws 99, and he may not be able to throw it through a door, but that scout can say, 'Hey, this guy's got a great arm, he throws hard, all he needs is someone to tweak him a little.'

"It's safe. But that guy that throws 92, 93, sinking fastball, decent control and movement on the ball? That's the guy I love."

Duncan—who had been a power-hitting catcher in his 11 years as a player—loves the sinker for a very logical reason. The easiest way to score runs, he reasons, is with extra-base hits. Except for hard grounders right down the line, almost every extra-base hit is a ball in the air. Pitchers, therefore, should live at the bottom of the strike zone with a hard slider, hard curve, changeup—or, most reliable, a two-seam sinker.

Duncan built those pitchers in St. Louis, helping the Cardinals become consistent contenders and two-time champions in the early part of this century. He encouraged Chris Carpenter, a league-average pitcher in Toronto, to use more sinking fastballs, and Carpenter became a star, passing on the gospel to teammates like Adam Wainwright, who continued to spread the message.

In 2011, Duncan's final season as a full-time pitching coach, the Cardinals won the World Series. That season, according to Baseball Savant, major league pitchers threw more than 167,000 pitches that were classified as two-seam fastballs or sinkers. The Cardinals' staff ranked second in the majors in such pitches, throwing them more than 34 percent of the time.

Not all old coaches are as enthusiastic as Duncan. Bill Fischer started and relieved for four teams in the 1950s and '60s, distinguished by how often batters put his pitches in play. Fischer holds the record for most consecutive innings without a walk, with 84⅓ in 1962, and averaged just 3.4 strikeouts per nine innings. Coaches told him to throw two-seam fastballs, not four-seamers, and he followed orders. But he never liked the results, and when Fischer became a coach he vowed his pitchers would be different.

"I had Roger Clemens," Fischer said in 2017, at age 86, still in full uniform at the Royals' spring training camp, rambling through the back fields in Surprise, Arizona, on a golf cart with his name on it.

"The first year in Boston, he struggled, his arm was bothering him. I said, 'How do you hold your fastball?' He said, 'With the seams.' I said, 'Roger, you gotta turn that ball around in your hand and throw four-seamers.' He said, 'I pitched this way in college and I had success, I want to do it the same way.' He was a hardheaded son of a bitch.

"So we went to Sarasota to play an exhibition game and Tom Seaver was gonna pitch against him; Tom was with the White Sox. I said, 'Tom, I got a guy I'd like you to talk to,' so I took him over there. First thing Tom Seaver said is: 'I'm gonna talk to you, and I don't want you to open your mouth till I tell you. Kid, how do you hold your fastball?' He said, 'With the seams.' Tom said, 'Well, you might as well go home right now because you ain't gonna be worth a shit. You want to be good?'"

Fischer laughed: "Roger listened this time. After that I had no trouble with him anymore. He went all four-seam fastball, he got faster and faster and faster. Holy Christ!"

Seaver did understand the value of the sinker. In his book *The Art of Pitching* he explains that low pitches are effective because the batter cannot hit a ball squarely if he sees only its top half. He describes how he turns the ball on its side a little, applies pressure with the outside of his index fingertip, instead of from the middle finger, and lets the ball move down and in on a right-hander. But this "turned two-seam fastball," as Seaver called it, was not his preferred option. He saved it, he wrote, for "when the good riding fastball has deserted me."

The two-seamer is fine if it's all you've got, and it's handy for a double play. A few Hall of Famers were known more for sinkers than four-seamers, like Grover Cleveland Alexander, Bob Lemon, Don

Drysdale, and Greg Maddux, who mastered everything. Maddux didn't even call it a sinker or a two-seamer, and didn't think about diminished velocity.

"Whatever," Maddux says. "I called it a fastball—a two-seam fastball that runs in front a little bit. That was just my fastball. I threw as hard as I could."

Maddux envisioned an X on both edges of the plate, and tried to throw pitches that followed those lines: in and away on one side, in and away on the other side. With four possibilities—*both* directions on *both* sides—the hitter could never account for them all. His only hope would be to read the movement, yet with Maddux, the pitch would go right for the sweet spot and then veer away, as if magnetically repelled. Steve Stone, the Cy Young Award winner who broadcast Cubs games when Maddux reached the majors, said this action sent Maddux to Cooperstown.

"Late movement," Stone said. "If you have gradual movement, they're gonna knock the crap out of you. Late movement is the whole thing."

Maddux called the sinker "the furthest strike from the hitter's eyes—a little bit harder to see, a little bit harder to hit." His successor in baiting hitters with it would be Roy Halladay, a Cy Young Award winner for the Blue Jays and the Phillies. The pitchers had strikingly similar rate statistics: Maddux averaged 8.5 hits allowed per nine innings, 1.8 walks per nine, 6.1 strikeouts per nine; for Halladay, it was 8.7, 1.9, and 6.9.

Demoted to Class A in 2001, after 33 starts across three seasons in the majors, Halladay reinvented himself, dropping his arm angle to three-quarters, which made his fastball naturally scoot a few inches to the third base side. This was a relief to Halladay, because the straighter fastball unnerved him; he felt he had to be too perfect with it. The sinker—coupled with the cutter, which he perfected later in his career—helped free Halladay from anxiety.

"Before I felt like if I wasn't on the corners, I was in trouble," Halladay said in March 2017. "With the sinker I could basically start it middle of the plate and just let it run. And as a young pitcher not able to really throw the ball anywhere I wanted all the time, it allowed me to throw a sinker on that side that was running to their hands, and then a cutter that was either running away from a righty or into a lefty. Everything was running away from the plate.

"So it really just gave me so much—it gave me the ability to be aggressive, to go after guys and challenge them, knowing that the ball's moving. Even if I could get it to move three or four inches going either direction, I'm missing the barrel, and that was my only goal. I wanted them to swing at every pitch, I wanted them to put it in play, but I was trying to stay off the barrel."

Luke Scott, then of the Orioles, once demonstrated this for me by his locker at Camden Yards. I was covering the Yankees and a pitcher named Darrell Rasner had gotten off to a good start. Rasner was not overpowering, but for a while he was quite effective and I asked Scott why. He explained why pitches off the barrel are hit so weakly, which I knew but had never seen illustrated quite this way.

Scott held a brown bat in the air, perpendicular to the ground. In his other hand he held a pink bat, parallel to the ground. Holding the brown bat steady, he lightly tapped the pink bat against it, starting around the middle and proceeding down. For several inches, the brown bat barely moved.

Then, for only two or three inches just before the name on the barrel, it jumped, as if spring-loaded. It was like finding the jelly inside a doughnut—*this* part was different. *This* was the sweet spot. And then, for the last few inches, the bat seemed dead again.

Connecting squarely on the barrel can make the ball seem weightless. So when it runs off that sweet spot, and the hitter buries it into the ground, the ball can seem heavy, unable to be lifted, like an anchor plunging to the bottom of the sea.

Here's how catcher Mickey Owen described the sinker of Bill McGee, a sidearmer for the Cardinals in the 1930s and '40s, to *Baseball Magazine* in 1941: "He throws a ball that seems like a cannon ball when it comes into a catching mitt." Some three decades later, the Yankees' Thurman Munson said Mel Stottlemyre's sinker felt like it weighed 100 pounds.

Randy Jones, Brandon Webb, Dallas Keuchel, and Rick Porcello won Cy Young Awards by throwing heavy sinkers, and Chien-Ming Wang was a runner-up. Kevin Brown made six All-Star teams and earned baseball's first $100 million contract with a sinker that brimmed with rage.

"He looked vicious," said Torii Hunter, the former star outfielder. "I mean, he looked like a cowboy that wants to draw on you on the mound. He cut his sleeves, he was jacked. He had that sinker with teeth. It was coming at you like this"—Hunter chomped his teeth vigorously, like a rabid dog—"ready to bite your bat off."

If forced to choose, a sinkerballer wants movement over velocity. For some, the terminology is important. Brad Ziegler, a longtime reliever, makes a conscious effort not to think of his sinker as a fastball—because "fastball," to Ziegler, means "try to throw it hard." The harder he throws, the flatter his pitch becomes, and that means a line drive or worse.

Avoid the barrel, and the pitcher will usually win the encounter. An even better plan is to avoid the bat entirely, but that's not always possible against the world's best hitters, and seeking strikeouts is an easy way to run a high pitch count. Halladay—a seven-time league leader in complete games—couldn't fathom why so many pitchers throw balls with two strikes. He knew *why*—they want to entice a jumpy hitter to swing at something he can't touch—but he also knew that good hitters take those pitches.

"I felt like with two strikes—0–2, 1–2—if they didn't swing at it, it was gonna be strike three," Halladay said. "I wanted something that they either had to swing at and put in play, or it was gonna be a strike. It's changed a lot in the way people think about pitching: they want to stay just off the plate and avoid contact."

Orel Hershiser used a term that defines the sinker mentality: *bat stimulus.* Hershiser, a slightly built Dodgers righty, won 204 games but is best known for a glorious two-month stretch in 1988. He finished that regular season with a record 59 consecutive scoreless innings, then started the postseason with eight more. His breathtaking ledger from that September and October: an 8-0 record, 0.46 ERA, eight complete games and seven shutouts in 11 starts, plus a save. He was MVP of the NLCS and the World Series, lifted to the sky after vanquishing a powerful Oakland team to win the Dodgers' last title. Hershiser's mind-set, described decades later over lunch before a Dodger broadcast, is the perfect distillation of the sinkerballer's creed.

"Because I didn't really consider myself a strikeout pitcher, I thought, 'OK, then really it's about contact—but it's *really* about weak contact,'" Hershiser says. "And then it's also about pitch count and being able to complete games and get deep into games. So what you're looking for is early, weak contact, and the best way to get that is movement.

"But you also have to give the hitter something to start the bat. So for me it was about bat stimulus. I've got to give him something visually that he likes, and then I've got to make it move. Greg Maddux would say, 'Make strikes look like balls and make balls look like strikes.' That's pitching. And there's two ways to really get a hitter out, which is to convince him what's coming and throw the opposite, or convince him what's coming, throw it, and put it in a hard place to hit."

Moving down and tailing off the plate, the sinker is a model of expedience, producing quick outs or, at worst, a bunch of singles. To Rogers, the Expos' first great pitcher, down and in to a righty was the magic quadrant of the strike zone. He wanted his sinkers there, and his fingers pointed the way. Rogers's goal was to drive the ball down to that area, and by pointing there when he threw, he accentuated the pressure on the ball with his index finger.

One of Rogers's earliest coaches was Cal McLish, an old right-hander from Oklahoma who was part Choctaw, part Cherokee and had perhaps the most mellifluous full name in the annals of baseball: Calvin Coolidge Julius Caesar Tuskahoma McLish. His message to Rogers was simple: "All right, son, just get out in front and get whippy!"

Rogers did not know what that meant, and McLish never had much to add—but there was a lot of truth in it. McLish had thrown sinkers and knew the late life essential to the pitch came from a whippy sort of arm action at release, an almost imperceptible turning over of the wrist.

The one McLish lesson that did help Rogers was a primer on the slider. It was a pressure pitch, the coach explained; turn the fingers in and apply pressure on the middle finger, and you've got a slider, sweeping down and away from a right-hander. In that case, Rogers thought, shouldn't the reverse hold true for a sinker?

He already had calluses on his index finger, and the middle finger just seemed to be getting in the way when Rogers pronated his wrist as he let the ball go. What if he shifted his fingers slightly, so the index finger applied pressure on the outer side of the left seam, and the middle finger sat on the white, touching no seams, just along for the ride?

That adjustment sent Rogers on his way, and he became a preeminent ground ball specialist. Elbow surgery in 1978 helped refine his mechanics, and also caused just enough drop in velocity to give his sinker even more fade.

This was the pitch Rogers threw in the decisive fifth game of the 1981 NLCS, with the season on the line against the Dodgers. He had been a playoff star that fall, beating the Phillies twice, the Dodgers once, and collecting 80 of a possible 81 outs—though just 10 by strikeout, typical of a sinkerballer. Now he was on in relief, for the top of the ninth inning of a 1–1 game at frigid Olympic Stadium.

It was a Monday—Blue Monday, as it has forever been known in Montreal, describing four things at once: the mood of the fans, the day of the week, the winning team's color, and the hero of the game. Rogers faced four batters. Steve Garvey popped to second. Ron Cey flied out to deep left. Then came Rick Monday, with Pedro Guerrero on deck.

"I did not throw a single pitch mechanically correct until the three pitches to Guerrero, after the adrenaline was out of my system," Rogers said. "I was just overthrowing everything. I was a top-down pitcher. I had to be tall and then down, tall and then down. And I was losing the angle of the mound because I was so pumped up in the bullpen. I was throwing the ball hard, as hard as I could throw it, maybe 91."

Rogers said he was not bothered by pitching in relief. It was just his excitement, with a pennant at stake, that hurt him. He wishes he had faced Monday with a man on base.

"It probably would have been a great service to me if either Cey or Garvey had gotten a base hit, because what would it have done? You go in the stretch," Rogers said. "Then it takes the windup out of the picture, and that's what I was overdoing."

An overthrown sinker never has time to dive into that special quadrant, the one where Rogers imagined his finger pointing. Monday swung hard at the 3–1 pitch and smoked it high over center field. It cleared the blue wall as he rounded first, leaping and punching the icy air with his fist.

Guerrero struck out, but it didn't matter. The Dodgers got the final three outs to win the NL title, on their way to a World Series victory. The Expos never made the playoffs again. The sinker had sunk them.

———————

Montreal could have used a closer like Zach Britton. In 2016, Britton converted all 47 save chances for the Orioles, plus another in the All-Star Game, which he finished by using his sinker for a double play grounder from slugger Nolan Arenado. Britton's 0.54 ERA that season was the lowest ever for a pitcher with at least 65 innings.

Britton honed his sinker by using a contraption first created by Branch Rickey, the visionary architect of the Brooklyn Dodgers. One of Rickey's most promising pitchers in the late 1940s was Rex Barney, a hard-throwing right-hander who fired a no-hitter in 1948 and twice started games in the World Series. He was also among the wildest pitchers in baseball history, and Rickey devised a system of strings for the bullpen mound in Vero Beach, Florida, to help his control.

"Creating a visible strike zone in the pitcher's mind, regardless of where the batter may be standing in the batter's box, helps a pitcher throw to the intended spot," Rickey wrote, in personal papers that were later published. "Pitching to the strings will accelerate the mastery of control, and pitchers, particularly the young ones, should be given ample opportunity to use them."

Rickey gave specific installation instructions: two six-foot poles driven 12 inches into the ground, with a system of strings to be moved up or down to pinpoint a particular zone. The Dodgers had just moved their spring operations to Vero Beach, and the Rex Barney strings became a fixture there, long after he was gone.

Barney never did find his control; he threw his last pitch in 1950 but stayed in the game for decades, serving as the Orioles' public address announcer until his death in 1997. Ten years after that, a young Britton was toiling in the Baltimore farm system when a coach, Calvin Maduro, tried to teach him a cutter. Maduro used an unconventional, curveball-like grip—but when Britton tried it, the pitch would not obey. It was supposed to move in on a righty, but instead darted down and away. Maduro was dumbfounded but told Britton to go with it.

"Pitching's so weird, because everyone's arm action is different," Britton says. "Even though it may look the same, it's different—their bodies are different, the way they put pressure on the ball is different. That grip is a good sinker for me. If I gripped it like a two-seamer, it probably wouldn't even move."

Britton's sinker got him to the majors, but he mostly struggled as a starter. He switched to the bullpen in spring training 2014, when the Orioles introduced a new pitching coach, Dave Wallace. Britton had worked with strings before; Rick Peterson, the Orioles' former minor league pitching guru, also believes in them. But in Wallace, Britton had a genuine Dodgers disciple to guide him.

Wallace had a brief major league career in the 1970s and established himself as a coach in the Dodgers' system. He used the strings—portable now, if still cumbersome—as a tool in other jobs, with the Mets and the Braves. In the spring of 2014, Wallace and Dom Chiti, the bullpen coach, encouraged Britton to use the strings for every bullpen session, and to throw only sinkers.

Britton had been too wild as a starter. He needed better command of his sinker, and Wallace moved the knots within the strings to an area about six inches square, low and away. That is the critical spot, to Wallace; get the ball down and away, consistently, and everything else will be easy by comparison. He has another name for his tiny zone: a quality major league strike.

"We usually give a guy 20 throws, and a lot of guys don't get 10," Wallace says. "But what you find out is if they get eight, there's another five or six that are real close, because of the level of concentration."

For Britton, it was a revelation. Visualization, he found, was everything. If he wanted to throw the sinker for a strike, he would aim it at the equipment logo on the catcher's chest protector, just below the neck, and the movement would take it to the zone. If he wanted to throw it for a ball, he would aim it at the catcher's shin guards, and the movement would carry it to the dirt, for a chase.

Soon enough, Britton was threading his sinker through the strings about seven out of 10 tries. He took the pitch into games, and familiar hitters, used to getting ahead of him, were suddenly behind in the count. That made them vulnerable to his sinker off the plate—and

Britton knew how to get it there, because he knew how his ball should behave.

"That drill really helped me understand what my pitch is actually doing," Britton says.

———————

Orel Hershiser had worked with the strings as a young pitcher for the Dodgers, and his intellect helped him last 18 seasons in the majors. For much of that time he kept a copy of Robert K. Adair's book, *The Physics of Baseball*, in his travel bag. Yet he also grasped the benefits of a rudimentary teaching tool.

"The strings are amazing," he says. "They're stationary, and as a pitcher, your head's not always still. So you might think you just threw a good pitch, but you don't actually know. Or maybe you're being led to believe it was good by the catcher, the way he caught it—but you didn't necessarily see where the catcher's set up, or maybe the catcher's lazy. But with the strings, when the ball hits it right there on the corner, it rattles, and you know you just threw a ball and it hit the corner.

"Your vision can lie to you, and the strings helped you get your eyes lined up, that you're actually throwing a correct pitch. It's the combination of the visual, mental, and physical."

That is what Ferguson Jenkins had discovered, too, as a teenager in Chatham, Ontario, in the late 1950s. Every Tuesday and Thursday in the winter, Jenkins would throw to a strike zone of movable strings at a local gymnasium—not at full strength, just hard enough to study and internalize the way his ball should move.

Jenkins would become the greatest pitcher in Chicago Cubs history. With command of a sinker allowing him to last deep in games, Jenkins threw at least 289 innings in seven different seasons, mostly for the Cubs. Every time he did, he earned at least 20 wins.

"I used the top of the ball, where the printing's at, and my fingers were close together," Jenkins says. "A great pulling pitch. All you do is pull it backwards. Pull it hard, and you get that sink."

Jenkins was 284–226 with a 3.34 ERA and made the Hall of Fame. Tommy John was 288–231 with the same ERA, and has never come

close. John is mostly known for the revolutionary 1974 elbow surgery·
that bears his name, but he also honed his pitching savvy with strings.

When John was a boy in Indiana, he scavenged for soda bottles
and used the redemption money on a pitching book by Bob Feller. In
it, Feller described how to set up a strike zone made of strings, like
Rickey's contraption at Dodgertown. John's father built it for him in
the backyard.

"The top string would be mid-thigh or just above mid-thigh; the
bottom string would be about six inches below the knee; the inside
string would be on the outside half of the plate and the outside string
would be about six to eight inches off the plate," he says. "That was
my strike zone, and that's what I threw to. I didn't want the high
strike—I wanted to concentrate on throwing the ball low and away,
low and away."

At 18 John signed with Cleveland, and at 20 he was pitching in the
majors, throwing nothing but sinking fastballs and curves. He gripped
both the same way and always pitched in a hurry: *get the ball and throw
it,* no time to fiddle with grips. In his seventh full season, with the
White Sox, John learned a slider from new pitching coach Johnny Sain.
He practiced it so much that his fastball suffered, and John turned to
Ray Berres, an old catcher who had been his first pitching coach in
Chicago.

"I was hoping you would call," Berres barked. "Stick that fucking
slider up your ass! Never add a pitch if it's gonna make your existing
pitches worse!"

After Dr. Frank Jobe's famous operation in 1974—in which he
used a tendon from John's forearm to replace his torn ulnar collateral
ligament—John pitched for 14 more seasons. He was 46 when he made
his 700th and final career start. Only one other lefty, Steve Carlton,
has ever made more.

———————

To impart even more sink, while adding a dash of funk to make up for
diminished velocity, some pitchers drop to a submarine angle. Usually,
though, it's nobody's first choice.

Darren O'Day figured his baseball career was over when he failed to make the team as a freshman at the University of Florida. But a friend asked him to play for a men's league the next summer, and as O'Day played catch with his brother to get ready, he fooled around with a sidearm angle. Just like that, he had the kind of sinking action he never could get overhand. He went on to become an All-Star setup man for Baltimore.

"If you throw it right, you can get an element of topspin that you can't get overhand, and you're usually not throwing quite as hard, either, so the ball's going to sink more," O'Day says. "The big thing about it is hitters just aren't used to seeing it, so they can't pick up the spin as easily."

An unfamiliar motion can help a pitcher enormously; some recent aces, like Clayton Kershaw, Max Scherzer, Jake Arrieta, Madison Bumgarner, and Chris Sale, use deliveries so distinct that hitters have little basis for comparison. And just a split second of indecision further shifts the advantage to the pitcher.

Submariners are not as rare as knuckleballers, but they belong in a similar category. They do something different, hear predictable taunts from opposing fans—"This isn't softball" is a popular one, Brad Ziegler says—and frustrate hitters with a method most players use as a lark.

On a team flight with the Tigers in 1995, the Hall of Famer Al Kaline approached Mike Myers, a soft-throwing, overmatched rookie. Kaline noticed that Myers was around the strike zone a lot and thought he needed a different look to succeed. He asked Myers if he had ever dropped his arm angle. Of course, Myers replied.

"I always threw sidearm in the outfield anyway, just screwing around, for fun," Myers says. "Like how every second baseman throws a knuckleball."

Myers tried the low angle—not quite submarine, where the pitcher releases from so low that his knuckles almost scrape the dirt, but close enough—and it worked. He led the majors in appearances the next two seasons and would pitch almost 900 career games. Hitters would tell Myers that his 80-mile-an-hour sinker looked about 15 mph faster because he set it up with slow, Frisbee-like sliders.

The forefather of all modern sidearm slingers is Grover Cleveland Alexander, who went by Pete and was also called "Ol' Low & Away." Alexander—born in 1887, during the first of President Cleveland's nonconsecutive terms—earned 373 victories, tied with Christy Mathewson for third all-time. Alexander, who pitched mostly for the Phillies and the Cubs, had a reputation as one of the game's fastest workers. That was consistent with his pitch, the sinker bearing down and in on right-handers.

"What's the use of doin' in three pitches what you can do in one?" he said, as quoted by Martin Quigley in *The Crooked Pitch*. Indeed, Alexander was so efficient that he led his league in innings seven times and twice won both ends of a doubleheader, both times with two complete games. A teammate and opponent, Hans Lobert, described Alexander's best pitch this way to Lawrence Ritter in *The Glory of Their Times:*

"He had little short fingers and he threw a very heavy ball. Once, later on, when I'd moved over to the Giants, Alex hit me over the heart with a pitched ball and it bore in like a lump of lead hitting you. I couldn't get my breath for ten minutes afterward. Matty was just as fast, but he threw a much lighter ball."

(Ivan Rodriguez, the Hall of Fame catcher, described a similar sensation many years later. The fastest pitcher he ever caught, Rodriguez said, was the Tigers' Joel Zumaya, whose ball felt light. But when Rodriguez caught sinkers from a young Kevin Brown in Texas, the ball felt so heavy he worried it would shatter his thumb—inside his glove.)

Alexander surely threw harder than most of his era, but also understood the advantage of being unusual. As he said in *Baseball Magazine,* in an undated clip quoted by Rob Neyer, "I believe that the side arm motion is much more baffling to the batter than the overhand delivery. For that reason I have developed the side arm delivery and have cultivated it so that I have it down pretty well."

In 1926, at age 39, Alexander clinched the Cardinals' first World Series with a performance so heroic that Ronald Reagan would play him in a 1952 film, *The Winning Team,* chronicling Alexander's triumph over alcoholism and epilepsy. In the series, Alexander beat the Yankees in Games 2 and 6, then came into Game 7 from the bullpen and struck out Tony Lazzeri with the bases loaded. That's the end of the movie, but it was really just the end of the seventh inning; the game actually ended when Babe Ruth, of all people, was caught stealing second. Ruth's rationale was the ultimate compliment to Alexander: he needed to be in scoring position, he believed, because there was no way the Yankees could get two more singles to score him from first. And good luck hitting that sinker in the air for extra bases.

The Yankees recovered in grand style, sweeping Pittsburgh in the 1927 World Series to cement their status as the most fearsome team of all time. Their pitching star was another sidearming sinkerballer: Wilcy Moore, a 30-year-old rookie, who had turned to the style after breaking his arm two years earlier, closed out Game 1 and went the distance in the finale.

Moore was a hybrid, a spot starter who also finished games in relief. He led the AL in saves three times—before that statistic was created—and was an early forerunner of the sidearming late-inning stoppers who would follow decades later. Two, Kent Tekulve and Dan Quisenberry, are forever intertwined. Neither threw hard, but neither was defined that way, either.

"Watching Quisenberry as a kid, they didn't have radar guns on the TV," says Brad Ziegler, who grew up in Kansas City and would imitate Quisenberry with Wiffle balls. "It wasn't about that at the time. It was about getting outs. You get outs, you've got a shot to pitch."

Submarine pitchers generally work only in relief, so the manager can pick their spots (say, to get a double play) and take advantage of their durability—which comes mainly from not throwing very hard or throwing many pitches. Everyone in the ballpark knows the aim of a submariner: to sink the ball and get the batter to hit it on the ground. By inviting contact, though, a pitcher also invites chaos if those grounders find holes. Some teams would rather avoid the style altogether.

It should be no surprise, then, that Tekulve and Quisenberry were not drafted. Neither, for that matter, was O'Day. Ziegler was released and pitched for an independent team before the A's signed him and eventually changed his angle. Those four submariners overcame the collective rejection to pitch about 3,000 games in the majors.

Before he could pitch in his first, in 1974, Tekulve had to listen to an old scout over beers after a game in Double-A. Tekulve had thrown sidearm all his life and found immediate success in the minors with the Pirates. But the scout, George Detore, told him his sinker would never trick big league hitters unless it moved better in the strike zone.

More sophisticated hitters, Detore insisted, would take his good sinkers, which were off the plate, and hammer the flat ones in the middle.

"So I started experimenting with stuff," Tekulve says. "The first thing you do is you go up to three-quarters, like a normal human being—but I went up there and it was a total disaster. If I was throwing it 82 miles per hour, it was a lot, and it was perfectly straight. Eighty-two miles per hour and perfectly straight is defined as batting practice. So that didn't work."

From three-quarters, Tekulve was missing his topspin, the furious rotating action that propelled the ball down and forced hitters to bury it into the dirt. Throwing in the outfield a bit later, he thought of Ted Abernathy, a longtime major leaguer who had pitched for Tekulve's hometown Reds. Tekulve swung his arm lower, almost to the ground—and unlocked the pitch that would make him the game's all-time leader in relief appearances when he retired in 1989.

"The very first one I threw, I knew—*this is it,*" Tekulve said. He was throwing it harder, and the ball was diving at precisely the right spot: three feet in front of the plate, after the hitter had committed himself to swing, a fat strike until its final tumble. "From that day forward, I knew what the sinker was and what it was gonna be—and it was gonna be good."

Tekulve was 27 by the time he made his debut. He soon became an expert on angles and grips and their effects on the movement of a baseball delivered from below. If he raised his fingers by 45 degrees—instead of pointing them straight down—Tekulve could produce a more dramatic tailing action into a right-hander. "The revolutions still matched up," he says, matter-of-factly, meaning that the moment of deception, the critical three-foot mark, would still be the same.

Tekulve would close out the 1970s, saving Game 7 of the World Series for the Pirates in his 101st appearance of the season. Tekulve's final sinker did not do much—he described its flight to me with a farting noise—but Baltimore's Pat Kelly could only lift a harmless fly ball to center. As the Orioles nursed their defeat, their first base coach, Jim Frey, could not shake the memory of Tekulve's quirky dominance. Named as the new manager of the Royals, Frey decided to find his own version. At an off-season banquet, he asked Tekulve for a favor.

The Royals' bullpen in 1979 had allowed more than five runs per nine innings. Its best performer, oddly, was a rookie with a funny name and a sidearm delivery. He had managed only 13 strikeouts in 40 innings, but his control and ability to generate grounders offered promise. Frey wondered if Tekulve could help Quisenberry with his mechanics in spring training.

Quisenberry had started throwing sidearm as a senior at the University of La Verne, in California, because his arm had grown tired from the workload of 194 innings. But the motion ran in his family: Quisenberry's older brother, Marty, had been a submarine pitcher who was scouted, though not signed, by the Royals.

When no team drafted Dan, either, his coach called the scout who had once shown interest in Marty. The Royals, it turned out, needed a pitcher for their Class A team in Waterloo, Iowa. Their bonus offer was a Royals bat, pen, and lapel button. Quisenberry accepted.

"I was really pretty excited," he told *Sports Illustrated*, "especially about the lapel button."

Quisenberry started and finished his first game for Waterloo in 1975. It was the only start of a career that lasted until 1990. Quisenberry became a star, as he would tell it, immediately following his tutorials with Tekulve—one in Fort Myers and another in Bradenton in that spring of 1980.

"We want this guy to be like you," Frey told Tekulve, as Quisenberry recounted it to Roger Angell. "He throws a little like you already, but basically he doesn't have shit."

Quisenberry went on to tell Angell all the ways Tekulve helped him: how to bend at the waist and extend his front leg, how to land with a hop to keep from falling over. He was wild and uncomfortable, he said, bouncing balls everywhere. But the coaches liked the extra movement on his sinker.

By the World Series, in which Quisenberry pitched in all six games of the Royals' loss to the Phillies, he had taken to calling the sinker his "Titanic pitch"—it sinks to the bottom—and crediting Tekulve with his transformation. Years later, Tekulve said Quisenberry was simply being kind.

"I did not change very much at all with Quisenberry," Tekulve says. "He was pretty much in the right place. He had the sink late. He didn't throw it as hard, but he didn't have as many revolutions, so therefore he still had it sinking at the right spot. There were only a couple of very minor things I suggested to him, and I think probably what benefited him more than anything else, as a young guy coming in, was having somebody who had just had success in the last World Series—somebody that did it—tell him, 'Hey, you're right.'"

Many years later, Tekulve would encourage Ziegler in a similar way, reminding him not to fear hitters, because they never like to face a submariner. That was clearly true for Quisenberry, who thanked Tekulve by sending a pair of plaid socks—the quintessential gift for Dad—to Three Rivers Stadium as a Father's Day gift in 1980.

That season began a stretch of six in which Quisenberry averaged more than 35 saves. He did his best to live up to the contract he made with his sinkers.

"Have I ever told you about my agreement with the ball?" Quisenberry asked Angell, who said no. "Well, our deal is that I'm not going to throw you very hard as long as you promise to move around when you get near the plate, *because I want you back.* So if you do your part, we'll get to play some more."

The Cubs retired No. 31 in honor of two pitchers, Greg Maddux and Ferguson Jenkins, who both finished their careers with more than 3,000 strikeouts and fewer than 1,000 walks. Only two others in history—Curt Schilling and Pedro Martinez—have ever done this, and Jenkins was the first.

Jenkins joined the Cubs in a trade from the Phillies in April 1966, the same month Maddux was born. He was 23 and had made a few relief appearances, but no starts. That July the Cubs signed another former Phillie, Robin Roberts, for the final stop of his Hall of Fame career.

Roberts was 39, the oldest player in the National League, and he also helped coach the Cubs' pitchers. He preached the importance of the sinker to Jenkins, imparting two main lessons culled from more than 600 starts in the majors: the hitter wants a ball up over the plate, and doesn't really want to swing at the first pitch. With such impeccable control, Jenkins forced hitters to swing early, for fear of falling behind. He knew how he wanted them to hit.

"A sinker down over the plate, and down around the knees, was something that was gonna help me get guys to hit on top of the ball—not through the ball," Jenkins says. "And I had a good infield, guys with good gloves who knew what to do."

With Ron Santo at third, Don Kessinger at short, Glenn Beckert at second, and Ernie Banks at first, Jenkins had far better infielders and a smoother playing surface than he'd ever had in the minors. That eased his transition after his trade, and he won 20 games in 1967, his first full season as a starter. From that year through 1980, Jenkins would lead the majors in victories.

He did it, essentially, by becoming Roberts's clone. The sinker allowed them both to zip quickly through innings. Their control made them prone to home runs—only Jamie Moyer surrendered more than Roberts and Jenkins—but it tended to minimize damage. Jenkins also hated allowing walks because he much preferred to pitch from the windup.

Maddux did much of his bullpen work from the stretch, reasoning that his pitches with men on base would matter most. He joined the Cubs as a rookie in 1986, three years after Jenkins retired, and took his stylistic cues from Hershiser, another right-hander with a similar build and intuition about the craft. Asked in 2015 why he trusted his two-seamer and used it so often, Maddux replied: "Well, I saw Hershiser do it."

Maddux watched Hershiser whenever he could, delighting in the way he defied the traditional wisdom of coaches, who warned against pitching down and in to left-handers.

"I guess I was just stubborn enough not to believe them," Maddux says. "It was a pitch I was capable of throwing, and I saw Hershiser use it. As a young player I thought, 'Well, I'm going to do it, too.'"

Maddux's first role model was his older brother, Mike, who would have a long career as a major league reliever and coach. As teenagers in Las Vegas, they were tutored by a retired scout named Ralph Medar. He believed they would play professionally but knew that was not the main goal.

"In order to have success at a high level, you're going to rely more on movement than velocity," Maddux says, quoting Medar. "He taught me at a young age it was movement, location, the ability to change speeds—*and then* velocity, in that order, which I think still holds true today."

Medar switched Maddux from a four-seam fastball grip to a two-seam grip, and lowered his arm angle from high- to low-three-quarters. Maddux became entranced by the movement of his fastball, which would start at the hip of a left-hander and curl back to clip the inside corner for a strike. He would execute a pitch and ask Medar how it moved, not how fast it went.

Maddux was a senior in high school when Medar died of a heart attack. But the Cubs' scouting report on Maddux, before the 1984 draft, reflected the lessons Medar had imparted: "He throws 86–89 consistently with very good movement," wrote the scout, Doug Mapson. "His movement isn't a gradual tailing type but a quick, explosive, bat-breaking kink."

Mapson wrote that if Maddux (then just 5 foot 11, and almost done growing) were more physically imposing, he could have been the first overall pick. The Cubs passed on him anyway at No. 3, taking a strapping college left-hander, Drew Hall, who would win just nine games in his career. They grabbed Maddux in the second round (at pick number 31) and he would win 355—the most of anyone who started his career after Jackie Robinson integrated the majors in 1947.

"Maddux had the 100-mile-an-hour mind," says his agent, Scott Boras, who first saw Maddux in high school. "He had insights to the game that people with raw physical talents weren't even close to."

Pitching for the Braves in 1995, Maddux began the World Series by beating Hershiser and the Indians with surgical mastery: a complete game two-hitter on 95 pitches, with no walks or earned runs. He was at his best, soon to win his fourth consecutive Cy Young Award and, for the second season in a row, scoring at least 260 in ERA+, a metric that measures ERA against league average, adjusting for ballpark factors. Only one pitcher—Bob Gibson in 1968—had come close to that figure in the last 80 years. Close, but not better.

While some aces overpowered hitters with muscle (Roger Clemens, Randy Johnson), Maddux simply gripped his best pitch the usual way, along the narrow seams, "nothing different than a kid in Little League," he says. He was a virtuoso at calling his own game, knowing precisely how to read hitters' swings; on the bench, he would predict exactly where a batter would hit a ball. He set up hitters to get themselves out, and the sinker was his kill shot, best fired with two strikes.

"I usually threw it after a cutter," he says. "I had a cutter that I would start for a strike and end up as a ball, and I had a fastball that started in as a ball and ended up as a strike. I very rarely ever threw that two-seam fastball inside unless I threw a cutter or two before it. A hitter remembers the last pitch probably better than any pitch he's seen out of my hand."

Maddux started throwing the cutter in earnest in 1992. He was off to a very good start in his career, with the first four of his record 16 consecutive 15-win seasons, but he needed a complementary pitch to make his sinker more effective. He tried the cutter against the first batter he faced that year, the Phillies' Lenny Dykstra. It came in on Dykstra but did not dart back over the plate, as usual. Instead, it kept slicing.

"He checked his swing and it hit him on the wrist—and it broke his wrist," Maddux says. "Lenny said to me, 'Hey, when did you start throwing a cutter? I thought it was gonna move back over the plate!' That was when I recognized: 'OK, yeah, this is gonna work.'"

Maddux won that game, on his way to 20 victories in his first Cy Young season. He moved to the Braves in free agency and returned to the Cubs in 2004, when he earned his 300th victory. He remembers the precise moment, with the Dodgers at age 42, when he knew it was time to go.

"I threw this ball, it was absolutely perfect," Maddux says. "It came out of my hand just the way it's supposed to, down and away, painted the corner, and I took a peek up there at the radar gun and it said '82.' And I went, 'Whoa.' It was a strike. I mean, it was a meaningless 1–0 fastball. It wasn't like strike three. It was just, everything was absolutely perfect and I just—I lost too much speed.

"Do you have to throw hard to win? No. Do you need to throw hard enough to compete? Absolutely. And I think I just lost too much speed to be able to go out there and compete."

Maddux has never called velocity meaningless. It ranks fourth on Ralph Medar's list, but it is still on there. Maddux personified efficiency: six times, he threw a nine-inning shutout in fewer than 90 pitches, doubling the total of any other pitcher in the last 30 years. But he does rank tenth in career strikeouts, with 3,371, and he never wanted hitters to connect.

If they did, at least, Maddux's best pitch was the balm. It took the sting out of contact. On the day he was introduced as a Hall of Famer, in January 2014, Maddux summarized the essence of his success: "Have a good moving fastball that does something the last 10 feet, and be able to locate. That's what gave me an opportunity to win."

Maddux won more times than anyone alive, through precision, intuition, and unrelenting confidence in a pitch that exemplifies restraint. If a pitcher trusts brains over brawn, trusts his defense, and trusts the long game—even today—he will understand this succinct summary of the virtues of a sinking fastball.

"You throw strikes," Maddux says, "and they stay in front of the outfielders when they hit it."

————

At least, they used to. Pitchers from Maddux's generation—like Derek Lowe, the former Boston standout—have noticed the decline of their best pitch. They still praise its virtues but acknowledge that hitters have adjusted.

"The strike zone's changed, and the swing path of hitters has changed," Lowe says. "A lot of these hitters are taught to swing down-to-up, so [the sinker] goes right into the current swing path. The game today is velocity, so a lot of people say, 'If I could throw 95 with a four-seamer or 92 with a two-seamer, I'm gonna throw 95.' It is a dying art."

In 2017, major league pitchers threw almost 23,000 fewer two-seamers and sinkers than they had in 2011. Of the 10 playoff teams in 2017, only one ranked in the top third in percentage of two-seamers and sinkers: the Twins, who lost the AL Wild Card Game. Most teams, like the champion Astros (twenty-first), ranked in the bottom third of such pitches.

Charlie Morton collected the final out of that season on a grounder to second by the Dodgers' Corey Seager. That was fitting for Morton, a 33-year-old veteran whose sinkers had earned him the nickname Ground Chuck, but it was also misleading. Morton—the first pitcher ever to win two Game 7s in the same postseason—had a career year by throwing harder than ever before, elevating his fastball and using more curves. He had grown tired of relying on batted balls to succeed.

"I was a sinker guy, throwing 60, 70 percent sinkers, and they were hitting my sinker," Morton explained during the ALCS. "So the game plan has changed. The idea that I'm going to make these guys put the ball in play and try to induce soft contact, that's out the window....

"Lefties, I'm not trying to do that. I'm not trying to let them hit the ball. At least, I'm not trying to encourage them to hit the ball. Before, the assumption [was that if] you have a good sinker, you can get the ball on the ground. That wasn't the case.

"Lots of four-seams, curveballs, and cutters."

Morton was only reacting to the adjustments many hitters made in the middle of the decade, when teams started aggressively shifting infielders to gobble up grounders, and the balls themselves suddenly turned livelier. Major League Baseball denied any changes to the ball, but the fundamental calculus of hitting had evolved. Batters finally seemed to understand the folly of hitting down on the ball, their popular philosophy echoing Dave Duncan: *there's no slug on the ground.*

"You see hitters trying to do damage more on certain pitches that, in the past, it was accepted they weren't gonna try to do damage on—like the sinker," the veteran Brandon McCarthy says. "More guys are capable of hitting that and elevating it. Not everyone's successful at it, but it's a different approach than we saw years ago. Historically, there were guys that were pure roll-over candidates down there. They were easy outs. Now they can elevate that ball, get under it, and drive it."

More than ever, it seems, teams want fastballs with a high spin rate, the kind that stay true through the zone, rather than sinkers. With coaches emphasizing a swing's launch angle and downplaying the risk of strikeouts, sinkers, as Lowe says, fall right into the barrel of the bat. Al Kaline says modern hitters know where to look for the ball, because the shoulders-to-knees strike zone of his day is long gone.

"Pitchers can't hit the corners all the time, and that's why there's so many home runs, because the hitters have a very small strike zone to look at right now," says Kaline, a 3,000-hit man for the Tigers. "That's why you see everybody uppercutting the ball, because they know everything's gonna be down low."

Hitters set a record with 6,105 home runs in 2017, and they continued their assault in the World Series with a record 25 in seven games. Yet pitchers who had made a living with sinkers still believed in the pitch. Can't today's hitter just dig it out of the dirt and golf it into the stands?

"No, not a good one," says Tommy John, who would still rather throw a sinking fastball at 86 mph than a straight one at 93. "I mean, I couldn't pitch to these guys today, because I'm 75 years old. But I would take my chances with 'em. They don't see pitchers like that anymore."

———

Most pitchers want the other fastball, at least at first. Curt Schilling stumbled through three organizations until 1992, when the Phillies' pitching coach, Johnny Podres, asked to see his fastball. Schilling used a two-seam grip, the only one he had ever known. Podres suggested a four-seamer, and Schilling, who craved power and precision, found the pitch he'd been missing.

Yet he also knew, from studying a rival, that velocity was not everything. A darting, well-placed sinker led a superior pitcher's portfolio.

"Early in my career I tried to figure out why Greg Maddux was so much better than me," says Schilling, who threw much harder. "He was good because he changed speeds, number one, and he made the ball move in both directions on both sides of the plate. You could not sit on a spot; you could not sit on a pitch. I knew I wasn't gonna throw a two-seamer at that point, so my game plan became: *find the hitter's hole and throw the ball there.* To do that, I needed to throw the four-seamer, because I needed to know where the ball was gonna be when it crossed the plate."

Schilling envied the Maddux two-seamer, but once he found the four-seam fastball, he never threw the old one again. He figured it was wiser to devote his attention to one kind of fastball, not divide it between two. The decision reinforces the image of the two-seamer as the little brother of fastballs, a weaker version of the same thing that still wants in on the action. He can't survive on brute strength, so he has to be cunning. He might have a chance to play, but given a choice, you wouldn't pick him first.

No coach would change a pitcher who can make the ball sink violently, down and away from the opposite-hand hitter, like a bowling ball spinning toward the gutter. But the general rule, now more than ever, is that pitchers sink the ball because they have to.

If you've got a big fastball, you'd better use it.

THE
CHANGEUP

A Dollar Bill Hooked on a Fishing Line

The changeup is an artistic pitch," Bobby Ojeda says, and not all pitchers are artists. Anyone would envy its results, those feeble, flailing hacks off the front foot from a hitter fooled by a pitcher's arm speed. But every changeup is the product of hard-won patience, and the maturity to accept a counterintuitive mind-set. The hitter brings a bat to the cage match. The pitcher brings a feather duster.

Ojeda pitched 15 seasons in the majors after learning the changeup from Johnny Podres, who used it to bring the Brooklyn Dodgers their only championship, in 1955. It was Ojeda's lone off-speed option, because the curveball shredded his elbow. For pitchers with other choices, the delicate brushstrokes of the changeup can be maddening to master.

"Most guys, if they're trying to learn something and it's not instant success, they just stick it in their back pocket," says Jamie Moyer, the everlasting lefty who learned his changeup at Saint Joseph's University from Kevin Quirk, an alum who was pitching in the minors. "I don't know how many times I threw the changeup over the guy I was playing catch with, either over his head or five feet in front of him, because the grip was so awkward for me. But you spend enough time with it, it becomes part of you. I play catch with my son in the driveway now, and I go right to it. It's not quite the same pitch, but that feel comes back."

Between innings, while warming up, pitchers signal for the changeup by opening their glove hand as if gripping a grapefruit. They might then pull the glove back an inch or two, as if pulling the string on a toy.

Think of a dollar bill hooked on a fishing line, resting on the ground. The pitcher is the guy who yanks it back, just out of reach of the sucker who thought he'd found easy money. That is the changeup.

Throwing it takes not just guile and artistry but courage. Consider your trusty, hardworking index finger. Now try throwing a baseball without using it very much. If that finger could talk, it would question your sanity: *You sure you don't need me for this?* The pitcher must block out that noise.

"I stood on the mound in instructional league and Johnny helped me with the grip," says Frank Viola, another 15-year lefty who learned from Podres. "We played around with it and he said, 'Throw it.' I kid you not: I don't think I got it halfway to home plate. It just went straight into the ground. And I'm like, 'You gotta be kidding me, Johnny, there's no way!' He just said, 'Trust me, it's gonna come together.'"

After several years of practice, it did come together for Viola, just as it has for so many others with the right combination of genetics, gumption, and guts. Cole Hamels, a star lefty for the Phillies and the Rangers, thinks of turning off his most important muscles to do it.

"It's like you dead-arm it," Hamels says. "That's what I try to tell people: fastballs are strong, changeups are dead. So if you can grasp that concept of how to control and deaden something in your body, then you're able to get the basic idea."

Arm speed sells the pitch. The hitter sees fastball from the motion of the arm and the spin of the ball, which sputters as it crosses the plate, fading away from a right-handed hitter when thrown by a lefty, and vice versa. It is typically 10 miles an hour slower than the same pitcher's fastball, a cousin of the screwball, splitter, and sinker that has grown in acceptance as pitchers use it more.

Throwing slowly to disrupt hitters is nothing new. Long before Bugs Bunny did it in a famous 1946 cartoon—the term "Bugs Bunny changeup" still evokes a helpless slugger swatting at air—Connie Mack made it the secret weapon for his Philadelphia A's.

Down the stretch in 1929, with the A's sure of winning the pennant, Mack called an aging pitcher, Howard Ehmke, into his office at Shibe Park. He sat Ehmke down and told him they would have to part. The crestfallen Ehmke, who was 35 and in his fourteenth major league season, replied that he had always wanted to pitch in the World Series.

"Mr. Mack," he declared, "there is one great game left in this old arm."

Mack was delighted to hear it, and shared his plan. What he meant, he told Ehmke, was that he wanted him to stay behind on the next A's road trip, to study the Chicago Cubs as they played the Phillies. The A's would be meeting the Cubs in the World Series, and Mack wanted Ehmke—not the great Lefty Grove—to start the opener.

As Red Smith related in a tribute to Ehmke, Cubs manager Joe McCarthy had a premonition of what Mack might do. As McCarthy told another writer, Ring Lardner, "We can hit speed. But they've got one guy over there I'm afraid of. He's what I call a junk pitcher."

It was Ehmke, and his array of slow-moving pitches baffled the powerful Cubs and their three future Hall of Fame hitters—Rogers Hornsby, Hack Wilson, and Kiki Cuyler. Ehmke set a then–World Series record with 13 strikeouts in a complete game, 3–1 victory. It was the last game Ehmke ever won, and the A's prevailed in five.

The changeup goes against a hitter's macho instinct. The fact that it is marketed as a fastball, but in fact is something else, was once seen, by some, as a sign of weakness by a pitcher afraid of a challenge. This is absurd, because it takes a special kind of nerve to throw slowly on purpose. But not too long ago, a pitcher who beat a hitter with a changeup could expect an insult in return.

On August 1, 1978, the Reds' Pete Rose came to the plate with two out in the top of the ninth inning at Atlanta–Fulton County Stadium. Rose had hit in 44 consecutive games, the longest streak since Joe DiMaggio's record of 56 in 1941. He was hitless in the game, a blowout loss to the Braves, and was facing Gene Garber, a sidearming closer with a peculiar habit of turning his body completely to the center fielder while delivering a pitch. This was not the quirk that bothered Rose, though. What bothered him is that, with two strikes, Garber threw him a changeup. Rose whiffed to end the streak.

"A 16–4 game and Garber's pitching me like it was the seventh game of the World Series," Rose fumed to reporters later. "In that situation, most guys try to throw hard, or get you with sliders. They won't try to jerk you around."

For Garber, it was clear what he would throw with the crowd on its feet and history in the balance. The changeup was his best pitch, as it would become for more and more pitchers in the coming years. As Mario Soto, a star for the Reds in the early 1980s, would say in 2015: "That is *the* pitch right now in baseball. Any pitcher in the major leagues right now that doesn't have a good changeup, he's gonna get in trouble."

Even the hard throwers envy it. Sometimes, the fruitless pursuit of a changeup becomes a joke; every spring training, the Yankees' Mariano Rivera would report that he was trying to learn a changeup, to laughs from the beat writers. The hot-tempered Kevin Brown even tried to pick it up from Moyer and Doug Jones, his cerebral changeup-throwing Orioles teammates, in 1995.

"We went to Boston for a four-game series and Kevin said, 'Show me how to throw a changeup, I think I could throw a good one,'" Jones says. "I told him, 'You'll need a year and a half to really be consistent, but I'll show you some really simple ways to throw it and we'll see what it looks like.' And for four days we'd play catch every day, and he would throw a good one and then two bad ones, and a good one and three bad ones, then a good one. And after four days, he said, 'I can't throw the changeup, I quit.' I said, 'Well, OK.' He really didn't want a changeup. But that's how we learn things."

Jones learned his changeup, or at least observed its grip for the first time, from a future fictional closer. Willie Mueller pitched briefly for the Brewers in 1978 and 1981 but is best known for a role in *Major League* as Duke Simpson, the menacing Yankees reliever. Bob Uecker, playing broadcaster Harry Doyle, noted that Duke was so mean, he threw at his own kid in a father-son game.

Like Mueller, Jones pitched for Milwaukee only briefly—four games in April 1982, just long enough to say that he had reached the majors, and to know he didn't belong. The Brewers let him go two years later, after a rough season spent mostly at Double-A. Jones was 27 and satisfied that he had at least worn a big league uniform. It was more than he could have expected in high school, when he threw so softly that his father—a sprint-car driver, no less—told him speed was overrated: "Remember, the harder you throw the ball, the less time you have to duck."

Jones never threw hard. He had carved out a professional career with a well-located sinker, but could not master the changeup. Mueller threw it to him one day while playing catch in the outfield, and Jones asked to see the grip. It was the first time he had seen a three-finger changeup, with the middle and ring fingers on top. It planted a seed.

In 1985 Jones found work with the Indians, driving a beat-up Camaro from Southern California to spring training in Tucson. He broke down in Blythe, talked his way into a parts store that had closed, bought a carburetor, and chugged in at two in the morning. Jones turned the car over to a friend of a friend who sold things on consignment. The extra cash helped.

He made a team: Double-A again, in Waterbury, Connecticut. One night in New Britain, Jones was told to pitch the last three innings of a game. He wore himself out firing fastballs—such as they were—in his first inning. How would he get through two more? He thought of the changeup, and it worked. Jones struck out five of the next six batters. He was on his way, even if the Indians didn't notice for a while.

A few weeks later, manager Jack Aker—an old fireman for the Kansas City A's—met with Jones in the bullpen. His bosses had told him to ask Jones if he wanted to coach the next season.

"I about fell off the bench," Jones says. "I didn't know whether to be flattered or insulted. I said, 'I think I've figured out something, and I'd like to run with it right now. But thanks for asking.'"

His persistence paid off. Jones returned to the majors in September 1986—more than four years after his previous game—and found so many ways to manipulate his changeup that he really had three variations, including one that would start at the hip of a left-handed hitter, then loop softly over the inside corner for a strike.

His deception helped him earn a spot on five All-Star teams, if not much respect. In 1988 Jones became the first pitcher ever to earn a save in 15 consecutive appearances. Topps commemorated the feat with a "Record Breaker" card that featured Chris Codiroli—a different Indians righty with a walrus mustache—on the front. In 2006, Jones received only two votes for the Hall of Fame and was dropped from the ballot. The same year, Bruce Sutter received 400 votes to gain induction. Their final career save totals: Jones 303, Sutter 300.

Jones is hardly the only changeup artist to be underestimated. Jamie Moyer, too, was urged to become a coach while pitching in the minors. He declined the offer and, at 49 years old in 2012, became the oldest pitcher in major league history to record a win. Moyer finished with 269 victories, one more than Jim Palmer. But like Jones, Moyer, too, slipped off the Hall of Fame ballot after just one year.

———————

In the courtyard outside the Hall of Fame Library are statues 60 feet, 6 inches apart: Johnny Podres and Roy Campanella, the hallowed Brooklyn battery of 1955. Podres beat the Yankees twice in that World Series, on his twenty-third birthday in Game 3 and again in Game 7, with a 2–0 shutout in the Bronx.

The statues, linked by a stone pathway in the grass and sculpted by Stanley Bleifeld, symbolize the unity of pitcher and catcher. Yet before the cathartic final pitch of 1955, Podres and Campanella disagreed.

"Campy had called for a fast ball, but I'd shaken him off," Podres wrote that winter, in a piece for *The Saturday Evening Post*. "It was the only time I did that the entire Series."

Podres would spend decades as a coach proving the wisdom of his uncanny instincts. He chose wisely for the winning pitch—a changeup, dutifully beaten into the ground by Elston Howard. Pee Wee Reese scooped it at shortstop, fired to Gil Hodges at first base, and the Bums at last were kings. As the World Series MVP, Podres got a Corvette.

Four days later, he was back home in upstate Mineville, New York. It was there that his high school principal had once persuaded a friend who scouted for the Dodgers to come see the town's young phenom. Podres responded by throwing a no-hitter against Ticonderoga, enticing the Dodgers to offer him $6,000—more than his father's annual salary working in the mines. After the World Series, a hometown parade brought more gifts: a new shanty for ice fishing, and a 24-inch television set for Podres's mother. She put it in the room where Johnny was born.

Podres would help pitch the Dodgers to more championships in Los Angeles, and he worked for the organization when they won another in 1988. Owner Peter O'Malley was so elated then that he treated the organization to a vacation in Rome for a week. Podres quickly grew restless.

"We were going to Pompeii, my wife and I on the bus with Pods, and he said, 'Hey, Guy, let's go to the race track,'" says Guy Conti, another pitching coach in the Dodgers' system. "I said, 'Pods, my wife would kill me if I got off this bus and decided, in Pompeii, to go to the race track!' But that was him. He was just a down-to-earth man. He wasn't no big shot, he was just Johnny Podres."

Podres retired from playing after the 1969 season—when he pitched, naturally, for the Padres—but he could throw the changeup for decades, demonstrating it for his pupils with the Padres, Dodgers, Red Sox, Twins, and Phillies. Conti marveled at the way Podres could whip his left arm, as if throwing a fastball, and then spit out a pitch that seemed to suspend itself in midair. Logically, you knew it was impossible, but Podres's pitching could defy reason.

"He was convinced his changeup rose, and you didn't doubt him," Bobby Ojeda says. "It's against the laws of physics that any ball rises; they don't rise, it's impossible. But he was convinced he rotated the shit out of that changeup so much that it rose."

Ojeda did not know Podres's background when he first started working with him as a Red Sox farmhand in Elmira, New York, in 1978. But he could tell that this was a true baseball guy: a big gut, a cigarette, and a no-nonsense presence, gruff but encouraging, that commanded respect and awe. He's probably done a lot in this game, Ojeda thought, because he really knows his stuff.

Twenty years later, not much had changed. Ryan Madson was 17 years old, assigned to Martinsville, Virginia, for rookie ball with the Phillies. Madson already threw a changeup, taught to him by Fletch Jernigan, a coach he had met at age nine who learned the grip from a story he read in the *Orange County Register*. Madson would throw the pitch and Podres would make a big show, taking off his cap, stopping the bullpen session. "Did you see that!" he would say, as Madson beamed. He knew then that he had a real weapon—and Podres, most likely, had discovered something besides a major league changeup.

"He had a knack to be able to tell real early in a young pitcher's career, in the minor leagues, whether he'd be able to pitch in the big leagues or not," says Dave Wallace, who coached with Podres in the Dodgers' system. "He recognized character, makeup, competitiveness, balls—whatever you want to call it, he just knew."

Wallace turns his voice to a smoker's growl, imitating Podres:

"He would say to me: 'That guy's gonna pitch in the big leagues!'—or he would say, 'Wait till the lights come on and he's gonna melt!'" Wallace shook his head. "It might take a couple of weeks or a month, but he had an innate ability to recognize if you had 'it' or not. It was unbelievable."

If Podres believed in you, he would not give up. He understood that every pitcher—even those of identical height and weight—has a different physiology. But if a pitcher had "it," Podres would persist until he brought it out.

In time, the Podres changeup would have a profound impact on cities starved for championships, just as it had on Brooklyn in 1955. Viola would use it in 1987 to bring the Minnesota Twins their first World Series crown. Pedro Martinez—who learned it from Conti, who learned it from Podres—would use it to help the Boston Red Sox win the 2004 World Series, their first title in 86 years.

In 2005, a half century after his own precious moment, Podres shared his memories with Jim Salisbury of *The Philadelphia Inquirer.* His best pitch in Game 7 was the fastball, he said, "hard stuff all day" in the Bronx shadows until that final changeup to Howard. He was glad the ground ball went to Reese, the veteran captain, who had played for the Dodgers since Podres was in grade school.

"I know it meant a lot to a lot of people," said Podres, who would die in 2008, at age 75. "Sometimes when I'm home doing nothing, I put the video in. I get the feeling that I'm young again. What a time that was."

————

Stu Miller never closed out a World Series. In popular lore, he is best known for a balk in a 1961 All-Star Game at windswept Candlestick Park. Miller was not really blown off the mound—he swayed a bit— but the incident came to symbolize the notorious conditions then for baseball in San Francisco.

Jim Palmer, the Hall of Famer for the Orioles, has a more fitting memory of Miller from 1965. The Orioles called Miller "Bullet," mocking his low- to mid-80s fastball. But the pitch looked a lot harder because Miller paired it with his generation's best changeup.

"I'm 19, I'm in the bullpen, and we're at Dodger Stadium playing the Angels," Palmer says. "I'm standing at home plate, pretending I'm a hitter. He's throwing his changeup and I know it's coming. I'm striding—*and then he throws a fastball*, up and in, and I thought I was gonna have a heart attack. The difference between his fastball and changeup was unbelievable."

Palmer can still see the Yankees' Tom Tresh (2-for-22 against Miller) swinging wildly, and futilely, at Miller's changeups—while Mickey Mantle knelt in the on-deck circle, laughing. Mantle hit his 500th homer off Miller, but otherwise was 2-for-17. Harmon Killebrew, the mighty Twins slugger, was just as bad.

"I can't remember anybody else throwing like that," says the Yankees' Bobby Richardson, who also struggled with Miller. "He'd turn his neck and you'd be out in front of everything. John Blanchard would sit on the bench and say, 'I'm not going up there, he's gonna make me look foolish.'"

Miller bobbed his head as he delivered the pitch, adding an extra dash of hesitation and confusion. It was not on purpose, he would insist, but it helped the effectiveness of a pitch he learned in Class D with the Cardinals at the urging of manager Vedie Himsl.

"He said, 'You have to come up with a change-up. And the key is to make it look like a fastball,'" Miller told Dan Brown of the *San Jose Mercury News*. "That's all he said. And I thought, 'That sounds good.' I went out and threw one and he said, 'Oh, my gosh.' It came that naturally."

Miller pitched 16 seasons, mostly for the Giants and Orioles. He had 153 saves, won a league ERA title, and left an impression of invincibility on a pitcher bound for Cooperstown.

"Of all the guys that I've seen—Mariano, Jeff Reardon, Eckersley—you could load the bases up, and unless Tony Oliva was hitting, I'd take Stu Miller and his changeup over any of them," Palmer says. "Over any reliever I've ever seen. You could not time it. It was just incredible."

(Oliva, a three-time batting champion, hit .538 off Miller. In baseball there is always an exception.)

Miller pitched for the Orioles' first championship team in 1966. Their third World Series title—and last, to date—came in 1983. Catcher Rick Dempsey was the most valuable player and Scott McGregor pitched a shutout in the clincher. Both had come to Baltimore seven years earlier in a trade with the Yankees. It was not the Yankees' only contribution.

As a high school pitcher in El Segundo, California, McGregor learned a changeup from Tom Morgan, a Yankee reliever from the 1950s who scouted in Southern California. McGregor modified the grip to a palmball, a pitch thrown pretty much as it sounds: from deep in the palm, enveloped in fingers. It spun the same as his fastball, but nearly 15 mph slower.

As a Yankees farmhand, though, McGregor threw fastballs, curveballs, and occasional cutters. It got him to Triple-A, but his manager there, the future Hall of Famer Bobby Cox, stressed that he would not reach his potential unless he developed his changeup. McGregor knew how to throw the pitch but could not quite grasp the mind-set.

"The hard thing to do is go to the big leagues and say, 'OK, I'm gonna throw it a little slower,'" McGregor says. "You go, 'Really? I figure I gotta throw it harder.' But they don't care how hard you throw it. You've just got to learn how to get the change of speeds."

For McGregor that meant three distinct speeds—curveball, fastball, changeup—from the same arm motion. His was a fun windup to imitate: he would raise his hands over his head, swing them down over his right knee, and then spread them behind his back, like a bird taking flight, pausing there before whipping his left arm through. Earl Weaver, McGregor's first manager with the Orioles, had implored him to keep his curveball below 70 miles an hour, and the "funky-ass deceptive motion," as McGregor calls it, was the only way to do it.

With it, though, McGregor had his repertoire: a fastball in the 80s, a changeup in the 70s, and a curve in the 60s. Ken Singleton, the Orioles' right fielder, marveled at how all the pitches looked the same from his vantage point, and hitters were also confused. In McGregor's eight-year prime (1978–85), only Ron Guidry won more games in the AL.

McGregor starred in the 1979 postseason, but the Orioles blew a three-games-to-one lead in the World Series and lost to Pittsburgh. Four years later, they held the same lead before Game 5 at a different Pennsylvania ballpark, Veterans Stadium in Philadelphia. McGregor strode through the visiting dugout and told his teammates not to worry: "I got this," he said.

He threw only one curveball—to bait Joe Morgan, who had homered twice off curves in the series—and otherwise mixed changeups and fastballs in a 5–0 triumph. There were 67,064 fans at the Vet for the twilight start, the highest attendance for a World Series game in the last half century, yet few crowds could ever have been so quiet. I was there, and by the end, McGregor had so thoroughly humbled the Phillies that many fans had left. I scrambled to the front row behind first base for the final inning, and watched McGregor's oddly subdued reaction when Cal Ripken Jr. snagged Garry Maddox's soft liner to end it.

"They show the last out and the kids always tease me," says McGregor, now the Orioles' pitching rehab coordinator in Sarasota, Florida. "They go, 'Show us what you did, Mac!' Because I throw it, I put my glove under my arm and give a little fist pump. You're in such a mode where you can't think about it. I kept pushing it out of my brain the whole time. I couldn't think, 'If we win this thing, we're the world champs!'"

McGregor was just 29, but in five years he was finished. Arm speed comes from a sturdy shoulder, and by 1987 his was loose and sore, incapable of producing the speed variance that had made him a star. When he took the mound at the Metrodome on April 27, 1988, the Orioles were 0–19 for the season. As the Twins ravaged McGregor, Ripken came to the mound and asked if he was throwing the changeup.

"They're all the same speed anymore," McGregor told his shortstop. "Just back up a little bit. You might be a little safer."

There was a runner on base with two out in the fourth inning when manager Frank Robinson removed McGregor—just in time. Had the next batter homered off him, McGregor's ERA would have been stuck at 4.00 forever. Instead he finished at 3.99, with a career record 30 games above .500, a World Series ring, and the memory of overpowering hitters his way.

"I tell the guys, 'The changeup is a power pitch,' and they just look at me," McGregor says. "I go, 'You challenge them, balls-out throwing it, and you'd be surprised. You give it that effort and they go to hit it and it's not there? They got no chance.'"

Frank Viola did not face McGregor that final day at the Metrodome, but it was his home park, and he was at the top of his profession. Viola had just won the World Series MVP award for the Twins, beating the Cardinals in the first and seventh games the previous fall. He was on his way to winning the American League Cy Young Award, the first by a left-handed Minnesota changeup maestro, with two more to follow in the 2000s by Johan Santana.

The Twins had drafted Viola in the second round in 1981, just after his famous duel with Ron Darling in an NCAA tournament game at Yale Field. Darling fired 11 no-hit innings for Yale until allowing a bloop single in the twelfth. Viola twirled 11 shutout innings for St. John's to beat him, 1–0.

Viola did not throw a changeup then—"He didn't need it," Darling says—just a moving fastball, a curve, and an occasional slider. But the mix was enough to earn Viola an invitation to spring training in 1982. The Twins were terrible, and Viola had more polish than most of their pitchers. By June he was in the majors—nominally, anyway.

That season Viola had a 5.21 ERA. In 1983 he led the majors in earned runs allowed. He needed a put-away pitch, and before the next season Podres introduced the changeup. After those first few tentative tries, they spent more than a year playing with grips. Viola needed to believe in the pitch before he could find the nerve to use it. But because his results were improving, even without it, there seemed to be no urgency.

Then midway through the 1985 season, the Twins hired Ray Miller, the former Baltimore pitching coach, as their manager. By early September Podres was gone, grumbling that Miller did not like him because Podres knew more about pitching than he did.

Podres knew enough to deliver one vital message to Viola as he left the clubhouse: "Don't you ever give up on that changeup!" Viola did as instructed, and could not believe what he'd been missing. Sometimes he would call home and ask his father, in wonder, "How did I ever get here without this?"

Viola tried to throw his changeup 10 to 15 miles per hour slower than his fastball. He rested his middle and ring fingers on top of the ball and applied pressure with his pinkie, below the left seam. He formed the OK symbol—the "circle" in "circle change"—with his index

"He was just a crusty old dude," Andy Pettitte said of Hoyt Wilhelm, the Hall of Fame knuckleballer who later coached in the Yankees' farm system. "I loved him to death."

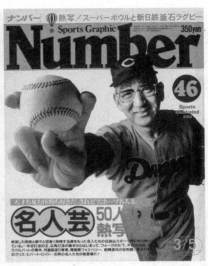

Shigeru Sugishita, known as the God of Forkballs, inspired generations of Japanese pitchers to use the splitter.

Phil Niekro, a 318-game winner, knuckled his way to a staggering 5,404 innings pitched, the most of anyone born after 1887.

For Bruce Sutter, 1979 was a bittersweet year: he won the NL Cy Young Award but lost his mentor, Fred Martin, who taught him the split-finger fastball.

BROWN vs. MATHEWSON
GREATEST TREAT OF THE YEAR for BASEBALL FANS

CINCINNATI, OHIO, SEPT. 1, 1916.

"YOU CAN POSITIVELY COUNT ON MY PITCHING AGAINST BROWN ON SEPT. 4th."

CHRISTY MATHEWSON,
MANAGER CINCINNATI REDS.

"THREE FINGERED" BROWN

BROWN'S TWIRLING HAND

CHRISTY MATHEWSON

CHICAGO, ILL. "MORDECAI BROWN WILL BE READY TO BATTLE AGAINST MATHEWSON LABOR DAY."

JOE TINKER, MANAGER CUBS.

— 1916 —

First Game at 1:30 P.M. **DOUBLE HEADER LABOR DAY** First Game at 1:30 P.M.
WEEGHMAN PARK

STARS OF MANY YEARS TO PITCH FOR CHICAGO CUBS AND CINCINNATI REDS

NORTH CLARK AND ADDISON STREETS.

THE DAILY NEWS BOYS BAND WILL RENDER MUSIC

RESERVED SEATS AT A. G. SPALDING & BROS. 28 S WABASH AVE. TEL. CEN. 446.

Christy Mathewson's fadeaway and Three Finger Brown's curveball were early-century marvels. This was the final career game for both, with Mathewson beating Brown, 10–8.

The screwball might have caused Carl Hubbell's notorious inverted pitching arm. It also earned him two MVP awards and a spot in Cooperstown.

Warren Spahn, throwing a ceremonial first pitch before the 1999 World Series in Atlanta, earned 363 victories, a record for a lefty, with a screwball that helped him thrive into his forties.

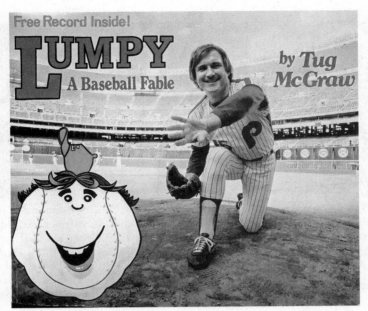

The irrepressible Tug McGraw twists his throwing hand inward, just as he would on his screwball, for the cover of his children's book in 1981.

Fernando Valenzuela, whose screwball captivated baseball in 1981, presents Clayton Kershaw with the first of his three Cy Young Awards in April 2012.

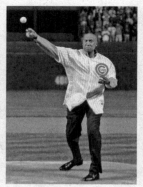

The sidearming Grover Cleveland Alexander won 373 games with a sinker that "bore in like a lump of lead," according to a rival.

Fergie Jenkins—the first pitcher ever to finish with more than 3,000 strikeouts and fewer than 1,000 walks—delivers the ceremonial first pitch before a 2008 playoff game at Wrigley Field.

Kent Tekulve, the yellow submariner, helped the Pirates win their last title in 1979. When he retired 10 years later, he had made more relief appearances than any other pitcher in history.

Among them, Tom Glavine, John Smoltz, and Greg Maddux earned 648 victories and six Cy Young Awards for the Braves.

Pitchers for the 1967 Tigers—including changeup master and future coach Johnny Podres (second from left, hand on hip)—get a spring training lesson from the great Johnny Sain.

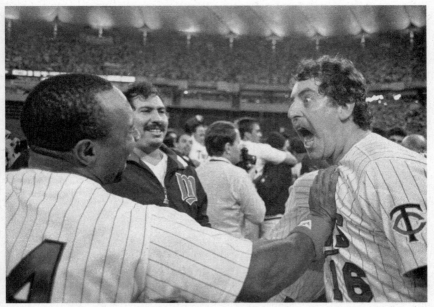

Armed with a changeup he learned from Johnny Podres, the Twins' Frank Viola (right, with teammates Kirby Puckett and Juan Berenguer) lit up the Metrodome by winning twice in the 1987 World Series.

"His hands were just ridiculously long," Curt Schilling said of Pedro Martinez, his Red Sox teammate, shown here in the shadows at Angel Stadium in 2003.

Jamie Moyer tosses a changeup for the Rockies in 2012, the year he turned fifty.

Stephen Strasburg, with his dominant index finger on the side of the ball, delivers a changeup for the Nationals in 2012.

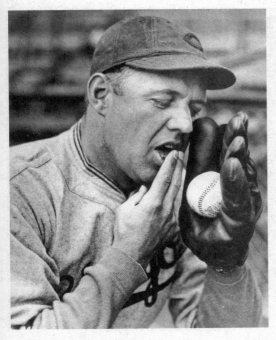

The last legal spitballer, Burleigh Grimes, won Game 7 of the 1931 World Series for the Cardinals after his father brought him his favorite slippery elm bark from Wisconsin.

Adjusting his cap—or loading up for a spitter? Gaylord Perry always kept hitters guessing.

An anguished Bob Stanley, moments after his wild pitch helped doom the Red Sox in Game 6 of the 1986 World Series. He said it wasn't a spitter; the Mets still aren't sure.

"All of a sudden it's over, and it's kind of like, 'Well, now what?,'" said Roy Halladay in 2017, recalling his emotions after his playoff no-hitter. "You want to keep going."

Mariano Rivera, whose cutter made him a legend, earned a record postseason 42 saves—matching his hallowed uniform number.

finger and thumb while hooking the right seam. To take still more speed off the pitch, he would tuck it further back in his palm. To Viola, the changeup allowed him to dominate, even if hitters felt differently.

"You wouldn't believe the feedback you'd get from hitters during a game," he says. "You might strike a guy out on a changeup and they're yelling at you from the dugout: 'Throw it like a man!'"

Viola could laugh off the taunting by pointing to his record. In his first seven seasons throwing the changeup, only one pitcher in the majors, Roger Clemens, won more games.

The changeup was so good that Viola could give it away and still win. When the Twins traded Viola to the Mets in 1989—several years before interleague play—Toronto pitcher Todd Stottlemyre gave some friendly advice to his father, Mel, the Mets' pitching coach. The Blue Jays' hitters, Todd reported, had noticed that Viola would lift his right index finger off his glove when he dug inside to grip his changeup. Yet even with this intelligence, the Blue Jays had lost twice to Viola that season.

Viola would make two All-Star teams for the Mets and retire in 1996. Fifteen years later, he embarked on a second career as a coach in their organization, building off lessons from Podres. One of his prospects at Triple-A in 2014 was Noah Syndergaard, a hulking right-hander with a monster fastball but little trust in his secondary pitches.

Viola told Syndergaard about a game he pitched for the Twins. Podres instructed the catcher not to move all day. Throw whatever he calls, Podres told Viola, and watch what happens. Viola listened, succeeded deep into the game, and came off the mound to see Podres smiling.

"Son, what'd you learn?" Podres asked him.

"I guess my stuff's pretty good."

"You've got to learn to trust it," Podres replied.

Syndergaard absorbed the lessons and made it through his first full season at the highest minor league level. The next spring he was in the majors, and Viola spoke with pride about his progress.

"Look at him now," he said. "It's nothing different. It's just confidence in knowing that he cannot be afraid to throw a 2–1 changeup if the catcher's calling it. If the catcher's got enough confidence in Noah to put it down, Noah's gotta say, 'Hey, if he's got confidence, I've gotta have confidence, too.' And that's what makes you the pitcher you're going to become."

Syndergaard would use more and more changeups as the season went on. His final victory of a standout rookie year came in the World Series.

———

Before he was known mostly as the older brother of a Hall of Famer, Ramon Martinez was a star for the Dodgers. He signed with them in 1984, at age 16, and soon developed a changeup. His long fingers made the pitch feel natural, and Martinez went on to win 135 games and toss 20 shutouts—three more than Pedro.

Martinez learned his changeup from Johnny Podres, recognizing it instantly. It was the primary weapon of his hero in the Dominican Republic.

"Mario Soto, he was my idol growing up, the guy that I watched, but I never got in touch with him," Ramon Martinez says. "It wasn't like I could see him and ask him, 'How do you throw the changeup?' Now it's easier; we can go and talk to the kids and teach them how to throw the changeup or breaking pitch. But at that time, to meet Mario Soto, it would be tougher."

Juan Marichal was the first Hall of Famer from the Dominican Republic. He was Soto's idol and the most prominent Dominican pitcher until Pedro Martinez. In between were World Series stars like Joaquin Andujar and Jose Rijo. Soto never got there, joining the Reds just after their titles in the 1970s. But his changeup endures.

"The best changeup I've ever seen in baseball, *the best*—and he threw 95, too—was Mario Soto," says Mike Brito, the famed scout in the white Panama hat who operated the radar gun behind home plate at Dodger Stadium for decades. "When he was on top of his pitches, nobody could hit him."

Soto was 23 years old and pitching irregularly out of the Reds' bullpen in 1979. That September, he was called into a one-run game in the fifth inning with the Braves' Dale Murphy at the plate.

"It was a 3–2 count and Johnny Bench keeps calling fastball, fastball, fastball, and then slider," Soto says. "I said, 'No,' and he got mad at me.

He said, 'What do you want to do?' I said, 'I want to throw a changeup.' He said, 'Changeup, you're crazy!' But I threw that then, and that ball just dropped straight down. It dropped so much and I struck him out. From there on I say: 'No more sliders.'"

Soto had learned the changeup from Scott Breeden, a Reds minor league coach. At his best, he could sink it to the right, cut it to the left, or make it drop. He honed the pitch meticulously at spring training in Tampa, reporting to the Reds' complex around 6 a.m. and dropping changeups into a target he had drawn on the back of the concrete center field wall.

Tom Seaver, the ace of the staff, noticed Soto's diligence and became his teacher. Seaver threw his changeup along the seams, somewhat like his sinker, while Soto threw his across the seams and applied pressure with his knuckles. Soto kept his own grip but embraced the finer points Seaver imparted.

"Do you try to throw strikes with every pitch?" Seaver once asked.

"Yeah," Soto said, to Seaver's dismay. "Why not?"

"Because you have pretty good control. You want to take advantage of that."

No one had ever explained to Soto the value in pairing stuff with command. Before that, he said, he had simply tried to throw a strike with every pitch; that is the definition of control. Yet simply finding the zone, he learned, was not the point. Putting your pitches where you wanted them to go—in *or* out of the strike zone, tricking hitters into swinging at stuff they could not handle—was the definition of command. That was an art.

That same realization hit Pedro Martinez at his first All-Star Game, with the Expos in 1996. On the bench in the right field bullpen in Philadelphia, he marveled at the warm-up of Tom Glavine, the Atlanta left-hander squarely in his prime as a master of the off-speed pitch. From close range, Martinez noticed Glavine directing his changeups and curves to precise locations, in and away. Martinez threw those same pitches, but never like that. The license to locate, as shown by a peer, was a revelation.

"To me, that was so important, because I normally would rely on the difference in speeds between the fastball and the changeup," Martinez says. "I was never worried about spotting the changeup or spotting the breaking ball. A lot of people tell me, 'Oh Pedro, you were so gifted.' I say, 'No, I was just a patch of a lot of players. I wasn't born with all this.'"

The next season, Martinez began one of the most remarkable stretches a pitcher has ever had. In a time of extreme slugging, Martinez led the majors in earned run average five times in seven years. His ERA from 1997 to 2003 was 2.20. The major league ERA for those seasons was 4.48. In simple terms, Martinez was twice as good as the average major league pitcher.

Curt Schilling was his teammate on the curse-breaking 2004 Red Sox, the second time Schilling rode shotgun to a World Series title with a winner of multiple Cy Youngs. In Arizona, he had seen Randy Johnson dominate with brute force: hard fastballs, hard sliders, endless ferocity. Martinez, Schilling said, was all feel. He was an intimidator, for sure, but succeeded by adjusting to what he saw and outwitting the hitter.

Extraordinary vision sharpened those powers of observation, and Martinez's body—deemed by the Dodgers to be too small for a starter—helped him execute his plans. Being shorter than Ramon gave him better balance, and while he was not quite double-jointed ("Almost," he says), Martinez could bend his fingers over the back of his hand for maximum flexibility.

"His hands were just ridiculously long," Schilling says. "That's one of the reasons why he had such a good changeup. Bigger fingers allow you more control over the baseball. It's the same as basketball, right? If you have big hands in basketball it's an enormous advantage. Now think about a ball one-tenth that size, how much more of an advantage you have with bigger hands. I think, to some guys, throwing a baseball is like throwing a golf ball, or a tennis ball.

"That's one of the things I implore people when they're drafting pitchers: look at their hands. Because a guy with small hands is what he is, and maybe he might have velocity, but his stuff is not gonna change that much. Whereas a guy with big hands, you could teach him anything you want."

You could, but it still might take a while to find something that works. Ramon Martinez's fingers were even longer than Pedro's, and he threw his changeup with his index, middle, and ring fingers on top of the ball. Pedro tried the same grip after signing with the Dodgers, with mediocre results.

He was 18 years old at extended spring training in 1990 when Guy Conti taught him the circle change he had learned from Podres. With his index finger hugging the left side of the ball and the fingertip tucked beside his thumb, Martinez wrapped his third and fourth fingers across the four seams. The pitch felt unnatural at first, but within two weeks it was behaving as Conti wanted. It would look like a strike to a lefty before slashing down and away, out of the zone. And it would look like a ball to a righty, who would give up on it, only to see the pitch veer back in to clip the outside corner.

Conti was entranced by Martinez from the first time he saw him in the Dominican Republic, in a group of other young and unfamiliar pitchers. Conti knew the Dodgers had signed Ramon Martinez's brother, but saw nobody with Ramon's 6-foot-4 build. He found Pedro, who is five inches shorter, by the sound of his fastball, the way his fingers snapped off the seams as he let it go. He figured the kid must be special.

Soon they formed a lifelong bond. Martinez calls Conti his white daddy. Conti calls Martinez a borderline genius. That intellect showed up in Martinez's understanding of the changeup and the subtleties of using his fingers to locate it.

"By taking that index finger off the ball, you take 50 percent of your velocity off," Conti explains. "Now, throw as hard as you can. You're only gonna throw it with 50 percent of your velocity. That middle finger is gonna be the only thing that really propels the ball.

"So what we did—which he could do, because his fingers were long like Ramon's—was we moved the ball even further. He was throwing that changeup *with the inside* of the middle finger and the fourth finger. Most pitchers couldn't get such a grip on it, but he could do that, and he could jerk that ball in there. It was really a funky grip, but he got it."

Pedro Martinez—like virtually every pitcher—emphasizes that a well-located fastball is the most important pitch in baseball. His changeup was used to accentuate the fastball, and it was only good because his fastball was good. Yet even after his sterling 1999 regular season, when he was 23–4 with a 2.07 ERA and 313 strikeouts, Martinez evolved.

He had strained a lat muscle against Cleveland in the first game of the playoffs that October. When the decisive fifth game began in a blizzard of offense at Jacobs Field—it was 8–8 in the middle of the fourth—Martinez arrived from the bullpen to spin six no-hit innings. His performance gave the Red Sox their first postseason series victory since 1986, and he did it without throwing a fastball. The Indians feared it, but it never came. Martinez unplugged a thunderous lineup with finesse.

"That's where I used everything I learned from Maddux, from Glavine, from my brother, from Roger Clemens, from Nolan Ryan, all the people I used to see pitch, that's when I came out to display everything," Martinez says. "Because up to that point, I was a power pitcher. I was someone that would rely on 80 percent fastballs and blow it by you. And that day I didn't have it, so I had to run to different sources. I had to run to the changeup, I had to run to the little cutter, I had to run to the curveball, I had to rely on location, and that's when everything came together. For me, pitching at 87 and pitching at 97 was pretty much the same, except that I knew how to do it on either side—power or just, you know, outsmarting you."

The 2000 season would be even better: a third Cy Young Award, a 1.74 ERA, and a WHIP (walks plus hits per inning pitched) of 0.737, the best in baseball history for a pitcher who qualified for the ERA title. It also included the game of which Martinez is most proud.

It was August 24, 2000, late in a stretch of 20 games in a row for the Red Sox without a break, in the heat of a pennant race with the Yankees. Boston's bullpen was exhausted and the team was beginning a road trip in Kansas City against the lowly Royals. For the only time he could remember, Martinez says, he was asked before a game to pitch at least eight innings.

Then he gave up five runs in the first.

Single, single, pop out. Single, single, double. Strikeout, double, ground out. The next inning, he gave up a homer. There was no way to explain it, Martinez says, and no advance warning of such a beating. But he persevered because his team needed him and he somehow got the game to the ninth, helping the Red Sox win. "That was as satisfying to me as probably winning a game in the World Series," Martinez says.

He would do that, finally, four years later in St. Louis. Martinez fired seven shutout innings in Game 3, bringing his team to the precipice of the title. He never pitched again for the Red Sox, but wears their cap in bronze on his plaque in Cooperstown.

Two plaques in the Hall credit pitchers specifically for their success with the "change of pace"—Tim Keefe, a 342-game winner in the 1800s, and Joe Williams, a Negro Leagues star from 1910 to 1932. But Martinez's was the first to include "change-up" in the text, and likely not the last. Someday, perhaps, there will be those inspired by Martinez, like Felix Hernandez, who had been in the majors four seasons before deciding to teach himself a changeup. Hernandez was already a star, but said Martinez and Freddy Garcia had shown what an effective weapon the pitch could be.

"I tried to throw it because I wanted to take it to the next level," Hernandez says. "I wanted to be the best I can be."

Hernandez holds the pitch like a two-seam fastball, with an extra finger (the middle one) on the white part of the ball between the narrow seams. Some hitters consider it a splitter or a sinker, because it dives down—and sometimes in—to a righty and tends to be only three or four miles an hour slower than his fastball.

"He doesn't throw strikes," says Evan Longoria, "but his stuff is so good that he gets guys to swing, just because you *think* it's a strike."

Longoria batted cleanup for the Rays on August 15, 2012, when Hernandez threw a perfect game at Safeco Field, finishing by freezing Sean Rodriguez on a sinking changeup—*at 92!*—for the final out. Hernandez had fallen behind 2–0, and then pulled even with sliders.

"I said, 'All right, now he's definitely coming back heater,'" Rodriguez says. "Nope. Off-speed. Tip your cap."

Martinez threw nine perfect innings once, in 1995, but the game was still scoreless and he gave up a double to lead off the tenth. He never threw an official no-hitter, but his two hitless innings to start the 1999 All-Star Game, in which he struck out five of six hitters at Fenway Park, was a touchstone moment for his fans back home.

"You remember that All-Star Game?" says Kelvin Herrera, the star reliever who was nine that summer. "Filthy!"

Herrera says his country came to a stop when Martinez pitched; it felt like a national holiday every five days. In time Herrera would come to throw changeups under pressure in October, and earn a World Series ring of his own with the Royals. But he understood that Martinez's pitch was a singular sensation.

"If you see Pedro's hand, it's like, so flexible," he says. "Pedro's changeup is unique. You cannot have that one."

———

The best pure hitter to make his debut after 1939—that is, after Ted Williams—was Tony Gwynn. Across two decades for the Padres, from 1982 to 2001, Gwynn hit .338 and won eight batting titles. He came to bat 323 times against Greg Maddux, Tom Glavine, John Smoltz, and Pedro Martinez, and struck out just three times.

Yet Glavine held Gwynn to a .303 average—outstanding for most hitters, but far below Gwynn's standards. Gwynn thought Glavine's changeup never seemed to reach the plate. When Glavine complimented Gwynn on his plate coverage, Gwynn responded this way:

"You make it tough on me because lefties aren't supposed to throw changeups to lefties, and you do."

Glavine, who won 305 games in his Hall of Fame career, was not alone in that strategy; it also worked well for Jamie Moyer, among others. But it defies convention for a left-hander to throw a slow pitch down and in to a lefty—the danger zone for pitchers, exactly where many left-handed hitters want it. Glavine said he still had not mastered that skill in 1991, when he won his first Cy Young Award.

The caricature of Glavine is that he lived on the outside corner and rode soft stuff to Cooperstown. His athleticism tends to be downplayed. As a high school senior in Billerica, Massachusetts, Glavine was chosen in two drafts: in the second round by the Braves and in the fourth, as a center, by the NHL's Los Angeles Kings. Five rounds later, the Kings took Luc Robitaille, a future Hall of Famer.

Glavine got to pro ball without a changeup. Two years later, in Double-A, he was using a forkball and winning. The Braves had signed a veteran catcher, Ned Yost, to guide their pitching prospects. Yost was unimpressed by Glavine's forkball, which bounced at the plate but fooled anxious, overmatched hitters. Their conversations went like this:

Yost: "Tommy, you gotta get a changeup."

Glavine: "Changeup? My split's awesome."

Yost: "Tommy, your split sucks. You get to Triple-A and the big leagues, those guys are gonna freakin' spit on that thing and it's gonna be worthless for you. You gotta get a changeup."

"Well, he didn't believe me," said Yost, whose plainspoken bluntness would one day help him as a manager. "He went to Triple-A and started getting his ass whupped, and I remember he lost 17 games his first or second year in the big leagues with that split. He started throwing that changeup and it took him to the Hall of Fame."

Glavine's first hint that Yost was right came from Bo Jackson, then a Memphis Chick, who launched a mammoth blast off Glavine's forkball in the summer of 1986. His 7–17 record for the Braves in '88 also signaled his need for a true out pitch—and it rolled right up to him the next spring in West Palm Beach, Florida. In the outfield during batting practice one day, Glavine picked up a ball that slipped in his hand as he went to toss it back. Gripping it with his middle and ring fingers—not his index finger—Glavine's toss faded down and to the left, just the way a lefty's changeup should.

He quickly deduced the happy accident: removing his index finger from the top of the ball was like stepping off the accelerator. With just the third and fourth fingers to guide the pitch, Glavine had a built-in change of speed. He no longer had to slow his arm down to produce it.

"I could throw that pitch as hard as I wanted to, and it just didn't come out the same," Glavine says. "That's the reason it was so deceptive, because my arm speed and everything was exactly the same as it was on my fastball. I didn't have to manipulate anything." By 1991 the pitch had become Glavine's safety valve: on days when his other stuff was lacking, the changeup was always there, giving him a chance to win. Yet he still did not consider himself a complete pitcher. As good as his changeup was, he obeyed the old taboo—and it frustrated him.

"I didn't handle lefties the way I handled righties, in large part because I didn't throw my changeup to lefties," Glavine says. "So I was eliminating my best pitch against left-handed hitters. I finally got fed up with it and said, 'Why can't I throw changeups to lefties? It's my best pitch.'"

Glavine started doing it, and the Braves kept winning. He sold himself on the idea for good in spring training in 1994, his first as a teammate of Fred McGriff, the left-handed slugger acquired the previous summer. Glavine asked McGriff, who had hit him well, what he thought about a lefty throwing changeups to a lefty.

"It seems like a good idea," McGriff said. "I don't know how I could keep it fair."

Glavine tried it in practice against McGriff, who unloaded on the pitch and crushed a long drive—but foul, over the first base seats. Just a loud strike.

"So that's kind of the mind-set that I had: if I can get it in there and throw it right, yeah they might kill it, but I just don't see how they can keep it fair, and it's one more thing for them to think about," Glavine says.

"It was the same with righties. I didn't pitch in all that much, but when I went in, it was always a fastball. Well, heck, if I can throw a changeup in to a right-hander and make him start thinking: *When it comes in here, I don't know if it's hard or soft,* just like they had to do when I was pitching away—man, that would open up a whole other can of worms for me.

"I remember one of the first times I threw it in to a right-hand hitter was Scott Rolen, when he was with the Phillies, and I saw him after the game and he's like, 'Are you kidding me? Now I gotta worry about *that* pitch inside? At least inside it was a matter of guessing, but I only had to guess hard. Now I gotta guess hard *or* soft? And I gotta guess *when* you're going in there?'

"So those are all the kinds of reactions I was looking for, and when I got them it was kind of like: 'OK, I'm onto something.'"

Glavine's continual evolution helped him pitch past his 42nd birthday. He even won another Cy Young Award, in 1998, when he narrowly edged another changeup master bound for Cooperstown.

————

The 1998 season was Trevor Hoffman's best. He led baseball with 53 saves, part of a career collection of 601. He earned the first of seven All-Star selections and helped the Padres win the pennant. The lyrics to Hoffman's anthem, "Hell's Bells" by AC/DC, forecast doom for all who dared to face him: thunder, hurricane, lightning, death.

With Hoffman, though, the intimidator's ultimate weapon—the blazing fastball—was a memory by then. It left him forever on a beach in Del Mar, California, in August 1994, just after the players' strike began. Tossing a football with friends, Hoffman dove for a pass in the surf and felt a pang in his shoulder. Then, in a beach volleyball game, he dove for a ball in the sand, like an outfielder in full extension for a sinking line drive. Hoffman heard a distinct *pfffft* sound, he says, "like air coming out of a tire." He had torn his rotator cuff.

The mid-90s fastball that had catapulted Hoffman to the majors in 1993—less than three years after converting from shortstop with the Reds in Class A—would never return. The long off-season gave Hoffman time to strengthen his arm so he could pitch in 1995 and delay surgery. It also gave him time to think.

"It expedited the transition every power pitcher has to make—they have to learn how to pitch and develop other pitches," Hoffman says. "I still felt like I was going to throw as hard, I still gave it the same effort level, but the gun didn't read it. It kind of forced me into thinking, 'What are you gonna do now to get people out?'"

Hoffman never started a game in the majors, but he had started just enough in the minors to be forced to experiment with secondary pitches. A Reds scout, Larry Barton, had shown him a grip for a circle change, but the pitch was ordinary, like his curveball and slider, and Hoffman did not trust it. He always feared it would slip from his hand.

With the Padres in 1994, Hoffman's catch partner was Donnie Elliott. They were not too different, a pair of right-handed relievers for a last-place team who had already played for a few organizations. Hoffman asked how Elliott threw his changeup, and learned the basis for a grip that would make him a star.

Elliott, who would pitch only once in the majors after 1994, had invented a grip in which his index finger and thumb pinched a seam on the left side of the ball. For Hoffman, it felt like sliding his body from the wooden arm of a couch to the soft pillows in the middle. The ball was centered better in his hand with Elliott's grip, allowing Hoffman to engage his thumb, index finger, and middle finger—the most reliable steering digits.

Hoffman could spot his diminished fastball with impeccable command, and he deadened his changeup by shoving it deeper in his palm. He began to use this combination in earnest in 1995, throwing a fastball around 90 miles an hour and a changeup, at times, around 72.

"He had so much of his hand on it," says Robin Ventura, who was 0-for-5 with four strikeouts against Hoffman. "He threw it, you'd see it, and then it would disappear for a second—and then it would keep coming."

Hoffman converted 88.8 percent of his career saves, a figure almost identical to Mariano Rivera's 89.1. But postseason success eluded Hoffman, who made it to the playoffs just four times in 18 seasons. He pitched only one game in the World Series and blew the save. All that time as a closer and he never experienced the defining moment of the position: leaping into the catcher's arms to end the baseball season.

Yet Hoffman's attitude about it could serve as a model for dealing with disappointment, and goes a long way to understanding the ethos of an athlete. Everyone wants to win a title, but perhaps more important is earning the chance to compete for it. Hoffman did that in 1998, even without a championship ring as the prize.

"I've kind of gotten over wishing for it," he says. "I had my opportunity. I was in the '98 World Series. We had Game 3 with a chance to close it down, and I didn't. It's not really a wish for another opportunity, having been there. I just didn't seize the moment."

The Padres had lost the first two games in New York against the dynastic Yankees, who had gone 114–48 in the regular season. Back in San Diego, the Padres led by a run in the top of the eighth with a runner on first and no outs. With AC/DC's bells clanging and 64,667 fans roaring and waving towels, Hoffman trotted in from the bullpen. He got one out, then issued a walk.

Scott Brosius came to the plate, having homered in his previous at-bat. He checked his swing on a curve for strike one, then took two changeups in the dirt for balls. Hoffman never threw him another.

After the second changeup, the Padres' pitching coach, Dave Stewart, visited his pitcher on the mound. Brosius pulled a fastball foul down the third base line, then smashed another—89 miles an hour—over the center field fence for a three-run homer. The Padres never recovered. Hoffman had been beaten, but not with his changeup.

"The 2–2 fastball that I threw to Scott Brosius in the World Series— that's probably the optimal time that I should have thrown it, and I didn't," Hoffman says. When nudged, he added why. "You know what? Dave Stewart came out one time the whole year, and it was in that moment. He came out and said, 'We need to be aggressive here.' I threw a pitch that I probably shouldn't have.

"But that's the way it goes. At least it was a strike. If he missed it or swung through it or took it, it was gonna be a strike."

It was, and it went a long way. The single most important changeup of Trevor Hoffman's career is the one he never threw.

Stephen Strasburg remembers sitting in the left field seats as a teenager at Petco Park and peeking into the Padres bullpen to watch Hoffman warm up. He recognized the artistry of Hoffman's changeup but could not repeat it quite that way.

"He let it fall off the fingertips and almost, like, paintbrush it down," Strasburg says. "You have to have a tremendous feel of the baseball to be able to do that, and for me, I have to throw everything off of my fastball. I have to throw everything as hard as I can."

Strasburg learned his changeup at San Diego State from the Aztecs' pitching coach, Rusty Filter, but there was no reason to use it much in games. The point would be to keep hitters off his high-90s fastball, but they never proved they could hit that pitch, anyway. Strasburg blitzed through college with 375 strikeouts in 243 innings. He was picked first in the 2009 draft by the Nationals, who promoted him to Washington a year later.

That season, Ivan Rodriguez caught all but one of Strasburg's starts. Rodriguez, who would retire the next season with the record for games caught, thought Strasburg's changeup was even better than his celebrated curveball. Strasburg threw it about 90 miles an hour, which was still sometimes 10 mph slower than his fastball.

Most major leaguers could handle that pitch, on its own, but not when they had to respect a changeup, too. Rodriguez encouraged Strasburg to finally use the pitch he had never needed.

"I trusted whatever he called, absolutely," Strasburg says. "I would throw it down and they'd be so geared up for the fastball, they'd see that and it'd disappear. I'd get a lot of swings and misses that way."

Another San Diego boy needed the changeup simply to have a chance. Cole Hamels—a high school freshman in the fall of 1998—had also watched and admired Hoffman while growing up in San Diego. He recognized the way Hoffman tormented hitters with a pitch they knew was coming. If Hamels's peers also noticed, they were not trying to learn it.

"Guys were really trying to learn split-fingers and sliders, anything else besides the changeup," Hamels says. "They wanted to see instant results, and the changeup's not instant results. While you're learning it, you're spiking it into the ground or you're hanging it and guys are crushing it. With a slider or a curveball, you see right away how it's really affecting a hitter. So guys are more attracted to the instant success as opposed to the long-term success, and you start to see that some guys just don't like to work as efficiently or as diligently as it takes to be able to succeed at something."

Hamels was playing the long game. He threw only 81 or 82 miles an hour as a freshman at Rancho Bernardo High School, and did not make the varsity team. But the school's star at the time, a junior named Matt Wheatland, was thriving with the changeup. Wheatland would play for Team USA at a tournament in Taiwan on his way to becoming a first-round draft pick of the Tigers. Hamels, sufficiently impressed, learned Wheatland's changeup from his coach, Mark Furtak.

Hamels thought the pitch might compensate for his late-blooming velocity and give him a varsity spot as a sophomore. He was right, but had no idea just how effective his changeup would be.

"We had a ton of scouts at all of our games, big tournament games, all these potential first-round picks—and I was able to make guys swing and miss by a mile," Hamels says. "And that's where I'm like, 'Hmm, that's weird. Why are they missing so bad?' So I'm like, 'OK, I'm gonna do it again,' and they would miss by a mile again. They're not making the adjustment. I was *bouncing* them and guys were swinging. I'm like, 'Well, I guess this pitch is really deceptive.'"

Hamels injured his left arm that summer when he ran into a parked car playing touch football. When he tried to pitch that night, he fractured his humerus bone. A few years earlier, Furtak had been at the game in San Diego when Tom Browning, the stalwart Reds left-hander, suffered the same injury. Browning had 123 career victories at that moment and never won again. Hamels feared for his future.

"This is not a normal arm," Furtak told doctors at the hospital. "You need to do something special."

Doctors inserted two rods in the humerus. Hamels missed a year. But he grew two inches, to 6 foot 3, and when he returned as a senior, he could finally throw his fastball in the low 90s. He trusted in his changeup throughout his recovery.

"For that whole year, I still kind of knew that would be the easiest pitch, because it's not a lot of stress on the area," Hamels says. "You're not trying to muscle and engage and jack everything around. So mentally, I was like: at least I know I can always throw *this* pitch."

He has never stopped. Hamels went undefeated as a senior in 2002 and signed with the Phillies as a first-round pick. Six years later, he was MVP of the World Series. Seven years after that, he was traded to the Rangers and led another team into October.

The stuff he had in high school, Hamels guessed, would not make him a first-round pick anymore. There is too much emphasis on velocity, he said, too many travel-ball programs he worries will burn out top prospects, endanger their arms, or both.

"Every generation's gonna get better and better; you never know when it's gonna stop," Hamels concedes. "But every generation's gonna keep pushing the limit."

There may well be a limit to how fast a human being can throw a baseball. There will never be a limit to the joys of fooling the world's best hitters with something slow.

THE
SPITBALL

Hit the Dry Side

The Brooklyn Dodgers met an old friend on a trip to St. Louis early in the 1955 season. Preacher Roe, a sly and slender lefty who had just retired to West Plains, Missouri, entertained his former teammates at the Chase Hotel. He needed their advice.

"We sat around a big table, all talking to Preacher," recalls Carl Erskine, a top Dodgers starter then. "He said, 'Fellas, I want to ask you a question: *Sports Illustrated* has offered me $2,000 to tell them how I threw the spitter. You think I should do that or not? With that $2,000 I can blacktop my driveway and I can fix up my house. I could really use that $2,000. What do you think?'

"The guys all said, 'Yeah, go ahead, Preach, sure, why not?' I did not. I admired Preacher. He was a great study to watch pitch. He was very clever and won a lot of games; he was really a pitcher's pitcher. So I didn't say yes to that. As we were leaving the dining room, Preacher said, 'I didn't hear you speak up.' I said, 'No, I didn't, Preacher. You were such an outstanding pitcher without the spitter, I'd hate to see you taint your whole career by talking about throwing it.'

"So anyway, Preacher did the article, he got the $2,000, and sometime later when I talked to Preach he said, 'Carl, you know what? I just ruined my chances for the Hall of Fame by admitting I threw the spitter, and you're the only one that advised me not to do it.' And I said, 'Well, Preacher, I saw you pitch, you were a pitcher's pitcher. You could have won without the spitter.'"

Maybe, maybe not. While Erskine believed in Roe, the man himself didn't: in his confession, Roe said he turned to the pitch after slumping to 4–15 with the Pirates in 1947. Reviving the spitter, which he had practiced with Harry Brecheen as a Cardinals farmhand, was his last chance. He made the most of it, becoming a regular All-Star, though not quite a Cooperstown candidate, for the Dodgers. Cheating only made sense.

"Why shouldn't I have?" Roe told Dick Young in the story. "I was about through when I decided to get me the pitch. 'If I get caught,' I told myself, 'they'll kick me out. If I don't, I'm through anyway, so how can I lose?'"

He didn't lose very often. Roe won so much—a .715 winning percentage over seven years with Brooklyn—that he guessed the spitter earned him $100,000. On the bench between innings, Roe would pop a stick of Beech-Nut gum in his mouth and announce, "I'm gonna get me a new batch of curveballs." In the game, he'd spit on the meaty part of his thumb while pretending to wipe his brow. Then, while hitching his belt, he'd subtly wipe his index and middle fingers on the saliva. Two wet fingers on top, a dry thumb underneath, and Roe was ready. He compared it to squeezing a peach pit or watermelon seed with your fingertips.

"The idea is to get part of your grip wet, and the other dry," he said. "When the ball leaves your hand, it slips off your wet fingers and clings, just tiny-like, to the dry part of your thumb. The ball jumps on account of it. If it's a good 'un, it drops like a dead duck just when it crosses the plate."

Roe's confession only confirmed his reputation. As Stan Musial wrote decades later, "I'd always be first-pitch hitting against Roe, because when he had two strikes on you, he'd usually load up, and I hated to get a shower." Anticipation of the spitter helped Roe, and he knew how to destroy evidence. He was never caught in the act.

"Preacher was a psychologist—he would psyche guys out," Erskine says. "They thought the spitter was coming every pitch, practically, and half the game they'd be saying to the umpire, 'Look at the ball, look at the ball!' So the umpire would call for the ball, and Preacher would stomp around and look at his hand like, 'Uh-oh, you probably got me this time,' and then instead of tossing the ball in, he'd roll it to the umpire on the ground!"

Like steroid users decades later, Roe stayed ahead of the cops and thrived. But his pang of regret to Erskine—at least for going public and bursting his cloud of mystery—showed that he knew what he had done. The specter of the dark arts would indeed follow Roe to his grave; when he died in 2008, the word "Spitball" appeared in the headline of his *New York Times* obituary.

Spitballs and scuffed balls are something like the Wonder Twins of pitches. They don't really belong in the team picture, like Superman, Batman, and the rest. But they're two of a kind, they're constantly shifting shapes, and lots of folks would rather not admit to their existence.

They're also illegal, but they didn't start that way. After two chaotic decades or so, the spitball was banned for 1920, the same year the country went dry under Prohibition. The rule simply turned the mound into a speakeasy, with many pitchers going undercover to get the same slippery edge as their predecessors.

The physics behind the spitball is simple enough: when the ball slides off wet fingers, it loses backspin and therefore rotates less—something like a knuckleball, which should not rotate at all, or a forkball tumbling in its final plunge.

Defacing the surface of a ball produces the same kind of effect—added movement, to the opposite side of the scuff. This also dates to the game's early days. Imagine what the baseballs looked like in the early twentieth century:

"We'd play a whole game with one ball, if it stayed in the park," said Wahoo Sam Crawford, a Hall of Famer who played from 1899 to 1917, in *The Glory of Their Times*. "Lopsided, and black, and full of tobacco and licorice stains. The pitchers used to have it all their way back then."

Crawford hit often against Jack Chesbro, who won 41 games for the Highlanders (now the Yankees) in 1904 while throwing almost nothing but spitters. Four years later, Ed Walsh of the White Sox won 40 and worked 464 innings; in between, he dominated the 1906 World Series. The spitter helped Walsh to a 1.82 career ERA—the best in baseball history for pitchers with at least 1,000 innings.

"I think that ball disintegrated on the way to the plate and the catcher put it back together again," Crawford said. "I swear, when it went past the plate it was just the spit went by."

Nineteenth-century pitchers experimented with spitballs, too. Bobby Mathews, a curveball pioneer of the 1870s and 1880s, would spit on his palm and apply the saliva to a specific area. Umpire Hank O'Day, who had been a pitcher in Mathews's time, wrote of this in *Baseball Magazine* in 1908: "In the course of two or three innings, the ball would be perfectly black except in the spot where it was rubbed and there it would be perfectly white."

Mathews had a few big years, but apparently not enough for his pitch to spread. For that, it took a playful and perceptive minor leaguer, George Hildebrand, who wasn't even a pitcher. Hildebrand—who later served 22 years as an AL umpire—played briefly in the outfield for Brooklyn in 1902, the same year he was teammates in Providence with a young righty named Frank Corridon. Fooling around with a wet and soggy ball while warming up on a drizzly day, Corridon pegged his catcher in the shins. Hildebrand noticed and encouraged Corridon to "shoot 'em in faster." Hildebrand and Corridon both continued experimenting with the pitch, and when Hildebrand joined a team in Sacramento later that season, he shared the idea with another pitcher.

That pitcher, Elmer Stricklett, would be the Johnny Appleseed of the spitball. When a group of major leaguers visited for an exhibition series, Stricklett captivated them with his spitball, and he proudly spread the secret. In spring training of 1904, he passed it on to two future Hall of Famers who propelled the pitch to prominence.

Stricklett pitched in the White Sox' chain then, but was loaned to a New Orleans team for an exhibition with the Yankees. Chesbro took notice of the spitball, and Stricklett encouraged him to learn it. Mostly, though, he had made Walsh his project that spring in Marlin, Texas. Walsh didn't even know what the spitball was when Stricklett suggested it.

"He showed me what he meant and threw the spitball, and I saw something!" Walsh would tell the *Courant Magazine* in 1956. "It broke two ways, straight down and out."

Stricklett instructed Walsh to place his fingers on a wet spot between the seams and let the ball slip out. The two were not teammates long—Stricklett pitched only once for Chicago—but Walsh worked on his parting gift for two years before deciding to trust it in 1906. Sharp-eyed opponents could tell when Walsh was about to throw a spitter, because his cap would bob from the movement of his jaw when he wet his fingertips behind his glove. But it couldn't have been much of a problem: for a seven-year stretch, through 1912, no pitcher had more strikeouts than Walsh, and only Christy Mathewson had more wins.

The spitter was legal throughout Walsh's career. Just before his death in 1959, he railed against the injustice of its ban to the *Fort Lauderdale News:*

"Everything else in the game favors the hitter. Livelier baseballs, smaller ball parks. They've practically got the poor pitchers working in strait jackets. Those guys have the right to make a living, too."

Walsh said curveballs, not spitters, hurt arms, and that knuckleballs were more prone to hit batters. He said he admired his successors for breaking an unjust law.

"Some people call 'em cheaters," Walsh said. "They're not. They're just guys doing everything they can to win."

That's one way to think about it. Satchel Paige offered another: "I never threw an illegal pitch," he said. "The trouble is, once in a while I toss one that ain't never been seen by this generation."

The ethics of spitters and scuffed balls offer a window to a kind of logic that seems convoluted, yet makes perfect sense to many in the game. To Keith Hernandez, whose Mets were flummoxed in the 1986 playoffs by Houston's Mike Scott, the method of subterfuge is everything: do something illicit away from the field—corking a bat, injecting steroids—and that's cheating. Do something on the field, in front of everyone, and get away with it? As Hernandez wrote in his book, *Pure Baseball:* "More power to you."

Orel Hershiser nods and laughs at the distinction between cheating and its benign cousin, gamesmanship. "Oh, I understand," he says, "if you can be a magician." Hershiser doesn't quite buy it, and offers this definition:

"A pitcher is cheating when he puts a certain spin on the ball but the ball does something unnatural for that spin. That's cheating. Because a hitter hits off of spin and release and trajectory, so he's reading all of those things and hitting what he predicts the ball is going to do because of what you've told him from the spin and the release and the trajectory. So if I put Vaseline on the ball, which creates a completely different spin for the release and trajectory, and that makes the ball dive because of that—OK, then that's cheating. If I cut the ball and the ball has a certain spin but now it does double the movement it should for that amount of spin, that's cheating."

When Larry Andersen would be accused of scuffing the ball, he felt both flattered and offended. It happened to Andersen frequently, because he played for the 1986 Astros and had wicked movement on his pitches. But he swears he left the funny stuff on the side.

"I could go out to the bullpen right now and scuff it and make it do stuff," Andersen says. "But mentally and emotionally, it wasn't right. I played with a lot of guys who didn't always go by the rules, but for me, I just couldn't do it. I couldn't get it out of my head that I was cheating if I did it."

As manager of the Chiba Lotte Marines, Bobby Valentine was mystified by his pitchers' attitude toward using a doctored ball. In Japan, it is just not done.

"The code of honor that all Japanese pitchers pitch by concerning the ball is that it has to be a perfect sphere," Valentine says. "So they use balls right out of the box. We rub 'em up to make 'em dirty, but if the ball is ever dirty there, if it's ever scuffed, if it ever has a piece of pine tar from the bat on it, it's illegal to throw—and they don't do illegal."

Pushing the legal limit is a personal decision, and players generally stay out of each other's way on those matters. That code explains the silence that helped stoke the steroid era; if you suspected your rival of juicing, you kept it to yourself—partly because you wouldn't want anyone snooping around your clubhouse, either.

For all the stories of players howling from the dugout about scuffing or spitball suspects, most of the time they kept quiet for one simple reason:

"Because there was always somebody on your team that probably did something, too," Joe Torre says. "Guys used to come back and bitch about it and you'd say, 'Hit the dry side.' What are you gonna do?"

Now, as the chief baseball officer for MLB, Torre must punish pitchers who flout the rules. Few cases come up, though, partly because players allow subtle rule-bending. Most will accept some chicanery—like applying something tacky to the pitcher's fingers, to get a better grip—as long as it's done right.

"Just don't make it blatant," says A. J. Ellis, the veteran catcher. "Because when you make it blatant you're basically saying that we don't care, we're not afraid of you, we're not afraid you guys are gonna get upset about this. We don't respect you; we don't really think you guys are worthy of hiding anything."

The movement to outlaw the spitter, and other forms of doctored baseballs, was rooted at least partly in business. In the 1919 regular season, Babe Ruth swatted 29 home runs in his final season with the Red Sox, stoking the public's appetite for offense. Taking away a pitcher's weapon could only help offense—which, in turn, would be popular with fans. And removing *that kind* of weapon, which was unsavory by nature, would signal that baseball was actively striving for a clean game. That, perhaps, could help the image of a sport still trying to appeal to a wealthier class of fan.

Mostly, though, the whole thing was just kind of gross.

"There is nothing very pleasant in the sight of a big fellow emptying the contents of his face upon a ball," wrote *Sporting Life* magazine. "There's something creepy and 'slimy' in the very suggestion of the spitball."

That piece—quoted by Dan Gutman in *It Ain't Cheatin' If You Don't Get Caught*—was written in 1908, and one of many columns pleading for an end to so-called freak deliveries. Pitchers were making a mockery of the game, as Rob Neyer has written, scrambling to top each other with new and creative ways to deface the ball. "Frankly," Neyer wrote, "it became a joke."

Barney Dreyfuss, the influential Pirates owner who helped create the first World Series, led the banishment brigade. Before the 1918 season, he warned pitcher Burleigh Grimes that the spitball would soon be banned, and told him to learn something new in the minors. When Grimes refused, Dreyfuss traded him to Brooklyn. Grimes would return to the Pirates after 10 years and 177 victories, and said decades later that pitchers basically ruined all the fun with their unrelenting hijinks.

"The real reason the spitter was barred," Grimes said, "was because pitchers were roughing the ball with pop bottle caps, sandpaper, emery and whatnot, ripping a stitch or two of the seam with razor blades and such, and discoloring the ball with tobacco, licorice, coffee and in other ways."

Sometimes, though, they made such discoveries by accident. Warming up under the stands on a rainy day in Atlanta in 1907, minor leaguer Russ Ford threw a pitch that struck a post behind his catcher, Ed Sweeney. When Sweeney returned the ball, Ford noticed a rough spot from where it had struck the post. When he pitched the ball again, it veered sharply, away from the scuffed side. Ford knew he was on to something, and worked on the pitch for two years, scuffing the ball with a jagged soda bottle and fooling his teammates in batting practice. Eventually Ford found safer ways to scuff; an umpire said he hid emery paper in a hole in his glove, and Ty Cobb believed he used an emery ring. Ford wanted hitters to think he was throwing the spitter. "He would deliberately show his finger to the batter," Cobb wrote in his memoirs, "and then wet it with salvia."

For a while, it worked. After a one-game cameo in 1909, Ford went 26–6 with a 1.65 ERA for the Highlanders in 1910—the only season ever by a Yankees pitcher with that many wins and such a low ERA. He managed to keep the pitch a secret until 1913, when Cy Falkenberg of Cleveland caught on. It spread from there, and after the Yankees' Ray Keating and the Cubs' Jimmy Lavender were found with emery paper on the mound in 1914, the pitch was banned. Ford and Falkenberg quickly faded from the scene.

A similar fate befell Hod Eller, who found a "shine ball" with the Reds in 1917. On a dark, damp day at the Polo Grounds, Eller noticed his pitch behaving strangely after he had vigorously rubbed off the dirt from one side. He quickly learned that by doing this and throwing hard, he could make the ball rise—three to four inches vertically, he said, somewhat dubiously, or five to six inches to the side.

"I used to reverse the break sometimes by holding the smooth spot on the under surface of the ball," Eller told *Baseball Magazine*. "You could get a terrific drop to the ball by holding it that way, somewhat like the break of a spit-ball and much more effective than the average curve."

The AL president Ban Johnson swiftly ordered an end to the shine ball, an edict as toothless as an 1897 rule forbidding players from defacing the ball. Life was grand for Eller, who went 19–9 in 1919 and beat the White Sox twice in the tainted World Series. Chicago's Eddie Cicotte also threw the shine ball—he rubbed it against colorless paraffin wax on his pants—but he conspired with gamblers to lose. So did Lefty Williams, whom Eller beat twice. Eller retired Shoeless Joe Jackson, another of the "Eight Men Out," on a grounder to end the farce in Game 8.

The Black Sox scandal would not explode until 1920, but the curious performances had at least stirred suspicion in the immediate aftermath. Coupled with the financial incentives in boosting offense, the atmosphere was ripe for a rule change. By spring training, this had become law:

At no time during the progress of the game shall the pitcher be allowed to: (1) Apply a foreign substance of any kind to the ball; (2) Expectorate either on the ball or his glove; (3) Rub the ball on his glove, person, or clothing; (4) Deface the ball in any manner; (5) or to deliver what is called the "shine" ball, "spit" ball, "mud" ball, or "emery" ball. For violation of any part of this rule the umpire shall at once order the pitcher from the game, and in addition he shall be automatically suspended for a period of 10 days, on notice from the president of the league.

Each team could designate up to two pitchers who would still be allowed to use the pitch in 1920. That year's World Series was a spitball extravaganza: Grimes tossed a shutout for Brooklyn and Stan Coveleski won three complete games to lead Cleveland to its first title. As the rule stood, though, Grimes, Coveleski, and the 15 other eligible spitballers would suddenly be forced to give up their best pitch forever.

In a letter to NL owners, Bill Doak, a 20-game winner for the Cardinals, argued that barring the pitch would "deprive all these pitchers of their greatest power," and Grimes made similar pleas through the press. They met a sympathetic audience: the NL voted 6–2 to allow the designated spitballers to use the pitch for the rest of their careers, and the AL soon agreed.

Three of the grandfathered spitballers—Coveleski, Grimes, and Red Faber, who used tobacco juice on the ball—wound up in the Hall of Fame. Grimes would be a World Series hero for the Cardinals in 1931, nearly spinning a no-hitter before President Hoover in Game 3 and then working into the ninth, despite severe abdominal pain, to win Game 7. Grimes's secret: original slippery elm bark imported by his father from his native Wisconsin. Grimes had run out of his supply, wrote his biographer, Joe Niese, and the drugstore-brand tablets in St. Louis made him nauseous.

Grimes outlasted all the other legal spitballers, retiring in 1934. Frank Shellenback, a marginal White Sox pitcher who was left off their list, flung legal spitters in the Pacific Coast League through 1938. That September, in Williamston, North Carolina, tenant farmers Evan and Ruby Perry welcomed a son named Gaylord into the world. He would master spitball skulduggery and ride its greasy path to Cooperstown.

"Ballplayers don't think a good spitballer is a criminal," Perry would write, many years later. "They think he's an artist."

———————

The ban on doctored baseballs simply sent the practice deeper underground. As a catcher for the Milwaukee Braves in the early 1960s, a young Joe Torre called spitters for a veteran, Lew Burdette. But that was all Torre knew.

"You didn't know where it was coming from," he says. "I mean, Burdette threw a spitter and I caught him, but I couldn't tell you where he got it, because he wouldn't tell anybody. I knew what it was going to do, but I had no clue where he got it."

Perhaps he got it from Grimes, though both men denied it. After his playing career, Grimes coached in the Yankees' minor league system in the late 1940s, just as Burdette was coming through. In a book interview with former commissioner Fay Vincent, Burdette said he asked Grimes how to throw a spitball, but Grimes refused to say.

"But I'll tell you one thing: you can go through gyrations and all," Grimes told him. "If you can get hitters—who are egotistical so-and-sos, you know—if you can get one of the first three guys in the first inning to go back and complain, by the fifth inning the batboy will be yelling, 'Look at the ball!'"

Burdette would fluster hitters by holding his hand in front of his mouth, touching his forehead, fiddling with the ball in his glove, adjusting his cap and wetting his fingertips on his tongue. After Grimes watched Burdette on TV, he told him, "You got it down good." Richie Ashburn complained constantly to Burdette, never cursing but accusing him on the field of throwing a "crapping spitter." Finally, Burdette complied, digging the ball into the dirt on the mound to overload one side with mud. It zagged under Ashburn's bat for strike three.

"Now that's a crapping spitter!" Burdette told him.

"I'll never complain again, Lew," Ashburn replied. "I'll never complain again."

Burdette was the hero of the 1957 World Series for the Milwaukee Braves, completing all three of his victories over the Yankees, including a Game 5 shutout against Whitey Ford. Ford had beaten Warren Spahn in the opener, and the two matched up twice again the next fall. Ford and Burdette had been teammates—under Grimes's tutelage—in the Yankees' farm system, and Burdette taught Ford his trick.

"Did you ever notice how many times Whitey used to tie his shoelace during the game?" Spahn told Vincent. "Because Burdette taught him how to throw a mud ball. And he'd wet the ball and put it on the ground and it was a little heavier on one side than the other, and he'd make the ball move because of that."

Spahn said he toyed with Burdette's spitter in the bullpen, but used it just once in a game and allowed a home run.

"Then I talked to Burdette about it and he says, 'You got to have two wet fingers and a dry thumb,'" Spahn said. "I remember him saying that so much."

In *Slick*, his 1987 memoir with Phil Pepe, Ford said Burdette taught him the mud ball late in his career; he gave no exact date, but hinted that it may have been 1963, when he went 24–7. Ford explained that he "needed something to help me survive," and said he would simply wet the ball with saliva and touch it to the dirt while grabbing the rosin bag. He threw the pitch as hard as he could, with the dirt on top as he released it. The pitch behaved like a screwball, sinking away from a righty but rotating more than a pure spitter. If a hitter asked for the ball before he threw it, Ford said, he would lightly brush it against his pants leg, knocking off the dirt.

The mud ball emboldened Ford. Seeking a new challenge, he thought of a way to scuff the ball while rubbing it up. One current major league pitching coach can do this with his fingernails, but Ford had a friend pay a jeweler $55 for a ring with a rasp—a half-inch long and a quarter-inch wide—welded onto it.

"Why would anybody have any use for something like this?" the jeweler asked the friend, who told him just to shut up and make it. The handiwork delighted Ford.

"I would put the part of the ring with the rasp underneath my finger," he wrote. "On top, I covered the ring with flesh-colored Band-Aids, so you couldn't tell from a distance that I had anything on my finger. Now it was easy to just rub the baseball against the rasp and scratch it on one side. One little nick was all it took to get the baseball to sail and dip like crazy."

Opponents suspected Ford, but umpires tended not to push too hard. Bill Fischer, a journeyman reliever of the era, recalls sweating profusely with the bases loaded one day in Cleveland. From behind he heard a voice: "This'd be a good time to load one up, Fish." It was the second base umpire. Now imagine the deference shown to a pitcher like Ford.

"There was one time when Whitey was scuffing up the ball and the umpire came out, and he knew," teammate Jim Bouton said a few years ago. "I forget who it was, but he was one of those old-timer guys who's not gonna be a wise guy or a big shot—this is Whitey Ford, he's one of the greats. A certain amount of respect is due.

"So he went to the mound and the conversation went, 'Uh, Whitey, I see the ring there. I tell you what, what you need to do is call time out and go in and change your jock strap. And when you come back, don't have the ring on.' He was giving him a cover to do that.

"That was just part of the deal: if you could sneak it in there, it was considered to be clever. It isn't a criminal offense or anything like that. If you could get away with it, then do it. And everybody else, if they could have done it, would have done the same thing."

Ford had other ways of getting an edge, sometimes literally. His catcher, Elston Howard, might scrape the ball against a sharpened clasp on his shin guards; a contemporary of Ford's, the Hall of Famer Jim Bunning, had used a similar technique with his belt buckle. Ford also mixed baby oil, turpentine, and resin to form a sticky substance he could use to grip the ball in cold weather. To conceal it, he hid it in a bottle of roll-on deodorant he would keep in his warm-up jacket. Boys being boys, Mickey Mantle once swiped the bottle, put it in Yogi Berra's locker, and howled as Berra got his arms stuck to his sides.

The most notorious AL cheater of the time, though, was probably John Wyatt, a reliever who earned 20 saves for Boston's Impossible Dream pennant winners of 1967. Wyatt was so committed to subterfuge that he was said to smother Vaseline nearly everywhere—even in his mouth. He finally came clean nearly 20 years later, to the *Fort Lauderdale Sun-Sentinel,* with some sound logic.

"I cheated, but I faced some tough hitters," Wyatt said. "Had to do something against those cats. They could make a guy look real bad."

———

In 1968, the year he threw 58⅔ consecutive scoreless innings, the Dodgers' Don Drysdale capitalized on his (accurate) reputation for throwing the occasional slippery pitch. In a commercial for Vitalis hair tonic, Drysdale looked in for the sign against a Giants hitter. When the hitter called time out, Drysdale casually removed his cap and ran his fingers through his hair.

"Greaseball! Greaseball!" cried Herman Franks, the Giants' manager, storming from his dugout. "See him rub his hair! He's gonna throw a greaseball, that's illegal!"

A disgusted Drysdale grimaced, tossed his glove on the grass, and retreated to the clubhouse. There, he found a bottle of Vitalis, returned to the mound and held the bottle high for all to see.

"Vitalis has no grease, and spreads easily through your hair," the announcer said. "If we all used Vitalis, we could help put an end to the greaseball."

Poor Gaylord Perry. He had the same idea as Drysdale, but his agent pitched it to the wrong company. Vaseline turned down Perry for an endorsement deal by sniffing: "We soothe babies' asses, not baseballs."

Ever resourceful, Perry found other ways to monetize his money pitch. In 1974, he published a confessional memoir, *Me and the Spitter*, with Bob Sudyk. If it hurt his Hall of Fame chances, the damage was minimal. When Perry retired in 1983, just two other pitchers, Walter Johnson and Steve Carlton, had 300 wins and 3,500 strikeouts. He made it to Cooperstown on his third try, in 1991.

As Grimes planted at least some seeds for Burdette's trickery, another legal spitballer helped Perry. After his long career in the Pacific Coast League, Frank Shellenback served as a supervisor and scout for the Giants. He taught the secrets of his illicit pitches to Bob Shaw—"I do *not* recommend their use," Shaw wrote in his pitching manual—and Shaw passed them on to Perry at Giants spring training in 1964. Watching Shaw throw his spitball, Perry wrote, "I knew how Tom Edison felt when he discovered the electric light."

"He wet his two fingers, placed them on top of the ball, wound and fired," Perry wrote. "And down it went."

In Shaw, a future pitching coach, Perry had found a seasoned and savvy mentor. By then Shaw had played seven seasons, won a World Series game, and saved an All-Star Game. He and Perry were inseparable.

"He was a good teammate," Perry said in 2018. "He told me how his career went, and I paid attention to him. He was an excellent setup pitcher. I learned a great deal by watching him set hitters up, good hitters that he got out very easily."

In the musty files of the library at the old *Sports Illustrated* offices in Manhattan, a sheet of notes for a 1973 article included a primer from Shaw on how pitchers load spitballs:

They apply whatever they use to the forehead, the back of the wrist, the forearm, the side of the pant leg, or the belt. The idea is to change the location, so when umpires look in one spot, it's not there. You can hit your glove and remove it from your wrist in one motion. You never load up with more than you can remove with one swipe. When you do apply it to the hand, you put it on the second and third fingers. That way, you can pick up the rosin bag with the thumb and index finger and not disturb your load.

Shaw detailed some of the loading agents: slippery-elm lozenges, saliva, Vaseline, or K-Y Jelly, the water-soluble lubricant. He said it was also essential to use plenty of mannerisms to bother the hitters. By 1973 Perry was expertly applying all these lessons, inspired by frank words from Shaw in the bullpen early in the 1964 season: "Gaylord, I don't think you've got enough right now to be a starting pitcher. There comes a time in a man's life when he must decide what's important. He must provide the best way he can for his family."

For Perry, a 25-year-old mop-up reliever, that meant putting the spitter into action. He had a 4.50 career ERA when he came in to pitch the bottom of the thirteenth in the second game of a doubleheader on May 31, 1964, against the Mets at Shea Stadium. Ten slippery, scoreless innings later, a baseball outlaw was born.

Perry would lick his fingers, legally, and pretend to dry them off with the rosin bag (a move he would practice with his daughter Amy's bean bag). When his mouth got dry, a teammate gave him a slippery-elm lozenge. When the first baseman, Orlando Cepeda, got a ball to end the inning, he rolled it on the grass to dry it off. When a fight broke out in the stands, diverting people's attention, Perry simply spit on the ball.

"Nice going, kid," Shaw told Perry. "You made it."

Perry called his spitter the super-sinker, and that is how it often behaved. It veered so hard, down and in on righties, that some refused to use their favorite bats for fear that Perry would break them. He learned to disrupt hitters with a series of six gyrations before the pitch, touching his hat, hair, ear, neck, wrist, and some part of his uniform.

Like any smooth criminal, he constantly searched for new strategies. At the 1966 All-Star Game, on a broiling day in St. Louis, Perry noticed Sandy Koufax with red-hot Capsolin rubbed on his pitching arm. Koufax needed the searing heat to distract him from his aching elbow; Perry needed it to sweat more.

"Capsolin is like putting on a blowtorch," says Dave Duncan, who caught Perry with Cleveland and later coached him with Seattle. "He'd lay on the training table and the trainer would smear his entire back with a coat of it. You couldn't even go in the room, it was so strong. Shoot, I don't know how he did it. I couldn't even put a drop of it on my shoulder without dying."

Perry was so furtive that, for a while, he strictly guarded his methods, even when another famous trickster begged him for his secrets at the 1970 All-Star Game. "Gaylord, tell me, where do you get it?" Richard Nixon asked, nudging Perry in the ribs with his elbow. "Mr. President," Perry replied, "there are some things you just can't tell the people for their own good."

Nixon erupted in laughter—Perry was, indeed, far better at concealing information than the president. When the book came out in 1974, Perry swore he was reformed, and Duncan says Perry indeed threw forkballs that season, not the spitters he had thrown the year before. But his spitball hiatus didn't last long.

Two years later, with the Rangers, Perry compared pitches with Bert Blyleven, a fellow future Hall of Famer. First Blyleven showed Perry his curveball.

"Then it was my turn to lube up in the bullpen, and it was like a new toy, like Christmas time," Blyleven says. "The ball's sinking, no seams, you know. The ball's slipping out of your hand, and all that slippage creates so much torque on your elbow, and the next day my elbow was barking. But Gaylord was a mule. He was a strong, strong son of a bitch."

Perry bounced to San Diego in 1978 and won his second Cy Young Award. He befriended a young setup man, John D'Acquisto, who encouraged Perry to run for exercise. Perry begged off. "I've got the magic pitch," he said, and D'Acquisto knew what made it work.

"You couldn't find it, because it was K-Y Jelly," D'Acquisto says. "K-Y Jelly dissipates, and he had it everywhere. There wasn't one spot, and it just looked like beads of sweat. Are you gonna throw a guy out for sweating? What Gaylord told me was, 'Johnny, you don't need much, just a little bit.' And I go, 'Yeah, but you've got it everywhere,' and he says, 'Well, that's so it doesn't look like you're getting it from one spot.'"

Three years later, D'Acquisto was trying to hang on with the Angels, who thought he was losing his velocity. He found a tube of K-Y Jelly in his locker, a flashing red light from the pitching coach, Tom Morgan. "You need to start using this," Morgan said, but D'Acquisto says he didn't have the right arm action to throw it. A year later, he had pitched his last game. If only he could have harnessed Perry's pitch.

"He was a beauty, man," D'Acquisto says. "He was a beauty."

––––––––––

Even in retirement, pitchers suspected of doctoring balls rarely like to talk about it. Don Sutton (who was sometimes called "Black & Decker," after the power tool company) once threatened to sue umpire Doug Harvey, who ejected him from a game for allegedly defacing a ball. Sutton was happy to talk about his curveball, but not about scuffing.

Phil Regan turned eighty in 2017 and was still coaching in the minors for the Mets. One morning that spring, I asked him about his well-known reputation for slick deliveries. This was a man who once dropped a Vaseline tube from his jacket pocket on the bases. Yet, at first, he demurred.

"Who told you that?" he barked, then dove into a story about a game at Wrigley Field on August 18, 1968. Pitching for the Cubs against Cincinnati, Regan was repeatedly cited for throwing illegal pitches. Twice, when the batter put the ball in play for an out, the plate umpire Chris Pelekoudas ordered him back to the plate to hit again. It was quite a scene, Regan said; his catcher was tossed from the game, but he kept pitching because the umpires found nothing on his cap or glove. The next day, league president Warren Giles flew to town for an emergency meeting and promptly undercut the umpires, holding a news conference and praising Regan as a "fine Christian gentleman." One little problem: the umpires were right about Regan.

"They said they called 14 illegal pitches," Regan said. "They missed three!"

Then he winked, smiled, and walked away.

Policing pitchers was a tedious and somewhat humiliating process for umpires, who could rarely catch pitchers in the act. Before that 1968 season, baseball had tried to strengthen the 1920 rule by decreeing that any pitcher going to his mouth before delivering a pitch would be ejected. The leagues hoped to eliminate fruitless mound searches and speed up the game, but by mid-March, after a rash of spring training ejections, the rule was amended again: the penalty would be a balk with runners on base, or a ball without, and a pitcher could still blow on his hand or lick his fingers, just not while standing on the dirt. Six years later, umpires were told they could issue a spitball warning without evidence, just by observing something strange in the flight of the ball.

Yet for all of that, few pitchers were actually caught in the act. One of the most notorious, and hapless, perpetrators ended up teaching pitching for a living: Rick Honeycutt, the future coach for the Dodgers. It was the last day of September in 1980, the end of an All-Star season gone awry. After starting 6–0, Honeycutt had gone 4–17 for the last-place Mariners. He was starting in Kansas City against the World Series–bound Royals. On his way to warm up in the bullpen, Honeycutt passed a bulletin board. Foolish inspiration struck.

"I saw a thumbtack and I was like, 'Well, I know that would scuff up a ball,'" Honeycutt says. "You hear about guys doing certain things, and you think, 'What the heck, why not?' It was just a stupid and idiotic move, really."

Honeycutt knew only the basics: when a ball is scuffed, you put the scuff on the opposite side of the way you want it to move. But he had never practiced it before, and had no plan for disguising the thumbtack. He tried to stick it through his glove, but when it wouldn't pierce the leather, he taped it on with a flesh-colored bandage.

For two innings, Honeycutt tried nothing. Then, with two out in the third, he scraped a ball and delivered it to Willie Wilson, who smacked it to right for a triple. On the next ball Honeycutt sliced, George Brett singled.

"Then Kunkel comes out," Honeycutt says. That would be Bill Kunkel, the very last umpire you'd want behind the plate if you were nervously trying to scuff a ball with no clue how to do it. Kunkel had pitched for the 1963 Yankees, with Whitey Ford.

"He said he'd loaded up a ball once in a while when he was pitching," says Jim Evans, a fellow AL umpire at the time. "We would chat and he would say, 'Here's a guy you gotta watch, this is what he does.'"

Honeycutt might not have been a suspect before, but these she-nanigans were just too obvious. Kunkel ejected him, and Honeycutt panicked. "They can't kick me out of the game forever, can they?" he asked a coach. Honeycutt was relieved to get a fine and the standard 10-day suspension, but he never pitched for the Mariners again. They traded the young lefty to Texas that winter and he went on to pitch 17 more seasons.

The opposite of Honeycutt, in every way, was Mike Scott. While Honeycutt was clumsy, ineffective, and easily caught, Scott was cunning, overpowering, and elusive. In four years as a Met, from 1979 to 1982, he was 14–27 with a 4.64 earned run average. He went to the Astros, won a Cy Young Award, nearly won another, notched 306 strikeouts in a season, threw a division-clinching no-hitter, and got his number retired.

Here is an alternate summary of Scott, from a former major league All-Star of the era who saw Scott's image on TV in the Fenway Park clubhouse in 2015: "Mike Scott, when he was with the Mets, he was the worst motherfucking pitcher in the league. As soon as he started scuffing, it all changed. He said 'split-finger.' Split-finger, my ass!"

The cranky ex-player was crudely accurate, in a way: in those first four seasons, among all major league pitchers with at least 350 innings, Scott was indeed dead last in the category ERA+—he performed nearly 25 percent worse than the average pitcher of the time. But Scott did learn a split-finger fastball, as described in that chapter. That was the pitch that dove into the dirt. The pitch that nearly vanquished the Mets in the 1986 NLCS was something different.

"It was like sandpaper, chicken scratch," Keith Hernandez says. "It was all right there, one side. It overloaded one side when he threw it, whichever side had the scratch, and he'd make it run this way, and he'd turn it over and make it run the other way. He was doing it on his fastball. It would move a foot and a half, trying to get you to chase. I never saw a guy whose fastball ran that much—and he threw 97, 98, and he knew exactly what he was doing with it, too."

In Game 1 of the NLCS, Scott shut out the Mets with 14 strikeouts. He threw another complete game four days later, allowing three hits and a run. The Mets collected every ball Scott pitched that came into their dugout, and claimed to have dozens scuffed in the same spot. Yet

Dutch Rennert, the plate umpire that night, said the Mets never asked him to check a ball that hadn't already hit the dirt. Rennert said he checked at least once an inning, and found nothing.

"I believe the pitches Mike Scott are throwing are legal, and I believe it with all my heart," Doug Harvey, who worked the plate for Game 1, told the writer George White. "During the season I must have checked 65 to 70 balls that Mike Scott threw, and not one showed any sign of scuff marks."

The Mets believed the umpires couldn't catch Scott because one of his fielders was scuffing the ball for him—and, Hernandez says, because Sutton's threatened lawsuit, in 1978, had essentially handcuffed baseball's cops. (Sutton withdrew it, having made his point when the league backed down without a fine or suspension.)

Only by winning Game 6 at the Astrodome, in 16 wild innings, did the Mets survive the series. Had they played a Game 7 and faced Scott—who was named Series MVP—they knew they had no chance.

"Mike Scott intimidated a ball club that did not get intimidated by anybody," said Bobby Ojeda, who won Game 2 of that series. "All he had to do was throw his glove on the mound and we'd go, 'OK, we don't want to play today.' But he was a master at making that thing work, which is kind of cheating, you know? But you've still gotta make it work. It's like Tom Brady with the deflated footballs. You've still gotta make the throw."

Alan Ashby, the Astros' catcher in that series, speaks in amazement about Scott's splitter, the way he didn't even have to spread his fingers very wide to get devastating action.

"But the splitter was a part of the arsenal," Ashby says. "It was a combination of stuff, and I'll leave it at that."

I suggested that maybe Scott does not get enough credit for how great he was, since he is so widely remembered for alleged scuffing. Ashby smiled, uncomfortably. He didn't know how to respond.

"Well, I don't know," Ashby replied. "He's got a Cy Young to enjoy. He's playing golf every day. Hard for me to answer and be real with you."

Scott has never admitted to scuffing, exactly, and rarely appears in public. The closest he came was in an MLB Network documentary about the 1986 postseason: "They can believe whatever they want to believe," Scott said. "Every ball that hits the ground has something on it. . . . I've thrown balls that were scuffed but I haven't scuffed every ball that I've thrown."

———————

The Mets went on to stage another epic sixth game in the World Series against Boston. Facing elimination at Shea, they were down to their last strike when a wild pitch by Bob Stanley skipped under Mookie Wilson's legs and past catcher Rich Gedman, scoring the tying run just before Bill Buckner's infamous error. Ron Darling said he has always assumed, because of the way the ball moved and Stanley's well-known reputation for throwing a spitter, that Stanley had, indeed, loaded one up for the fateful wild pitch. That's sort of how it sounded when I asked Gedman about it, during his final season in the majors with the Cardinals in 1992.

I had been captivated by the 1986 World Series—who wasn't?—and was writing a piece about it for my homemade magazine. I remember Gedman speaking very quietly and thoughtfully.

"You're probably the first guy that's asked me that since about a week after it happened," he said. "It was just one of those pitches that did something it normally doesn't do. Bob Stanley's a sinkerball pitcher. I was waiting for a sinker and got what appeared to be a cutter or a slider. I don't know if it was the grip on the ball or what.

"I look back and I see the pitch in my mind and there's no business I had missing that ball. But the pitch itself did not—it's like getting crossed up in a way. I felt like Bob Stanley took a lot of heat for no reason at all. If I had to see that pitch on TV, I'd say that was a passed ball and not a wild pitch. But I also know what happened."

Stanley has coached for years in the Blue Jays organization, and I saw him a while back at spring training. He talked about his sinker, and said he threw it about 90 percent of the time because breaking balls were harder on his arm. When I asked if he ever threw a spitter, Stanley was surprisingly candid.

"Yeah, I cheated, sure," he said, explaining that he simply loaded sweat on his fingers by wiping his brow. "You just grip the ball without any seams, just flat."

He talked a bit about how times had changed, how a pitcher like Perry—"Oh my God, he had all kinds of shit in his mouth," he said—would have a tougher time today. For Stanley, who pitched from 1977 to 1989, it was fairly easy.

"When I threw it, they never saw me do it," he said. "When I wanted them to think a spitter was coming, I'd throw 'em a palmball instead. I'd get away with it because I had a good sinker. They could never catch me because it was sweat, it wasn't like Vaseline. If they checked [someone else's] ball, they could feel the Vaseline, but this was just sweat—'I don't know, it dripped off my fingers.'"

He said he would only throw it with two strikes, never on the first pitch. That was my signal to go for it, to ask about the pitch I'd always wondered about, from the moment it left his hand to Gedman's heartfelt recollection to Darling's assertion. Here goes:

"What about the wild pitch in Game 6?" I asked. "That was with two strikes—was that a spitter?"

"That was a fastball in," Stanley said. "They set up outside, it went in."

Oh. Just an ordinary fastball.

In my mind, I could hear the losing horn from *The Price Is Right*, the jingle they play when someone falls short of the big prize. If a guy with a two-strike spitter really did let one slip at the absolute worst moment in 1986, I guess we'll never know.

————

The next year was a strange one, marked by a curious single-season spike in home runs and a cluster of ball-doctoring incidents in August. First was the Joe Niekro episode in Anaheim, when Niekro, then with the Twins, emptied his pockets for umpires and flung an emery board and sandpaper to the grass. A week later in Philadelphia, umpires found sandpaper glued to the glove of the Phillies' Kevin Gross. Both were suspended 10 games.

Later that month, the Yankees visited the Angels, starting Tommy John against Sutton. A year before, Sutton had earned his 300th victory for the Angels, cheekily telling reporters, "I've been trying legally, and illegally, to get here for years." Given his reputation, and the hot topic in baseball at the time, it was no wonder the Yankees' telecast zoomed in on Sutton throughout the game, focusing on a small patch on the palm of his left hand. When he rubbed up a ball with both hands, was Sutton defacing it?

Jim Palmer, the Hall of Fame Orioles pitcher, had always believed as much. When he lost to Sutton on the final day of the 1982 season, giving Sutton's Brewers the AL East title, Palmer said he noticed scratches across the name of the league president on the balls Sutton threw. At some point in their careers, Palmer said, Sutton told him how he scuffed.

"I said, 'How do you scuff a ball?'" Palmer says. "He said, 'Well, you use 180 sandpaper, you superglue it on your hand and you rub the ball up.' I said, 'I don't rub the ball up.' He said, 'Well, if you want to scratch the ball, you just put it there and rub the ball on it and you've got your scuff.'"

Sutton has denied a version of that story, but that method was on George Steinbrenner's mind as he watched the broadcast. Steinbrenner angrily, and repeatedly, called the Yankees' dugout until reaching manager Lou Piniella. He demanded that Piniella tell the umpires to check Sutton, but Piniella would not. He didn't want the umps checking John, too.

John and Sutton had been teammates, and John was also a frequent target of suspicion. He said he told Piniella to do whatever he wanted that night, because he was clean. And John knew what Sutton was up to, anyway.

"Sutton had a Band-Aid, and the reason he did was because he wanted the Yankee people to respond to him," John says. "I know he did, because I did the same thing to Tony La Russa."

John explained that Piniella had once argued about an Oakland pitcher the night before John's scheduled start. John expected La Russa, the A's manager, to retaliate by asking the umps to check him. That morning, he visited a baseball card store in New Jersey and bought a card of La Russa.

"I had it in my hip pocket and I had a Sharpie," John says. "I wanted the umpires to come out and check me. I was gonna back away, go into my pocket, draw my hand up, and flip the card on the ground. When they picked it up, I was gonna go over to Tony with the pen and say, 'Tony, would you sign this for me please?' But he never checked me! He messed up my time for fame. I would have been on Johnny Carson."

Brian Moehler had no such plans when umpires checked him at Tropicana Field in 1999. Moehler, a Tigers right-hander, was pitching well against the Devil Rays, who thought his pitches were moving suspiciously. Umpires inspected Moehler and may—or may not—have found sandpaper taped to his right thumb. He was suspended 10 days and did not appeal.

So, what was really on his thumb? Moehler still isn't saying.

"Well, it depends who you ask," he says. "One of the umpires said he saw something and the next one said he didn't, and they said they had some balls that had some scuffs on 'em."

Pause.

"Does that stuff go on?" he continues. "Yeah, it does. Do I sit here and say I know how to do it? Yeah, if I had gotten a scuffed ball, I had a pretty good idea how to do it. It's not something that's taught, but as a pitcher you kind of fool around with it, like someone with a knuckleball, you joke around with it, you get a scuffed ball that hits the track or something, you learn where the scuff is and which way to make the ball move.

"So have I ever had a ball that's scuffed that was given to me? I remember I had an umpire one time, the game had gotten out of hand and the ball had hit the track. They always check the balls, obviously, and he brings the ball to me and he goes, 'Have fun!' I was like, 'OK!' Was I aware of how to do it? Oh yeah, I was aware of how to do it. I think a lot of guys are."

Actually, Moehler says, in the moment he was more concerned about his glove, which had metal eyelets around the holes for the laces. Those were once standard on gloves, but are illegal now because pitchers could easily use them to scuff. Moehler got his glove back, no questions asked, and he used it for the rest of his career.

In some ways, he says, his crime helped him. After that, some hitters would always ask the umpires to check the ball.

"I would walk halfway to home plate, flip the ball to the umpire, and then when he gave me another ball I'd stand there and act like I was scuffing it up and walk back to the rubber," Moehler says. "If a hitter went up there thinking I was scuffing the baseball, I had an advantage. Because the hardest thing in sports is hitting a baseball, and he's gotta worry about doing that—but now in the back of his mind, he thinks I'm scuffing it."

Moehler ended up leading the AL in losses in 1999, with 16, and he finished his career well under .500. But he tricked hitters long enough to last 14 seasons in the majors, through 2010, and now scouts amateur talent in Georgia for the Red Sox. Friends say he would make a great pitching coach.

———

The mental edge of a scuffball suspect is nothing new. These words come from Chet Brewer, a star for the Kansas City Monarchs of the Negro National League in the late 1920s, but they sound timeless:

"A cut ball? I got credit for that," he told John Holway in *Black Diamonds*. "If I picked up a rough one, I didn't throw it out of the game. I didn't exactly put the cuts on it myself, but I could pitch it."

Brewer, who died in 1990, said that when he barnstormed against Swede Risberg, one of the banned members of the 1919 White Sox, the balls Risberg brought came pre-scratched. Knowing how to use a scratch was a matter of survival.

"When I learned the screwball, they said, 'Heck, he's scratching the ball,' so I knew that I was getting on them," Brewer added. "I'd face the outfield and rub the ball up, turn around, throw a screwball: 'Oh, he cut it!' But it was more a psychological thing."

Scuffing charges never dogged Mike Mussina, but like any smart pitcher, he would never reject a ball that came to him with a mark. This was Mussina's order for every catcher: if a ball hits the ground, *never* volunteer it to the umpire. Any ball that touches dirt, around the plate or the infield, might be a bar of gold in the pitcher's hand.

"Say a guy hits a ground ball to short and they throw it back to me from first base—as soon as I grab the ball, I'm running my thumb over these," Mussina says. He is holding a ball and referring to the white area within the horseshoe. "Do I have a sinker out of this ball? And if I find one I think's pretty good, I flip it to the other side to see if it's scuffed up on the wrong side."

By that he means the opposite side; if both horseshoe areas are scuffed, they'll counteract each other, to no advantage. If there's a scuff where the seams narrow—the sweet spot—it creates a four-seam sinker, a pitch that spins like a straight fastball but veers away, in the direction opposite the scuff.

But watch out for those high seams.

"If the seams are really high, even if I'm scuffed up just a little bit, they're gonna cause too much resistance naturally," Mussina says. "It's not gonna have enough of an effect to do anything."

A common lament among retired pitchers is that too many balls are now thrown out of play. To them, it underscores a lack of craftsmanship on the mound.

"I've literally seen teammates, when there's a scuff on the ball, they get rid of it," Jamie Moyer says. "They'll say, 'Oh, it does funny stuff,' and you go, 'Wait a minute, that funny stuff can be a benefit to you!' But they don't know how to do it."

Maybe not, but they also rarely get the chance. Hitters are conditioned to ask umpires to discard any ball that skips. Umpires and catchers know this, so catchers tend to have an almost reflexive response: they'll spear a ball from the dirt, transfer it quickly to their throwing hand, and hold it up for the ump to keep or reject.

Some fielders still try: catchers may deliberately short-hop their throws before innings, and outfielders may do the same on routine throws to the infield. But times have changed.

"When I played, a ball hit the dirt, it was still in play," says Chili Davis, who played from 1981 to 1999. "Today's game, if a catcher throws a ball down to second on a short hop, or a ball gets blocked in the dirt, that ball's out of the game. It's just automatic now."

Pitchers also seek ways to look natural while applying moisture or tackiness to their fingers. One former player, now a broadcaster, reached into his team's ball bag for me and pulled out a canister of colorless Tuf-Skin, a spray that helps secure athletic tape. With one spritz of Tuf-Skin on my arm, I had an invisible island of instant tackiness for my fingers. That's also why pitchers like putting clear BullFrog Sunscreen on their arms: grab the rosin bag, aimlessly touch the BullFrog spot, and you'll have just enough stickiness to help guide your pitches. One catcher said he has seen pitchers leave the dugout between innings and wrap their fingers around a ball coated with pine tar, leaving just enough residue on their hands to get a better grip when they return to the mound.

Next time you go to a game, notice all the surfaces a pitcher touches with his hand. Pitchers are fidgety creatures, constantly tugging and swiping and scratching their caps, their sleeves, their skin, *something*. Take a look at Corey Kluber, the two-time Cy Young winner for Cleveland who generates extraordinary movement with his pitches. Kluber grabs his tongue on the mound before every pitch—which has been legal again for years—then wipes his hand on the side of his pants.

"The way they rub the balls up now, they rub them all up in advance," Kluber says. "They're not rubbed up all day, and they sit in the bucket with all the dust and stuff, and they get so slippery. Just get a little bit of moisture on your hand, at least. You've still gotta wipe it off, obviously, but you get a little bit of moisture on your hand so the ball's not as dry."

Kluber does this no matter the weather, but such tactics are especially handy in the cold and at high altitude, where it's harder to generate moisture.

"I tell you what," says one NL veteran, "if they could get a camera behind the dugout in Colorado, it would be like a mad scientist's laboratory down there, people doing anything they can to find a grip."

Most players, even hitters, tend to accept this practice. A pitch can be an instrument of destruction, after all, and hitters would rather the pitcher know where it's going than accidentally fire a cue ball at their head. It is a fine distinction, to be sure, but this is the logic: tackiness helps command and finish on a pitch, and that's OK. Sandpaper or K-Y Jelly help enhance movement, and that's not.

"In the cold weather in Minnesota, you had to have something to grip the curveball," says Jim Kaat, who starred for the Twins in the 1960s. "Pitchers for years have lobbied: if hitters can use pine tar to grip the bat better—it doesn't help 'em hit it any farther—we should be able to use pine tar. It's not like a Vaseline ball or anything like that. It just helps you get a little better grip on it."

Then again, it comes back to discretion: in 2014, when the Yankees' Michael Pineda brazenly smeared pine tar on his neck on a chilly night at Fenway Park, it was so overt that the Red Sox felt compelled to object. Pineda got a 10-game suspension and widespread ridicule. But generally, as long as a pitcher is discreet, the other side has no problem with pine tar.

This was even true in perhaps the most famous case of pine tar on a pitcher. On a damp and windy day at the 1988 NLCS in New York, Mets manager Davey Johnson asked umpires to inspect the glove of Dodgers closer Jay Howell. Joe West, the plate umpire who took the glove, said Johnson was a reluctant whistleblower.

"Somebody saw it on TV, called the Mets, and the Mets' owners got together and sent a message down to Davey and said, 'Go check him,'" West says. "Davey didn't want to check him. I said, 'This is the playoffs, David.' He says, 'I know, but my boss is telling me I've got to check him, and I've gotta do what they say.'"

The Mets had been tipped off to Howell by Tucker Ashford, a minor league manager in their system who had played with Howell on the Yankees, and with Perry on the Padres. Perry often pitched with a smudge on his cap, and while watching Game 1, Ashford noticed that Howell did, too.

Howell was ejected from Game 3 and suspended for the next two games, but the Mets almost felt bad about it. Wally Backman, their second baseman, told reporters he felt Howell's infraction was less serious than the scuffing the Mets suspected Scott of two years earlier.

"Pine tar doesn't make you throw the ball harder," Backman said. "It doesn't make his curve break more. It's different than a guy using Vaseline or sandpaper. It's not up to me to pass judgment on the suspension, but I think the rule has to be rewritten or clarified."

All these years later, it never has been. In the 2006 World Series, at least, the penalty was less severe. When the Cardinals spotted a pine-tar-like smudge on the pitching palm of the Tigers' Kenny Rogers, La Russa asked the umpires to check. Rogers cleaned off his hand—he claimed it was dirt—and kept pitching, earning the Tigers' only victory of the series.

The next spring, I spent part of an exhibition game with Bob Feller as he signed autographs for fans in Winter Haven, Florida. One of them asked just what Rogers had been doing in that World Series game. Feller, as quick with opinions as he once was with fastballs, did not hesitate.

"He was trying to cheat," Feller said. "It's not the first time anyone's ever done it. They've been doing it from Day 1."

But how much do they really do it anymore? Pine tar is one thing—cheating by the letter of the law, yes, but not by the spirit. Whatever happened to the spitball, the Hall of Fame pitch of Chesbro and Walsh, Coveleski and Faber, Grimes and Perry? Richie Ashburn—he of the "crapping spitter" charge to Burdette—always thought of pitchers as shifty characters, never to be trusted. Where have all the scoundrels gone?

When I asked Perry in 2018 why more pitchers were not as, shall we say, *crafty* as they were in his day, he had a short but telling answer: "Well, maybe they don't need it." Dan Plesac, who pitched in more than 1,000 games, agreed.

"You're not looking for a Don Sutton now, a guy that can sink it and cut it and make the ball move," Plesac says. "If you don't have velocity, you can't pitch anymore. How many guys, how many real power pitchers, need to scuff the ball to be successful? Not many. You don't need to, if your stuff is that good."

Plesac works for MLB Network, founded in 2009, the hub of baseball's vast and ever-expanding visual empire. Every fan can watch games on the At Bat app. Every team has a bank of video screens, usually just off the dugout, showing every conceivable angle for replays and analysis. Good luck evading the most sophisticated alarm system in baseball history.

"When there's so many TV cameras, it's so hard to get away with it," says Jason Giambi, who played 20 seasons in the majors. "Obviously you're gonna get a few guys who've got pine tar in their glove and things like that to get a better grip on the ball. But the game has definitely evolved. You've got slow-motion, all these angles. Not only do you have players watching it, you've got the video guy down in the tunnel, and then your other video guys running the whole room upstairs.

"So you have so many sets of eyes on these guys, and especially if they see a pitch that looks really abnormal, the guy rewinds it 5,000 times: 'OK, what did he do different? Oh, he went to the side of his pants, he went to his belt, he went to the top of his hat.' Then they start to put together the timeline of every time he's pitched, does that ball do the same thing? What about his last start, his start before that? And before you know it, they've got it down—all right, go tell the umpire to check his hat, or check the side of his pants, or check inside his glove. You can't hide anymore."

But what if you could? What if maybe, just maybe, the next Preacher Roe was hiding in plain sight on a diamond near you, fiendishly fooling all the viewers and video technicians at the ballpark and beyond?

He could blacktop a lot of driveways by selling those secrets—and he'd probably keep the supplies after finishing the job. The sticky sealant just might come in handy.

THE
CUTTER

At the End, It Will Move

Roy Halladay threw the first no-hitter I ever saw, in Philadelphia for the opener of the 2010 playoffs. I was glad it was him. You never know if you'll see a no-hitter, and I felt honored to witness his moment. Halladay had enthralled me like nobody else when I covered the Yankees in the first decade of the 2000s, and he was the Blue Jays' ace. He made a lineup of seasoned stars look feeble, baiting them into check swings, weak pop-ups, and harmless ground balls.

"Toughest on me? Halladay, that sinker and cutter," said Derek Jeter, who batted .234 off Halladay. "I tried to just guess which way it's gonna go—and I always guessed wrong."

The playoff no-hitter, against the Cincinnati Reds, didn't feel random at all. All of us at Citizens Bank Park noticed something special going on, and even Halladay seemed to sense he might do it. After waiting 13 years to appear in the postseason, he looked like he could have kept going that way, forever.

"I was so ready for that opportunity, and I felt like I had prepared so long for it, it's just one of those where I felt like everything was on," he told me. "I was able to locate, I was able to work quick, I was able to do all the things I wanted to do. Those are few and far between."

Halladay and I spoke in March 2017 at a picnic table in Clearwater, Florida, in the shadow of the left field foul pole at the Phillies' spring training complex. He had just finished a morning session with the minor leaguers, coaching them on the mental side of pitching. He paused.

"But, you know, it's funny. When those actually happen it's so anti-climactic, because you're out there and it's simply just making pitches. And all of a sudden it's over, and it's kind of like, 'Well, now what?' You want to keep going. You feel like, 'Well, geez, there should be something more.'"

Eight months after our conversation, Halladay's family and friends gathered at that Clearwater ballpark to eulogize him. The son of a commercial pilot, he had learned to fly in retirement and reveled in the pursuit. Halladay was 40 years old and living his dream when he died, his small plane plunging upside down into shallow water in the Gulf of Mexico. He left behind a wife, two sons, and a legacy as a dedicated craftsman who strove constantly to improve.

Halladay always seemed very serious. You'd get to the ballpark four hours early and he'd be there, alone, running up the concrete steps like Rocky Balboa at the Art Museum. He never seemed much for conversation, but I had felt moved to shake his hand in the clubhouse before the 2008 All-Star Game in the Bronx, just to tell him I appreciated the way he went about it. He smiled and thanked me.

I didn't know it, but Halladay was in the process, right then, of reinventing himself for a brief but glorious final burst of success. He had already won a Cy Young Award and made five All-Star teams for Toronto. But he thought he could improve his cutter, which was not as consistent as he wanted. He suspected the problem was his thumb position, but he was not sure. Sharing a clubhouse with Mariano Rivera, he knew what to do.

Rivera was a legend by then, on his way to a record 652 career saves, five championships, and a 2.21 earned run average, the best of anyone born after 1889. He had become synonymous with the cutter, a pitch he found by accident but mastered like no other.

"Mariano really helped me," Halladay said. "When I got a chance to talk to him, sure enough, he told me that one of the keys for him was making sure he wrapped his thumb under and got it on the opposite side of the ball."

When Halladay was at his best, hitters had no time to tell which way his pitches would go. Would they bank this way for a sinker, or that way for a cutter?

To keep hitters honest, both pitches needed to be sharp. When he threw his sinker, with his index and middle fingers along the narrow seams, Halladay placed his thumb directly underneath his index finger on the bottom of the ball. When he threw his cutter, which he held with his index and middle fingers across the wide part of the seams, he had always put his thumb in the same spot.

Rivera showed Halladay his technique, bending his thumb at the knuckle and tucking it under the ball, so the nail was even with the middle finger, not the index finger. This kept the thumb pad from blocking the ball's spin as it left his hand, allowing the index and middle fingers to pull through, unimpeded, and send it on its path. I gave Halladay a ball and he wrapped it in Rivera's grip, holding his arm out straight.

"So now if you look at it from behind, you have all the ball sticking out on this side," he explained, and from the pitcher's perspective, you could see at least half the ball peeking out from the left side of the hand. The rest of the ball was covered up by Halladay's fingers.

"So now it's overloaded. It almost has to go that way. When I got my thumb underneath [the index finger], it was still centered. But as soon as I get it moved over, then all of a sudden, it overloads the ball on that side."

Did it feel natural right away?

"It took a little while," Halladay continued, "and it was so awkward at times that when it was really good, I traced my fingers on the ball with a pen. I just took a black ballpoint pen and traced it, right where my finger placement was, and I put it in my locker and just stored it and kept it with me. Well, the next spring, I was throwing it and it wasn't working, I wasn't getting results out of it. So I went back and picked up that ball and just grabbed it without looking at the marks. And sure enough, my thumb was back to here, where it felt comfortable.

"So I put it back on that mark where it was a little uncomfortable at first, but sure enough, it came right back. Then you get used to it, and you're like, 'OK.' But it was a pitch that you really had to monitor where you were, how you grip it, because you could get in bad habits just from long tossing. It's just an odd place to throw a ball."

Halladay beat the Yankees three times in the second half of the 2008 season; when Rivera's teammates learned of his generosity to a rival, they fined him in kangaroo court. For the next three seasons, one with Toronto and two with the Phillies, Halladay was never better. He went 57–26, won another Cy Young Award, threw a perfect game to go with the playoff no-hitter, and led all qualified pitchers in earned run average, at 2.53, while throwing the most innings.

A Phillies fan was so taken by Halladay that he started a blog called "I Want to Go to the Zoo with Roy Halladay"; when he retired, Halladay actually did go to the zoo with him. The site made "cutter" into a verb, and broke down Halladay's strikeouts into "cuttered" and "so cuttered." The pitch could not be ignored: in those first three seasons after the tip from Rivera, Halladay threw the cutter more often than he ever had before.

"I didn't get the Mariano cutter," Halladay insisted, but he never stopped trying to perfect it. He was never far from the baseball with Rivera's grip traced onto it.

"I'd keep it in my locker, and when we'd go on the road I put it in my travel bag," he said. "Stuck it in a shoe, wherever I went, and if I was struggling I'd just pick it up. I carried it the rest of my career."

Halladay retired after the 2013 season with three compressed discs in his back, a side effect of all that running he did between starts. He never reached the World Series, but found, to his surprise, that this did not really matter. In the end, all he wanted was a *chance* to win it, to prove to himself that he could be the same pitcher when the whole baseball world was watching. Maybe, he could be even better.

Halladay finished with a 203–105 record and a 3.38 ERA. In December 2018 he was scheduled to headline the Hall of Fame ballot, posthumously, with Mariano Rivera.

––––––

The first decade of baseball in the new century ended with a cutter. With two outs in the top of the ninth inning at Yankee Stadium, in Game 6 of the 2009 World Series, Rivera angled his tenth pitch to the Phillies' Shane Victorino just a bit lower than usual. It came in like a knee-high fastball, 91 miles an hour, and darted down and in—not much, but just enough for Victorino to pull a harmless grounder to second base for the final out. It was the fourth time Rivera had secured the last out of the World Series, more than anyone in baseball history.

The pitchers in that World Series highlighted the era's defining trick. Cliff Lee won Games 1 and 5. Rivera saved Games 2 and 4. Andy Pettitte won Games 3 and 6. All of them featured the cutter as their primary weapon. A month after their loss, the Phillies traded Lee and upgraded to Halladay. When they brought Lee back in 2011, they set a franchise record with 102 wins in the regular season.

Lee would pitch 13 years in the majors, with one Cy Young Award and a 7–3 postseason record. In his prime, nobody had better command. His fastball never averaged even 92 miles an hour, but it carried him through college and into the pros. It wouldn't have brought him much further without a cutter as a complement, in place of his ordinary slider.

"Cliff didn't throw hard, so what it did was it gave him another element of guys laying off his fastball," says Ace Adams, his pitching coach at Class A Jupiter in the Expos' farm system. "He threw 88 to 92, and when you have that late cutter instead of using a four-seamer in, that just jams 'em. They're looking for a fastball in a hitter's count and all of a sudden here comes a cutter and it's late, right on your hands. It blows their bat up. It gave him more leeway with his regular fastball. Now he could throw that thing right down the middle and let it run, and they couldn't sit on it because they knew he had this cutter. So that changed him."

Lee learned the cutter from Adams in 2001, and by the end of the next season, he was in the majors with Cleveland. Adams learned the pitch from Ray Fisher, a right-hander for the Yankees and the Reds from 1910 to 1920. When Fisher wasn't throwing the spitter—legal back then—he threw cutters. He started and lost Game 3 of the 1919 World Series, in Chicago's Comiskey Park against the infamous Black Sox, who had lost the first two games on their way to throwing the series.

After his pitching career, Fisher would spend decades as the head baseball coach at the University of Michigan, where the baseball field is named for him. He was retired by 1971, when Adams arrived at Michigan as a left-handed pitcher, but would help out the team almost every day, working with the pitchers at Yost Field House, where the hockey team now plays. Fisher was very thin and not quite six feet tall, but his hands were enormous; each one could hold five baseballs.

He was 84 then, too old to throw, but he could demonstrate technique, always emphasizing "wrist pop" to make the ball spin. Adams eagerly soaked up his tips and stories, and would walk to Fisher's house from his West Quad dorm in Ann Arbor to watch the World Series on TV. Fisher thought modern pitchers were soft, compared to those from his day, but he gladly analyzed their stuff for Adams, and shared memories of his time on that stage.

"They were blowing it on purpose and I still couldn't beat 'em," Fisher would say. "We all knew they were getting paid, and it actually made us a little nervous, because we knew they were trying to blow it and if we didn't beat 'em, it was embarrassing. So it wasn't fun. We knew it was going on, we heard everything. We didn't know everything behind the scenes, but we all knew. Damn right we knew."

Three of the White Sox who would be banned for life—Chick Gandil, Shoeless Joe Jackson, and Swede Risberg—had hits that led to runs off Fisher. Still, he did not pitch badly, allowing just two earned runs in seven and two-thirds World Series innings. There's no precise data on which pitches he threw, of course, but it's safe to say the cutter was among them, though Fisher always called it the cut fastball.

"He taught me to off-center it, hook my hand a quarter-turn, and let it rip," Adams says. "That's how I've always taught it. If you really throw it right, it goes across a little bit and then it goes down a little— just a little. And if you don't throw it right, if you get around it, it might break too early and it just goes across and might hang a little bit. But the ones that really have that lateness to it, it goes across and down and you really get a good rip down through your middle finger.

"Anyone can throw it—just off-center that son of a bitch, hook your hand, and let it fly, brother!"

The cutter lends itself to such excitement. It is meant to be thrown aggressively, and to act out the verb in its name. It aims to inflict damage, to take something whole and chop it up: the wood in the hitter's hands, yes, but also his confidence. A good inside cutter veers off course so late that the only way to hit it on the barrel is to pull it foul. The batter must guess where the pitch will end up; he does not have time to actually see its movement.

Pitchers, and not just Fisher, knew of this weapon long ago. Without video, we'll never know the exact movement on the extraordinary curveball of Hilton Smith, the Hall of Fame pitcher from the Negro

Leagues in the 1930s and '40s. But Smith could shape his breaking ball various ways; perhaps one moved like a cutter.

"We had to have two curveballs, a big one and a small one," Smith said in *Voices from the Great Black Baseball Leagues.* "Now they call it a slider, but those guys were throwing it years and years back."

Bob Shaw—who pitched for the White Sox in the 1959 World Series, their next after the Black Sox scandal—describes the cutter in his pitching manual as an offshoot of the slider, without using the term:

> When you don't have to throw a strike, break the ball flat and inside, belt-high. Percentages are that the batter will hit the ball foul if he makes contact. This is a good way to jam the hitter.

Billy Williams, the left-handed-hitting Hall of Famer who played most of his career for the Cubs in the 1960s, loved to drop his hands and attack the low slider. But just a slight adjustment, he said in 2015, turned that pitch into the toughest kind he faced: "It's a slider, but not down—coming in from a right-hander. It's belt-high, where you can't get extended. It's called a cutter now."

One of the most famous moments of baseball's black-and-white TV age—Bill Mazeroski's home run that won the 1960 World Series for the Pirates—came off a cutter.

"It was a high fastball; high cutter, really," says Ralph Terry, the Yankees pitcher who threw it. "It was moving a little."

The next Yankees pitcher to give up a World Series–ending hit also did it on a cutter. In Game 7 of the 2001 World Series, Luis Gonzalez floated a Rivera cutter into shallow left field for a single, winning the title for the Diamondbacks. By then, everyone knew what pitch Gonzalez had hit. Who knew they'd been throwing cutters so many decades before?

"Well," Terry says, smiling, "they just put a new name on it."

————

Chili Davis came to bat about 10,000 times in the majors. As a coach, he has studied countless more at-bats by his hitters. The cutter, he insists, has been around forever.

"Pitches have names now," he says. "They didn't have names back then. Back then it was fastball, breaking ball. You might have a curveball or a slider, some guys had better curveballs than others. You had the sinker guys, you knew the ball would sink and run away. And you had cutter guys—Dave Dravecky, Woodie Fryman, Jerry Reuss, Andy Pettitte, latter-day Mariano Rivera, even Jim Abbott threw a cutter.

"But you didn't walk out there and go, 'Hey, this guy, he's got a cutter, two-seamer, four-seamer, sinker. I mean, there's too many names for one pitch. It's a fastball—this guy can get into your kitchen if you let him, and he lives in there, because he's trying to break your bat. He's trying to crowd you, he's trying to jam you, and you knew that they could go out there, too. So basically you picked a side that you wanted to beat them on."

A fun example of the cutter's effectiveness was the pitch that ended the fourth game of the 2000 World Series. The Mets trailed the Yankees by one run, and with one more out they would fall behind three games to one. Matt Franco, a lefty, came up to pinch hit. He stood far from the plate, giving himself a little more room to clear his hands and connect with Rivera's best pitch.

The cutter would beat Franco, even though Rivera did not throw it. He and the catcher, Jorge Posada, recognized that with Franco standing way out there, he could never reach a four-seam fastball on the outside corner. So that is where Rivera put it, and Franco went down looking in his only World Series at-bat.

"I thought for sure he was going to come inside," Franco reflected the next spring. "He'd done it to me before, and I've seen it on TV a thousand times, just breaking bats with that cutter in. I wasn't going to get beat that way. He made two great pitches and there was basically no chance."

The cutter has that power. Nobody wants to face it, because it's so hard to square up no matter which way you hit. Mark Teixeira, a switch-hitter for 14 seasons, calls the cutter the pitch that equalizes everything. Deception is critical to every pitch, but the cutter changes its form so late that the hitter can feel helpless. It looks like a ball and zips into the strike zone, or it looks like a strike and bends in toward your belt.

"You almost have to commit and anticipate, but the problem with the cutter is you still have the velocity and it moves so late," Cal Ripken Jr. says. "If a ball spins, or a curveball starts at your front left shoulder and you know it breaks off, you can kind of gauge where it's gonna end up. But the cutter is more unpredictable in that it comes in like the fastball and sometimes it's just a little movement, sometimes it's bigger movement, sometimes it's a little later. And does it come in or go away? The sweet spot's only so wide, so you either hit on the end or you hit it in—but it hurts like hell either side."

For most pitchers, especially those who don't throw very hard, that kind of weak, uncomfortable contact is the whole point. Even for a pitcher who relies on other stuff, it can be essential. Marco Estrada was basically a league-average pitcher for parts of seven seasons, getting by with a changeup, a curveball, and a fastball with a high spin rate. He added a cutter in 2015, with Toronto, and led the AL in fewest hits per nine innings in each of his first two seasons with it.

"Back in the day when I'd fall behind, I'd have to go to a four-seam fastball that's about 88 miles an hour," Estrada said at the 2016 All-Star Game. "You're not gonna get away with much; you have to make sure you locate that pitch. Nowadays, if I fall behind and throw a cutter, I don't really have to be perfect with it, and I kind of want them to swing at it anyways. Maybe it'll cause weak contact, maybe a ground ball or a pop fly. It's just something with a little bit of movement that throws the hitters off."

Yet the hybrid nature of the pitch held back its spread for decades. It's not quite a fastball or a slider, so when a pitcher relies too heavily on his cutter, which requires pressure on one finger, he might lose velocity on his fastball, which requires pressure on two. This happened to Dan Haren, but Haren didn't mind; his fastballs at 90 and 91 were straight and hittable, and his cutters at 88 and 89 missed barrels. He loved the pitch, but for many, a slower, fastball-ish pitch is bound to be alarming.

Another problem, some coaches fear, is the umpire. When a startled hitter gives a theatrical response to the cutter's late action, the umpire might not call the pitch a strike. And because the cutter stays on or near the same plane as the fastball, without as much tilt as a slider, if it doesn't have much movement it's just an ordinary fastball begging to be crushed.

Then again, any pitch in the wrong location is dangerous for a pitcher. The advantage of the cutter is the timing of the action. Mark Melancon, a three-time All-Star closer, says he thinks about "literally cutting through the right half of the ball," and believes such conviction imparts the pitch with its ferocity. It's as if the pitch is just so determined to be a fastball that it won't give in and move until the very last moment.

"When you spin a bowling ball, it goes straight for three-quarters of the lane, and then that last quarter of the lane, it cuts—and that's when hitters' eyes can't actually catch up to the ball," Melancon says. "They can't see the last 13 to 15 feet. Hand-eye coordination isn't that good when a ball's coming in at that speed. They're literally guessing where it's going to end up, and not seeing where. They're anticipating but they can't physically see it."

Many pitchers find that their hand naturally finishes one way or the other, producing a cut or sink on their fastballs. Ron Darling, a righty, had no problem getting his fastball to run in on righties, but no matter what he tried, he could not get the opposite movement. Pitchers who mastered the sinker and cutter, like Halladay and Greg Maddux, conjured a delta effect in hitters' minds: the pitch would look the same for a while, but they never knew if it would take a left or right exit from the tunnel.

Before he learned to master the slider, perhaps as well as any pitcher ever, Steve Carlton threw a cutter. He thinks it's an ideal pitch to teach kids, because it generates the movement they want without the strain.

"All you do on the cutter is you load it up—say the top of the ball is 12 o'clock, you just load up your index finger and middle finger on the outside part of the ball, on the left or the right of what would be perceived as 12 o'clock—and throw it like your fastball, and it starts to cut on you," Carlton says. "That's fairly easy to do. That's how I teach kids, so that way you don't have to twist, because kids want to twist it to make it curve and dip and stuff like that."

When people ask Jon Lester about his cutter, they are often amazed by its simplicity. It is not what pitchers call a "feel pitch," one that requires precise, almost delicate, execution. Lester, one of the best big-game pitchers of recent times, says his hand naturally finishes inward and finger pressure takes care of the rest.

"I want to throw a fastball with my middle finger, basically; that's the feeling I want to feel," Lester says. "I don't want to say it's an easy pitch to learn—but it is."

———————

Jerry Reuss joined the Dodgers in a trade at the start of the 1979 season. The team had won the last two National League pennants, but stumbled to a losing record. Reuss went 7–14, turned 30, and lost his starting job.

Banished to the bullpen, where he would need just two pitches, Reuss focused on his fastball and curve. While throwing in the bullpen, his fastball started slicing in, late. Mark Cresse, the bullpen catcher, asked Reuss what he was doing. Quite by accident, Reuss said, he had been holding the ball a bit off-center and could feel it coming off the inside of his middle finger. He was putting it right where he wanted, too, and Cresse suggested he use it in games.

"I saw the reaction that the hitters gave," Reuss says. "They looked at the pitch and they looked out at me and I could see them squint their eyes as if to say, 'What was that?' And then I said, 'Whoa, we might have something here.'"

Hitters couldn't read the ball coming out of Reuss's hand; would it run, like the two-seamer he'd always thrown, or cut? Larry Bowa, the veteran Phillies shortstop, confronted Reuss one day: "I know you're cheating, and I'm gonna figure out how." Reuss humored him. He wasn't cheating, but he was glad to know he was in Bowa's head. With the cutter working, he could pitch more confidently with his other stuff. Never much of a strikeout guy anyway, Reuss embraced a pitch intended for weak contact, scribbling all the benefits on a legal pad as an unofficial contract with himself.

"It was one of those domino effect kinds of things," Reuss says. "You don't walk anybody if you get somebody out on three pitches. You're throwing strikes, and then it went into what happened defensively. I had a good defense behind me; there were some flaws, but each of them was made better because they played on their toes, they never got back on their heels. They would make plays for me that they weren't making for other pitchers that were going deeper into the count."

By shaving 10 or 20 pitches off each start, Reuss figured, he could be stronger later in the season and pitch a few more years. Both hunches were right. In 1980, Reuss would throw a no-hitter and win the *Sporting News'* comeback player of the year award. The next year he helped the Dodgers win a championship, shutting out Houston in the division series clincher and beating the Yankees' Ron Guidry, 2–1, with a five-hitter in Game 5 of the World Series. His first few seasons with the cutter were the best of a 22-year career that spanned four decades.

"I had a fabulous run, unlike anything else I had in my career," Reuss says. "And it was all due to the cutter."

Yet the cutter did not catch on. Surely others were throwing it, Reuss says, but he could not think of anyone. Many pitchers, it seems, developed cutters without knowing what they were really trying.

This is how it happened for a left-hander at the University of Michigan—what is it about that school and this pitch?—in the mid-1980s. The pitcher already had a natural cut to his fastball, and when he threw it with his index and middle fingers across the narrow seams, instead of with them, his middle finger caught the curve of a seam just as he finished, imparting more drastic inward movement.

Most people did not think of this pitch when they considered the pitcher, Jim Abbott, who was born without a right hand. He balanced his glove on his right arm as he delivered the pitch, then switched it to his left hand in case he needed to make a play. There has never been a pitcher like him, but it was not just courage and will that made Abbott an Olympian, a first-round draft pick by the Angels, and a 10-year major leaguer. It was the cutter.

"That little grip kind of became a pitch of its own," Abbott says. "And when I got up to professional baseball I heard people start referring to it as a cutter. It wasn't a slider, it wasn't a fastball, it was a cutter. And I said, 'Oh yeah, great—I have a cutter.'"

In 1989, his first pro season, Abbott went to spring training expecting an assignment to Double-A. But he made the Angels without a day in the minors, because his cutter was so explosive. Growing up in Flint, Michigan, Abbott had rooted for his catcher, the former Tiger Lance Parrish. Now he was hurting Parrish with a weapon that was ready for the majors.

"I rode one in on his thumb one day and he literally stood up and threw his glove on the ground, because his thumb hurt so much," Abbott says. "It was a striking experience, like: 'Man oh man, that's Lance!' And he started wearing this plastic thumb protector inside of his glove to stop it from running in on him. Definitely, some catchers didn't like it all that much."

Abbott won 40 games in his first three seasons with the Angels and peaked with a no-hitter for the Yankees in 1993. The final batter, the switch-hitting Carlos Baerga, chose to bat lefty against Abbott, to keep the cutter away instead of boring in. Abbott finessed him with a slider and Baerga grounded out to short.

The Yankees could have had another lefty with a cutter, Al Leiter, but by then they had traded him to Toronto. Leiter helped the Blue Jays win the World Series in relief that year, and two years later he began a decade-long run as a top-of-the-rotation starter, mostly for the Mets. With Toronto in 1995, he lost three times to the Rangers but still made a strong impression on their brawny lineup. After one of the games, Dean Palmer and others complimented him on his new pitch.

"When did you start throwing a cutter?" they said.

"A cutter?" replied Leiter, incredulous. "I throw a slider."

"Man, you can call it what you want," they said. "But that is a cutter."

For Leiter, it was a revelation. In his early years with the Yankees, Ron Guidry and Dave Righetti had emphasized the slider to complement his fastball and curve. In time, Leiter threw the pitch harder and harder—and when the Rangers called it something else, he realized it wasn't a slider anymore, but a fastball that cuts. To Leiter, that distinction is important.

"I've told minor league guys forever: 'When you're throwing your cutter, it's a *"fuck you"* pitch,'" says Leiter, whose enthusiasm for his craft is so endearing that you look right past the language. "You're offset and you're throwing it with every bit the same effort as your fastball. Remember: a cutter is not a power breaking ball. It is a cut fastball, and that's a different mind-set. You've gotta understand: 'OK, I'm throwing a fastball and it's gonna cut, so I've got the same aggressiveness—and that's different than a slider.' A slider's a smaller, power breaking ball."

The pitch now called the cutter was widely dismissed as flat and useless—faster than a slider should be, without the sharp, downward angle, and slower than a pitcher's best fastball, without the precise location. Some pitchers knew how to use it; Leiter remembers Catfish Hunter describing how he baited pull-happy right-handed power hitters by cutting his fastball to get lazy flies to right center. But throwing cutters on purpose, with encouragement from coaches, was just starting to catch on in Leiter's prime.

In the 2000 World Series, Leiter matched cutters twice with Andy Pettitte of the Yankees. Pettitte started using it the same year as Leiter, in 1995, with encouragement from Billy Connors, a coach who had worked in Chicago with Maddux. In his early years, Pettitte said, he angled the pitch more like a slider, boring in on the back foot of a right-handed hitter. Toward the end, with a different pitching coach, Larry Rothschild, Pettitte made it a pure cutter again to compensate for his fading fastball.

"I was getting in on guys, but I was still giving up a lot of jam-shot hits," Pettitte says. "I was getting so frustrated, and Larry was like, 'Well, why don't we try to cut it like you used to?' So my last year and a half I broke out my cutter on the belt again, and that was a game-changer for me. By that time I had so much command of my mechanics and such an idea of pitching, of what I wanted to do."

In those final seasons, Pettitte had a winning record and a 3.49 ERA—better than expected for a pitcher over 40 who had retired for a year before his comeback. A few years later Pettitte suggested that C. C. Sabathia use the cutter, and Sabathia reversed three years of decline by throwing it almost 30 percent of the time.

But the cutter's best salesman was a man who used the pitch to take the final, triumphant leap for an athlete: from star to stratosphere.

Mariano Rivera comes to the World Series every year now, as a favor to Major League Baseball, to present a reliever of the year award named for him. The setting is quite familiar, since Rivera may be the greatest October pitcher ever. His ERA, across 96 postseason appearances, was 0.70. He earned 42 saves, matching his uniform number.

Before a game in the 2016 World Series, under the right field bleachers at Wrigley Field, Rivera reflected on the spread of the cutter.

Why was everyone throwing his pitch? Even a humble man had to state the obvious.

"Well, because they saw what I did for so many years, I believe," Rivera said. "There's no other explanation."

And what, exactly, makes that pitch so devastating?

"It's the rotation," Rivera said. "For me, it was the four-seam fastball rotation. You think it is something that will be straight, and it's not. At the end, it will move. That's a true cutter. Most of the guys using the cutter, they're kind of like sliders, because it has that slider spin; it doesn't have a fastball spin. A true cutter, it has four-seam fastball spin, and it moves. They think they're swinging at something that looks like a fastball, but it's not—and it comes with power."

Power was Rivera's specialty in 1996, his first full season, when he helped the Yankees win the World Series as a setup man and fanned nearly 11 batters per nine innings. He never matched that figure again, because he never pitched another season without the cutter.

It came to Rivera before a game at Tiger Stadium in June 1997, while playing catch with teammate Ramiro Mendoza. Just as Mendoza reached for Rivera's throw, the ball zinged about a foot to his right. Rivera could not explain the movement—he was simply throwing his regular fastball, he said—and after more of the same, Mendoza gave up. Rivera sought out the bullpen catcher, Mike Borzello, who would have equipment to protect himself from this sudden, violent action.

"He threw it at first and I'm like, 'OK, what was that?'" says Borzello, who joined the Cubs' coaching staff in 2011. "We took that ball out—maybe it was scuffed—and he did it again. I go, 'What are you doing?' He goes, 'I don't know.' This was a guy who used to have pinpoint four-seam command. It was an easy catch. He threw 95, 96, but it was straight—and now it was cutting."

Rivera got the save that night, but the next day he was still unsettled. He told Borzello they needed more work. The "cutter," as such, was not really a pitch; at that point, Rivera had never even heard of the term. He missed his precision four-seamer.

"He used to be able to throw the ball wherever he wanted," Borzello says. "So even though he pitched mostly with a four-seamer, he could use all quadrants of the strike zone. And now he didn't know where the ball was going."

After 20 pitches or so, Rivera still could not straighten the fastball. He kept trying to find it, for two or three weeks, but his old four-seamer was now a cutter. It was a gift so bountiful, Rivera would write in his book, that it might as well have been a million pounds of fish overwhelming his father's nets back home in Panama. But he did not know what he had.

"I didn't even try to do it," Rivera says. "I didn't try to make it. The Lord gave it to me. You ask me: 'Why me?' Well, I don't know. I don't know why me. You've got to ask the Lord that question."

In time, with subtle changes to his grip and finger pressure, Rivera could place the cutter wherever he wanted. But as soon as he unwrapped his new gift, the factory settings worked just fine: in to lefties, away from righties, the movement too late for hitters to detect.

It was enough to defeat a man before he even got to the batter's box. Facing Rivera with one out to go in the 1998 World Series, the Padres' Mark Sweeney lugged his bat to the plate with an unshakable thought rattling around his brain: *Don't strike out to end this.* It was the only time in his career, Sweeney said, that such a pessimistic vision entered his mind as he prepared to hit. Sweeney succeeded—kind of—by punching a ground out to third and bringing Rivera to his knees in joy.

The Padres' closer that fall, Trevor Hoffman, had 601 career saves to rank second on the career list. He stands in awe of Rivera.

"When you talk about pitching, you want to simplify things," Hoffman says. "I would have loved to be able to go: OK, here's ol' number one, little cut on it, mid-90s forever. I'm gonna get inside your kitchen and break your bat for a left-hander, and I'm gonna get it on the edge of your bat for a right-hander. It was pretty amazing."

Even those who could hit Rivera, like Ichiro Suzuki (6-for-15 lifetime) routinely call his cutter the single toughest pitch they ever faced.

"If you say one pitch, then it's definitely Mariano Rivera's cutter, because you know it's coming and you still can't hit it," Suzuki says. "I think even if you take all the great pitchers that I've faced—besides the knuckleball, we'll put that aside—but even if they have a 100-mile-an-hour fastball and a split, if you knew the split was coming, you could do something with it. But in Mariano's case, you knew the cutter was coming, *you knew it was coming,* but it was still so tough."

The reason, to Lester, was that Rivera's cutter moved about two feet and did so later than anyone else's.

"Other guys' are back at 17, 18 feet from home plate, so there's longer to see the cut," he says. "Even though it's a smaller cut, there's longer to see it. That's what made Mariano's so unhittable: it was a four-seamer until it got to 12 feet. You have 12 feet to figure out how far that ball's gonna move."

Josh Donaldson ended the 2015 ALCS by bouncing a cutter from the Royals' Wade Davis to third base for the final out. It was a bitter ending for Donaldson, who would be named MVP of the American League, but the next spring he was convinced he'd been beaten by the best. Davis's cutter, he proclaimed, was the toughest pitch in baseball.

Maybe so—in that moment, anyway. But even Davis thinks Rivera's pitch was a cutter above his own.

"He's on a different planet," Davis says. "People have said he's the best because he mastered one pitch. It's like: no, he didn't master one pitch, he just threw a pitch that nobody else can throw. He had something that nobody sees. Hitters don't see that. You don't see a ball that moves like that, especially as accurate as it is. There'd be guys stepping in the box just waving at it, even later in his career, just waving at it. It's just a different pitch. That's why he's in a whole different category."

Rivera threw more than one pitch, and not just because of his extraordinary cutter command. He used a two-seamer effectively, especially near the end of his career, and always had the four-seamer to straighten a right-handed hitter who might be leaning over the plate. At the 2013 All-Star Game, he reminded the Giants' Sergio Romo—famous for his sweeping slider—to always protect his best pitch. Romo already knew this; he had ended the previous World Series with a tailing fastball down the middle to the Tigers' Miguel Cabrera, who was looking for the slider and never swung. Yet it thrilled Romo to hear the lesson reinforced from a master like Rivera.

"He protected that cutter the whole time," Romo says, "and nobody knew it."

The first two closers to eclipse Rivera's highest annual salary— $15 million—were Mark Melancon and Kenley Jansen, who both thrive with cutters. Neither learned the pitch from Rivera—Melancon, a former Yankee, got the most help from Brandon Lyon, a teammate with Houston—but Jansen's has a similar origin. He was throwing fastballs to Borzello, by then the Dodgers' bullpen catcher, without recognizing the natural weapon he held.

"Borzy caught Mariano, and he's the one who told me: 'You know your ball's cutting,'" says Jansen, a converted catcher. "That's when I started paying attention, and from there I realized the pitch was gonna become good for me. Because when I began, I always threw fastballs and I was like, 'Geez, why do they not hit that fastball?' I still didn't learn how to throw a secondary pitch, and they already put me in the big leagues without a secondary pitch. And then I find out my ball cuts."

Jansen's home mound, at Dodger Stadium, is right where Oakland's Dennis Eckersley stood as he faced a hobbled Kirk Gibson in the opener of the 1988 World Series. The right-handed Eckersley tried a backdoor slider to the left-handed Gibson, who famously swung on one leg to launch an indelible game-ending homer.

Somewhere in the stands that night was a 17-year-old from West Covina named Jason Giambi. In seven years he would be teammates with Eckersley, and later spend many years with Rivera on the Yankees. Before Rivera, Giambi says, the backdoor slider from Eckersley was about the only inward-moving pitch that a righty would throw to a lefty.

"Mariano really revolutionized the cutter inside, because that was always taboo for a right-handed pitcher, like, 'Oh, don't throw lefties in,'" Giambi says. "You could bank on it: it was sinkers down and away, changeups down and away, an occasional fastball inside to push you off the plate and then maybe like a runner—a running fastball at your hip to come back—but never was anybody talking about cutters in to lefties. Then Mariano took that fear away. Because he was so dominating, everybody was like, 'Shit, this guy's got one pitch and he's fucking dominating every lefty. I better learn it!'

"Because the advantage lefties had was, you would lean over the plate. If you really think about every pitch: changeup from a righty sinks down and away, a sinker sinks down and away, most guys' overhand breaking ball doesn't really break into you. There was Eck with the backdoor slider, but if you start to look, everything else is out over the plate—and Mo changed that. Everything started to be: *pound you in, pound you in* and then go away. So he really was a game-changer."

And if all that weren't enough, Giambi says, teams began to use more and more infield shifts toward the end of his career, which stretched through 2014. If lefties managed to pull the cutter fair on the ground, there was often another infielder stationed there to gobble it up.

Lots of cutters, lots of shifts, lots of misery for hitters.

"Now you're screwed," says Giambi, who was the oldest player in the league when he retired, a year after Rivera and apparently not a moment too soon.

————————

Stephen Strasburg pitches for a living, and only hits because National League rules require it. The first cutter he ever saw from a batter's box came in a major league game, from the All-Star left-hander Cole Hamels. It terrified him.

"It looked so good," says Strasburg, who hits right-handed. "I was squared out there for the bunt and that thing comes right in on your hand. Your heart stops a little bit. You see it, you see it, you see it—and then all of a sudden you're like that."

Strasburg mimicked himself in a panic, reeling back his bat as the ball screams in and plunks it for a foul. Even if he had faced cutters as an amateur, the feeling then would have been much different, because of what he held in his hand. A hitter with an aluminum bat can still get jammed and make solid contact, because the whole bat is a sweet spot. A hitter with a wood bat knows how vulnerable it is; Rivera was so famously destructive that the Twins gave him a rocking chair made from lumber shards as a retirement gift.

"In college, with aluminum bats, the effects of a cutter weren't as apparent," Abbott says. "It wasn't until I started facing wood bats in spring training of my rookie year—when I broke a lot of bats, and a lot of balls got in on right-handed hitters—that the talk started coming: 'Oh, wow, what a cutter!' The wood bats really showed it more dramatically, the effectiveness of the pitch."

Even if pitchers resist the cutter as amateurs, they are wise to learn it quickly in the pros. The pitch is so easy to pick up and makes young hitters so uncomfortable that it can help achieve instant results. In the first decade of the 2000s, veteran hitters say, the cutter was not even mentioned on most advance scouting reports. Now it is essential for many pitchers to advance.

"Because it's so hard to handle opposite-sided hitters, the remedy by most pitching coaches in most organizations is, 'OK, we'll teach him a cutter,'" Astros manager A. J. Hinch said. "And as matchup-oriented as we've become as an industry, in order for guys to stay in the game and not be replaced by a specialist, most pitchers have resorted to the cutter."

As the cutter evolves, pitchers have become increasingly bold in where they throw it. The Angels' Mike Trout, the best player of his generation, calls the cutter the toughest pitch he faces—but not the kind from a left-hander.

"The front-door cutter," says Trout, a right-handed hitter. "If they have a two-seamer in and then they run a cutter front-hip, it's tough."

That's a risky pitch, designed to start on the hitter's body and then clip the front edge of the plate for a strike. If it catches too much of the plate, without the full force of a fastball, it can go a long way, which partially explains the surge in home runs in the middle of the 2010s. A lot of experiments blow up.

"Guys are getting killed with cutters, because hitters are adjusting to them," said Dave Duncan, the retired pitching coach, in late 2017. "They've been thrown enough of them now that they're reading them, number one, and they're not swinging at the ones that are off the plate inside. They're waiting for that pitcher to make a mistake with it, and when he does, it's like a batting practice fastball. More and more pitchers are getting beat on cutters and going, 'Goddamn, that was a good cutter!' Well, it wasn't a good cutter, because it was a strike.

"Cutters are purpose pitches now more than anything else, unless you have that really freaky guy that has a cutter like Mariano Rivera. That's different. That's a different pitch."

In 2017, Jon Lester threw the highest percentage of cutters among qualified major league starters: 27.6 percent, according to FanGraphs. At his peak, after Rivera's tutorial, Halladay threw it more than 40 percent of the time. On that March afternoon in 2017, Halladay could tell that patterns were changing.

"You'd hear hitters say that was the one pitch that really changed the game for a long time—but for some reason it's rare now to see many more guys that are still throwing cutters," Halladay said. "I see a couple here and there, but talking to a lot of guys it's just something that's not done a lot."

FanGraphs data shows that cutter usage had indeed dipped, but only a bit; it peaked at 6.2 percent usage by all pitchers in 2014, and was down to 5.5 percent in 2017. Those rates could be influenced by the tracking technology, though, and the fact that the cutter is a hybrid. Computers and scouts won't identify it precisely every time, but hitters know it's there.

The decline has been so slight that Leiter, now a broadcaster, says he hasn't even noticed it. Pitchers do throw more curveballs now, to complement the trend of high fastballs. But the best cutters still shatter hitters' bats, soften their contact, and scramble their senses.

"There's an embarrassment factor," Leiter says. "It's not just an end-of-the-bat roller to shortstop or fly ball to right. It's a jam-shot, my finger stings, my hands are sore, and I'm pissed off because I just broke my favorite bat. The effectiveness of this pitch goes beyond actually having a result from it. I used to do it a lot of times—bust a guy in and just miss. Let him be conscious of smelling that 88- to 91-mile-an-hour cut. It's an 'Oh shit!' pitch."

It's not a fastball. It's not a slider. But thankfully, for hitters, the best one has already come and gone. There will never be another Mariano Rivera. Roy Halladay knew that, and so does Rivera's own son, a minor league pitcher who cannot imitate his father's famous pitch.

Mariano Rivera Jr., drafted by the Nationals in the fourth round in 2015, throws a fastball, a slider, and a changeup. He has tried to throw a cutter, without much luck. He might find it someday, but he is realistic. The pitch already had its prophet.

"If it comes, it comes," Rivera Jr. says. "But only he can do it like that."

Acknowledgments

Some authors told me it was torture to write a book. I'm very lucky, then, because I loved it. I had three full years to write and report on a lifelong passion. But the biggest reason for all the fun was the deep roster of people who helped and inspired me.

Many years ago, Tony Gwynn told me he learned something new at the ballpark every day. At that moment, I knew I would need many lifetimes to understand even a small fraction of what really goes on in the game. Thank you to every person interviewed here for being my teachers, and giving so generously of your time and insights.

Brad Lidge was my first interview for this book, and, with his candor, set the template for all the other conversations to follow. Some of the people I was privileged to cover as a beat writer—especially Mike Mussina, Gil Patterson, Jamie Moyer, Bryan Price, Jason Giambi, Mark Teixeira, Al Leiter, and Bobby Valentine—were especially helpful. Others who took a keen interest included A. J. Ellis, R. A. Dickey, Ron Darling, Mike Montgomery, Dan Haren, Brian Bannister, and John D'Acquisto. I am grateful to you all.

I was there for C. J. Nitkowski's first major league win, when he beat Curt Schilling at the Vet, and he was there for me throughout this process, a one-batter specialist turned one-line-at-a-time pitching consultant.

Other friends in baseball helped more than they probably realize, with words of encouragement and acts of kindness. Thank you to Mark Attanasio, Jerry Dipoto, Derek Falvey, Mike Ferrin, Sam

Mondry-Cohen, J. P. Martinez, Dayton Moore, Rob Neyer, and Gus Quattlebaum. And I owe a lifetime of thank-yous to Dave Montgomery.

After nearly every interview, as soon as I shut off my recorder, I would text Derrick Goold and Ben Shpigel to share my excitement. Every time, wherever they were in the world, they responded immediately, and genuinely, as true friends do. Not once did they send me the "Are you for real?" Bitmoji in return.

Alex Ellenthal entered the game around the eighth inning, and gets the save for his cheerful, prompt, and accurate work transcribing hours of interviews. Thanks to Gaku Tashiro, a true pro, for tracking down and interviewing the God of Forkballs, Shigeru Sugishita.

Some of my favorite days in the last few years were the ones spent at the Giamatti Research Center at the Baseball Hall of Fame. It sounds almost too good to be true—*a library with everything ever written about baseball!*—but it's even better than I could have imagined. Thank you to all my friends in Cooperstown for their help and hospitality, including Jeff Idelson, Brad Horn, Jon Shestakofsky, Craig Muder, Cassidy Lent, John Odell, Matt Rothenberg, John Horne, Jim Gates, Jeff Katz, and Chris, Jen, Rick, and Christine Hulse. Thanks to Bob Kendrick of the Negro Leagues Baseball Museum in Kansas City, and also to Jon Wertheim and Emma Span for letting me peruse the incredible trove of archives at the *Sports Illustrated* library—and to Jeff Pearlman for encouraging me to do so.

Besides the books listed in the Bibliography, I used information from other books and articles found at those libraries, and at the library in Wilton, Connecticut, where much of this book was written (at least when I wasn't writing at the Coffee Barn). I copied hundreds of pages of news clippings at the Hall of Fame, some from as far back as the 1800s, on dozens of pitchers and topics. I also consulted my own articles and articles on many websites (the SABR biographies at Baseball-Reference.com were especially helpful), viewed footage of old games and highlights online, and watched the video documentaries *Lefty: The Life & Times of Steve Carlton* (1994), *Knuckleball* (2012), and *Fastball* (2016). Most statistics come from Baseball-Reference.com and FanGraphs.

Thank you to the many folks who connected me to the voices you read in these pages, or provided help with photos. All of these people, and more, helped set up interviews or photo rights: Harvey Araton, Scott Boras, Rob Butcher, Greg Casterioto, Peter Chase, Gene Dias, Shelley Duncan, Lorraine Fisher, Steve Grande, Brad Hainje, Dan Hart, Tim Hevly, Jay Horwitz, Craig Hughner, Nate Janoso, Brad Lefton, Paul Lukas, Tony Massarotti, Valerie McGuire, Tim Mead, Adrienne Midgley, Laurel Prieb, Josh Rawitch, Matt Roebuck, Mike Sheehan, Bill Stetka, Bart Swain, Mike Teevan, Jim Trdinich, Rick Vaughn, Shana Wilson, and Jason Zillo. The forever-friendly Larry Shenk, who gave me my very first press pass, pointed the way to Steve Carlton, my baseball hero and the man I most wanted to interview.

My real hero, though, has always been Jayson Stark, who is the reason I do this and my standard for both writing and integrity. "Gods don't answer letters," John Updike once wrote, but I know that's wrong because Jayson answered mine when I was 14 years old. "You can't wear No. 32 for the Phillies," he wrote, "but writing about baseball is the next best thing." Boy, was he right.

Not only do I get to learn more about baseball every day, I get to do it around so many dedicated and talented media members whose work and friendship constantly inspire me. I'll always be indebted to those who gave me such a solid foundation in how to be a professional: Steve Insler, Paul Hagen, Bill Lyon, Scott Graham, Tim Kurkjian, Buster Olney, Bob Costas, George F. Will, Zack McMillin, Lee Jenkins, John Lowe, Peter Gammons, Mike DiGiovanna, Kevin Acee, Jim Street, Art Thiel, Dave Sheinin, Jack Curry, Dave Anderson, and George and Laura Vecsey. And I would never have survived a decade on the Met and Yankee beats without the camaraderie of pals like Peter Abraham, Dom Amore, Sam Borden, Pete Caldera, Ken Davidoff, Mark Feinsand, Dan Graziano, Bryan Hoch, George King, Andrew Marchand, Anthony McCarron, Sweeny Murti, Jesus Ortiz, T. J. Quinn, and so many more. Thanks also to my buddy Gar Ryness; the world needs more people who can imitate Bo Diaz's batting stance anytime, anywhere.

My closest friends in the world—The Posse, as we called ourselves on the mean streets of Fort Washington, Pennsylvania—keep me laughing every day: Joe Benjamin, Mike Daly, Jeff Decker, Mike McCuen, John Pasquarella, Tim Pies, and Jamie Trueblood. John and I started a little baseball magazine together at Germantown Academy in 1988, with Jamie as the art director and Tim as a columnist. I guess I took our project to the extreme.

Tim Roberts (the best seventy-fifth-round draft pick in Seattle Mariners history) and Dave Cote coached Little League with me for years. I cherished every moment and learned a lot about baseball, too. Nothing but "good game," guys.

I am proud to have spent nearly two decades at *The New York Times*, striving daily to live up to its standard of excellence. From the moment I met Neil Amdur, I wanted to work for him and make him proud. Thank you for taking a chance on a beat writer who wasn't old enough to rent a car at his first spring training. The unwavering support of editors like Bill Brink, Tom Jolly, Patty LaDuca, Naila Meyers, Carl Nelson, Gwen Knapp, Jason Stallman, and the late, great Janet Elder has meant everything. Colleagues Dave Waldstein, James Wagner, and Billy Witz uphold our tradition of smart, incisive *Times* baseball writing, while Fern Turkowitz and Terri Ann Glynn have made the whole place go with patience and smiles. The incomparable Jay Schreiber and I worked together on more than 5,000 articles, and I've never met anyone whose judgment and commitment I trust more. Thank you all.

Dan Shaughnessy of *The Boston Globe* is more than my favorite columnist; he's also a matchmaker. Dan introduced me to David Black, my agent, who took the time to understand my goals and motivations. I never could have done this without David's vision, guidance, and belief. Thank you for all of that, and most of all for connecting me with Bill Thomas, my editor at Doubleday, who called all the right pitches with the calmness and wisdom of a veteran catcher helping a rookie through the biggest game of his life. Big thanks to Bill's assistant, Margo Shickmanter, for all her essential work behind the scenes.

From the very first moment I stepped on a major league field, I wanted to be part of that world. I got there, quite literally, by kicking and screaming until my parents gave in. It was fireworks night at Veterans Stadium in 1982, and we had perfect seats for the show, 20 rows behind the third base dugout. But I was seven, and all I noticed was that fans from the upper deck in center field were leaving their seats to watch from the field. *From. The. Field.* I yelled and cried until my mom lifted me over the fence in foul ground, and I stood on the red rubber warning track for a few seconds, gazing up at the lights that ringed the top of the ballpark. After that, there was no going back, and ever since, my parents—John and Mimi—have continued to lift me up, nurturing my dreams in every possible way. More important, they have set a shining example for how to live.

My brother Tim hid my lucky hat before Game 4 of the 1983 World Series, but I love him anyway. My wonderful sister-in-law, Colleen, probably has no idea she's married to a thief who cost the Phillies a championship, but now she does. My brother Dave wears his hair like a member of those '83 Phillies, and I love him for it. Tim and Dave go by Bonesaw and Hoag now, and they're rock stars in Austin, Texas. Yes, they got all the talent.

I did throw a shutout in the 2006 media game at Fenway Park, and the next year I invited my father-in-law, Mike Lockhart, to see me dazzle 'em again. Instead, I gave up 10 runs and didn't make it out of the third inning. Thankfully, Mike has been nice enough to keep me in the family. My mother-in-law, Sue McHugh, is endlessly warm, loving, and accepting. To Tina, Jessica, Kate, Lizzy, Matt, and all of my aunts, uncles, cousins, and in-laws, thanks for always being there for me.

Shortly after I met my wife, Jen, the Yankees played the Braves in the 1999 World Series. She chose Mariano Rivera as her favorite player because his job was to end the games, which meant I could come home. Covering this sport keeps you away from the people you love, and without a patient, selfless, and understanding wife, I could never do it. Jen is beautiful, smart, compassionate, and kind, a dreamer who brings out the best in everyone she meets. Asking her to marry me was the easiest decision of my life, and she is the best role model our children could ever have.

I've written many thousands of words here, but nothing could properly describe how lucky I feel to be the father of four such amazing children—Lily, Mack, Caroline, and Rory, who make me proud every day, in so many ways. I love them more than they could ever know, and I admire them as people who make the world a whole lot brighter every day.

Bibliography

Most of the information in this book comes from more than 300 interviews conducted in person and by phone and email between January 2015 and March 2018. I also purchased and read dozens of books, including the following:

Abbott, Jim, and Tim Brown. *Imperfect.* New York: Ballantine, 2013.

Adair, Robert K., PhD. *The Physics of Baseball.* New York: HarperCollins, 2002.

Angell, Roger. *Late Innings.* New York: Ballantine, 1984.

———. *Season Ticket.* Boston: Houghton Mifflin, 1988.

Barney, Rex, with Norman L. Macht. *Rex Barney's Thank Youuuu.* Centreville, Md.: Tidewater Publishers, 1993.

Bouton, Jim. *Ball Four: The Final Pitch.* Champaign, Ill.: Sports Publishing, 2000.

Cairns, Bob. *Pen Men.* New York: St. Martin's Press, 1992.

Craig, Roger, with Vern Plagenhoef. *Inside Pitch.* Grand Rapids, Mich.: Wm. B. Eerdmans, 1984.

Darling, Ron. *The Complete Game.* New York: Vintage, 2010.

Dickson, Paul. *Baseball's Greatest Quotations.* New York: HarperCollins, 1991.

Feller, Bob, with Bill Gilbert. *Now Pitching Bob Feller.* New York: HarperCollins, 1990.

Ford, Whitey, with Phil Pepe. *Slick.* New York: William Morrow, 1987.

Freedman, Lew. *Knuckleball.* New York: Sports Publishing, 2015.

Gibson, Bob, and Reggie Jackson, with Lonnie Wheeler. *Sixty Feet, Six Inches.* New York: Doubleday, 2009.

Gibson, Bob, and Lonnie Wheeler. *Pitch by Pitch.* New York: Flatiron Books, 2015.

Grant, Jim "Mudcat," with Tom Sabellico and Pat O'Brien. *The Black Aces.* Farmingdale, N.Y.: The Black Aces, 2006.

Gutman, Dan. *It Ain't Cheatin' If You Don't Get Caught.* New York: Penguin, 1990.

Hart, Stan. *Scouting Reports.* New York: Macmillan, 1995.

Hernandez, Keith, and Mike Bryan. *Pure Baseball.* New York: HarperCollins, 1994.

Hershiser, Orel, and Jerry B. Jenkins. *Out of the Blue.* Brentwood, Tenn.: Wolgemuth & Hyatt, 1989.

Hollander, Zander. *The Complete Handbook of Baseball 1976.* New York: Signet, 1976.

———. *The Complete Handbook of Baseball 1987.* New York: Signet, 1987.

James, Bill, and Rob Neyer. *The Neyer/James Guide to Pitchers.* New York: Fireside, 2004.

Kahn, Roger. *The Head Game.* New York: Harcourt, 2000.

Knight, Molly. *The Best Team Money Can Buy.* New York: Simon & Schuster, 2015.

Kurkjian, Tim. *Is This a Great Game or What?* New York: St. Martin's Press, 2007.

Leavy, Jane. *Sandy Koufax: A Lefty's Legacy.* New York: HarperCollins, 2002.

Marichal, Juan, with Lew Freedman. *Juan Marichal.* Minneapolis: MVP Books, 2011.

Martinez, Pedro, and Michael Silverman. *Pedro.* New York: Houghton Mifflin Harcourt, 2015.

Mathewson, Christy. *Pitching in a Pinch.* New York: Penguin, 2013.

McCaffrey, Eugene V., and Roger A. McCaffrey. *Players' Choice.* New York: Facts on File Publications, 1987.

McGraw, Tug, with Don Yeager. *Ya Gotta Believe!* New York: Penguin, 2004.

Monteleone, John J., ed. *Branch Rickey's Little Blue Book.* New York: Macmillan, 1995.

Morris, Peter. *A Game of Inches.* Chicago: Ivan R. Dee, 2006.

Moyer, Jamie, with Larry Platt. *Just Tell Me I Can't.* New York: Grand Central Publishing, 2013.

Niekro, Phil, and Tom Bird. *Knuckle Balls.* New York: Freundlich Books, 1986.

Niese, Joe. *Burleigh Grimes: Baseball's Last Legal Spitballer.* Jefferson, N.C.: McFarland, 2013.

Palmer, Jim, and Alan Maimon. *Nine Innings to Success*. Chicago: Triumph, 2016.

Passan, Jeff. *The Arm*. New York: HarperCollins, 2016.

Pearlman, Jeff. *The Bad Guys Won!* New York: HarperCollins, 2004.

Peary, Danny. *We Played the Game*. New York: Hyperion, 1994.

Perry, Gaylord, with Bob Sudyk. *Me and the Spitter*. New York: Signet, 1974.

Quigley, Martin. *The Crooked Pitch*. Chapel Hill, N.C.: Algonquin Books, 1984.

Reuss, Jerry. *Bring in the Right-Hander!* Lincoln: University of Nebraska Press, 2014.

Richard, J. R., and Lew Freedman. *J.R. Richard: Still Throwing Heat*. Chicago: Triumph, 2015.

Ritter, Lawrence S. *The Glory of Their Times*. New York: William Morrow, 1984.

Ryan, Nolan, and Harvey Frommer. *Throwing Heat*. New York: Avon, 1990.

Seaver, Tom, with Lee Lowenfish. *The Art of Pitching*. New York: Hearst Books, 1984.

Shaw, Bob. *Pitching*. Chicago: Contemporary, 1972.

Smith, Red. *To Absent Friends*. New York: Atheneum, 1982.

Sowell, Mike. *The Pitch That Killed*. New York: Collier, 1989.

Stark, Jayson. *Wild Pitches*. Chicago: Triumph, 2014.

Terry, Ralph, with John Wooley. *Right Down the Middle*. Tulsa, Okla.: Mullerhaus Legacy, 2016.

Thorn, John, and John B. Holway. *The Pitcher*. New York: Prentice Hall, 1987.

Vincent, Fay. *We Would Have Played for Nothing*. New York: Simon & Schuster, 2008.

Wendel, Tim. *High Heat*. Cambridge, Mass.: Da Capo, 2010.

Westcott, Rich. *Masters of the Diamond*. Jefferson, N.C.: McFarland, 1994.

———. *Splendor on the Diamond*. Gainesville: University of Florida Press, 2000.

Will, George F. *Met at Work*. New York: Macmillan, 1990.

Williams, Ted, with John Underwood. *My Turn at Bat*. New York: Fireside, 1988.

Wright, Craig R., and Tom House. *The Diamond Appraised*. New York: Simon & Schuster, 1989.

Index

Illustration Credits

Page 4: (top left) National Baseball Hall of Fame and Museum, Cooperstown, N.Y.; (top middle) AP Photo/Pool, Steve Green; (top right) Courtesy of the Pittsburgh Pirates; (bottom) Icon Sportswire
Page 5: (top) AP Photo; (bottom) Gary Hershorn/Reuters Pictures
Page 6: Icon Sportswire
Page 7: (top) National Baseball Hall of Fame and Museum, Cooperstown, N.Y.; (bottom left) Courtesy of the Texas Rangers; (bottom right) AP Photo/Paul Benoit
Page 8: (top) Icon Sportswire; (bottom) AP Photo/Mel Evans